THE BATTLE FOR
INVESTMENT
SURVIVAL

INTRODUCING WILEY INVESTMENT CLASSICS

There are certain books that have redefined the way we see the worlds of finance and investing—books that deserve a place on every investor's shelf. *Wiley Investment Classics* will introduce you to these memorable books, which are just as relevant and vital today as when they were first published. Open a *Wiley Investment Classic* and rediscover the proven strategies, market philosophies, and definitive techniques that continue to stand the test of time.

THE BATTLE FOR
INVESTMENT
SURVIVAL

Gerald M. Loeb

Foreword by Ken Fisher

John Wiley & Sons, Inc.

Published by John Wiley & Sons, Inc., Hoboken, New Jersey
Published simultaneously in Canada
Originally published by Simon & Schuster, Inc.

Acknowledgments
Some of the articles contained in the following chapters originally appeared in
*Barron's, The Commercial and Financial Chronicle, Investor Magazine, Trust and
Estates, American* magazine, and in the NANA syndicated column, "Wall Street
Today." "A Layman Looks at Building" first appeared in the *Architectural Forum.*
The chapter "I Don't Sell—People Buy from Me," is from *How I Made the Sale
That Did the Most for Me*, compiled and edited by J. M. Hickerson, Prentice-Hall,
Inc., 1951.

For general information on our other products and services or for technical
support, please contact our Customer Care Department within the United States at
(800) 762-2974, outside the United States at (317) 572-3993 or fax (317) 572-4002.

Wiley also publishes its books in a variety of electronic formats. Some content that
appears in print may not be available in electronic books. For more information
about Wiley products, visit our web site at www.wiley.com.

ISBN-13 978-0-470-11003-4

Printed in the United States of America

10 9 8 7 6 5 4 3 2 1

CONTENTS

FOREWORD

This book was among the first ten on investing I ever read. Initially published in 1935, it went through umpteen reprints and was still a huge title in the 1960s when my own interests in capital markets were forming—hence why it was one of the first books I read. It remains important for anyone seriously interested in capital markets, financial journalism, or even their own personal investments—particularly if you're younger and weren't around to experience how different the world Loeb came from was from today's—even how different the 1960s were from today. Perhaps it was from Loeb, one of our early financial columnists, that I later got the inspiration to start haranguing *Forbes* for a column of my own.

I'm a fan of classic investment books. You may find that odd coming from someone who just authored a book about beating the market by finding the next new thing no one knows. But you can't find the next new thing if you don't know where you've come from. (You know what they say about those who fail to study history.) Without good historical perspective, you have no basis to know if anything is beyond reasonable to expect.

In the same way American history majors must study the Confederate States if they hope to understand the United States (if you assume the Confederates were bad eggs, you missed the most important parts of antebellum U.S. history), serious investors must understand market history. And if you want to understand the 1930 to 1960 market mentality without reading a history book, *The Battle for Investment Survival* is a great start.

Gerald M. Loeb's book is a wonderfully preserved slice of investing, and even American history. A battle for survival it certainly seemed in 1935. Compounding all the misery was a severe and lingering global depression, coming on the heels of the stock market crash of 1929, made vastly worse by egregious monetary mismanagement both in the United States and around the globe. Then, too, was the fear created as Congress passed a rash of legislation, including but not limited to the creation of the Securities and Exchange Commission (SEC), which many then (and some still do) thought dampened returns from excess regulation relative to what would have happened otherwise. Overseas, in the year prior to this tome's initial publication, Adolf Hitler named himself Führer and the Nazi party was on the march. As if Nazism weren't enough, communism and ensuing mayhem were also on the rise throughout Europe, supported by the Soviet Union. Here at home, it was daily survival itself for American Midwestern farmers as they barely eked out subsistence during the Dust Bowl, and many rode the rails seeking hope elsewhere, where it was likely just as bad.

Investors weren't starving but they were bloodied and disheartened. Life seemed bleak all around. And then a genial, baldheaded, bespectacled Loeb penned his upbeat little book. Reading more like a collection of loosely related essays or columns, Loeb offered approachable anecdotes about investing. *The Battle for Investment Survival* may seem an unlikely title for an "upbeat" book, but consider it this way: Battles can be won—which was exactly what Loeb wanted his readers to believe.

To a 1935 reader with meager liquid assets to invest, nothing was more terrifying than the prospect of buy and hold (rational though it may seem to a twenty-first century audience with history's perspective). In this world, following a severe market crash, Nazis, Stalinists, famine, and poverty at home, where polio still reigned, Loeb's preferred strategy of continual, in-and-out, concentrated "speculation" seemed radical, fresh, and far safer than buy and hold.

Modern readers might recoil at the thought of speculating. But keep in mind, one of the joys of reading books from a bygone era is language evolves. Watch any MGM movie from the 1940s and 1950s and you'll be struck by how commonplace words can morph drastically, in just a few decades. Loeb wrote in the style of the 1930s, like many other classic books of the day, and the book is filled with quaint words whose meanings have been lost or simply changed. A "customer's man" is a broker, a "tyro" is a neophyte, an expensive stock is "dear." He takes you to a different time because he came from a different time.

When I reread this book, I hear words I haven't heard used this way in a long time, like his use of the word "dabble" in markets, making the book more fun. He writes like an old friend thinking of you, with cute twists that still make sense today, like, "Don't learn on your main money."

In the 1930s, thanks in large part to Loeb, "speculating" did not have the sting it enjoys today. Today "speculators" are cowboys and dice rollers, taking huge risk, perhaps irresponsibly or even unethically. But, as you read, remember there's simply no connection between Loeb's meaning of speculation and today's. For Loeb, speculation was a way to survive in an often seemingly impossible world. It was only later the word took on today's meaning.

In 1935 (and, indeed, in following decades), speculation was a perfectly respectable alternative to buying and holding, or what Loeb ominously called "long pull" investing. (Substitute "haul" for "pull" and you get the meaning.) "Buy and hold" was not palatable to Loeb's audience, fresh from the ill effects of the crash and aftermath. Loeb in many ways was another alternative to avoiding the next 1929, in the same way Graham and Dodd's *Security Analysis* and later Ben Graham's *The Intelligent Investor* were.

Loeb advocated cutting losses, and aiming for short-term gains from a small selection of stocks. (Momentum investors can see the roots of their strategy in Loeb's treatise.) According to Loeb, have a few eggs, put them in one basket, and watch it closely. If the world was going to hell in a hand basket, ditch the basket. That did not have the negative connotation associated with speculating today.

Loeb also recommended "swapping," which to modern ears sounds eerily like "churning," another no-no for serious investors. Yet, by his standards and at that point in time, swapping made perfect sense for speculators. And he specifically cautioned against letting money ride in the stock market. If you spend more time out than in, Loeb reasoned, you miss out more on "dangerous markets," which sounded great to investors—and that was Loeb's end game.

That may not be sound investment advice to follow today, but that's not why this is a must-read for capital markets students. Rather, it paints a picture of the landscape from which we get the SEC, the National Association of Securities Dealers (NASD), the Investment Advisors Act of 1940, and the birth of value investing as championed by Graham and Dodd.

Loeb oozed enthusiasm for the market and did much to restore faith in capital markets to skittish investors. In the book he shared a favorite (and much repeated) anecdote about quitting his first job after just three days because he was forced to sell a bond he didn't believe in. (And the same thing happened in his second job! What are the odds?) He also shared self-deprecating tales of his meager beginnings and early missteps. Was any of it true? Who cares! They were good stories; people believed them, and they believed in him.

After famously quitting his first two jobs, he settled in at E.F. Hutton in 1924 at the tender age of 25. (Today, that name means nothing to young people, but when I was young, Hutton was a huge name.) Loeb was a partner by the time he was 30—a remarkable feat proving his exceptional ability to sell. E.F. Hutton knew what it was doing by promoting Loeb—he eventually became Hutton's mouthpiece and indeed synonymous with the firm itself. He was good for business. He had the ultimate sympathetic and trustworthy persona (and the fact his favored speculation strategy generated big commissions for the firm didn't hurt either). Remember those later TV ads—"My broker's E.F. Hutton, and he says . . ." That was Loeb they were talking about.

He was a trailblazer in other ways. Loeb was among the first to recommend against diversifying. He was for consolidating with just a few stocks—perhaps just six or so—putting him in good company with my father, Phil Fisher, and Warren Buffett. Though, I must point out, Warren Buffett frequently says one thing and does another and owns many more stocks than that and always did (and in my view is a great man who is most often misunderstood in just these kinds of ways). But concentrated investing today is having a revival.

Loeb was arguably its earliest proponent, two decades before my father was prominent in promoting it.

Loeb rose to prominence as the landscape was radically changing for investors, and he knew how to capitalize on it—he saw a need and filled it. His first printing of this book was pre–Investment Advisors Act of 1940. There were few investment advisors, and those that existed were unregulated. Mutual funds too were scarce. (He advises against them, as did Ben Graham.) Information and advice for investors were devilishly hard, not to mention expensive, to come by. Stockbrokers were the main source of information for investors.

That may seem hard to believe to investors today, who glean information from newsletters, Web sites, cable news, investment advisors, blogs—the sources are endless. Today, most financial columnists are not stockbrokers. Rather, they could be anything: money managers, analysts, economists, or just journalists. But in Loeb's day the broker, though still a salesperson, was also the main conduit for information.

Long before modern portfolio theory, he argued that markets are pretty efficient, although he didn't use that phraseology. Long before passive investing became common or even possible, he argued for why being passive is better than what most folks did. Even then he knew that most professionals don't beat the market. Long before the *Forbes* 400 list, where few people stay in the long term, he showed how hard it was to stay super rich. There is so much more in this book that Loeb describes before more modern methodologies molded today's vernacular; I won't belabor you with it here because you can read it for yourself.

Loeb died in 1974. He started out, as did my father and I, in San Francisco. Born just before the turn of the century to a French wine merchant and an unlucky gold miner's daughter in San Francisco, Loeb was raised poor. His parents went absolutely broke when the 1906 earthquake shattered his father's wine bottles. Loeb looked like an egghead. He had a round, bald head; black-framed glasses; and short, stubby fingers. He was a bachelor until late in life, marrying in 1946 after he was a big success and big name. He had no children. He gave very generously to charity, primarily in New York, which makes sense, but also where it best promoted his name because he was endlessly promotional (which isn't a bad thing in my mind—so am I. Our industry has always acted as if being promotional meant you don't have other skills, which isn't necessarily so.).

Loeb's hobbies were photography, automobiles (which was true of many of his generation), and architecture. I met Loeb only once, in 1972 in San Francisco, two years before he died. He came to visit my father. To me at the time he was an old man, and it was hard for my young self to see the greatness in him. It's pretty common for a young man who hasn't done much yet to be critical of an aging man who has but won't anymore because he's too old—and regrettably that's the way I saw him.

Because he was a native San Franciscan who made it big in New York, he always had a big image in my hometown. And maybe that, too, contributed to my noticing him so prominently when I was young. Once I wrote a cameo biography of Loeb and I wasn't generous with him, and I was wrong. I saw him then as the author of a big book who was otherwise only promotional. He was much more than that. I've been wrong a lot in life. That doesn't bother me. Being wrong is a normal part of life. But I do regret that I didn't then see the greatness in the man. It is because of that lack of vision on my part then that I'm eagerly writing this introduction now.

Loeb lived through incredible times and positively influenced a generation of investors in ways hard for young people today to fathom. Fortunately for him, arriving at Hutton in New York in 1924, he hadn't the experience or base to get blamed for the late 1920s. He became a partner in early 1929, just before the Crash. Nobody—and I repeat, nobody—was made a partner in those days at a major brokerage firm unless they could sell like hell. And Loeb could. But 1929 didn't break his spirit as it broke so many others. Most folks in that position would have washed out. Loeb was not and never would be a washout.

Early on, he learned he could amplify his selling with his writing. The first edition of this book sold over 250,000 copies, which was a whopping phenomenon for its day. There are precious few investment books even today that sell so well. Loeb sold a lot of books himself through direct-mail marketing. But 250,000—that's ten times more than my father's famous book, *Common Stocks and Uncommon Profits,* sold 23 years later. My father's book is more famous today because, since it came out, the world has evolved my father's way and there are more great recent investors who see it as an early influence on them. But it never sold as well. Loeb was nearly infinitely more famous in those days.

Loeb was one of the biggest investing names in America for almost 40 years, which is tough to do. He elevated the role of stockbroker as advice dispenser. He was selling stocks, but he was really selling the industry and the role of the broker to a bruised national psyche. And he was darn good at it.

This book is a good representation of the advice he dispensed: When to buy. When to sell. Know what you're buying. Have a good reason to buy or sell. Pitfalls to avoid. Some of the advice still makes sense. A lot of it doesn't anymore and maybe never did, but that is not the point and you will figure out which is which. When you read new investment books today, you still find lots of contradictions and plenty of nonsense. But Loeb's nonsense is time-tested nonsense, and you will see it for that and appreciate it. Why? Because Loeb almost single-handedly created a new genre—investing books for the Average Joe.

The book is riddled with folksy metaphors, designed to make investing more approachable to small-scale Depression-spooked investors. He instructed new investors to start small because "one must confine one's first efforts at cooking to boiling eggs; one does not begin with Baked Alaska." And he warned against "the new stock with a glamour or romance title and certainly the gratuitous ministrations of the 'boiler room' operator and 'sucker list' mailings." It's good advice, certainly, and expressed in a fun, flamboyant way today's business writers would certainly eschew. But why? If you want someone to follow your advice, you need them to listen to you first.

And listen to him they did. *Forbes* called Gerald Loeb "the most quoted man" on Wall Street, and he might have been. And with good reason—the man knew his audience and knew how to turn a phrase. Journalists loved Loeb for his ability to churn out quippy, easily digested quotes. His advice was made for sound bites. And brokers loved him for elevating their own status—in essence selling brokerage and encouraging high-turnover, high-commission investing.

But the primary reason the book is a must-read for any serious student of capital markets is the almost unique market history perspective it provides without being a history book. It is a classic time-period book that has become timeless. It is as much a time-period book as others classics of its era, such as Napoleon Hill's *Think and Grow Rich*, Dale Carnegie's *How to Win Friends and Influence People*, Robert Rhea's *The Dow Theory*, or John Maynard Keynes's *The General Theory of Employment, Interest and Money*. (By the way, many today criticize Keynes because they don't understand history, but any stock market student who doesn't read every bit of Keynes possible and study his biography is missing out on a lot. Keynes had a lot more Loeb in him than he did Graham or any more modern approach.)

This book gives you easy insight and overview into market history, sociology, and investor mentality in the 1930s, 1940s, and even the 1950s. (Loeb added more essays in later printings.) It comes from the death of 1920s growth stock investing, before modern growth stock investing evolved later with Rowe Price and my father. You must read it as a counterbalance to Graham and Dodd and the advent of value investing.

From this juncture, a variety of codified investing strategies were birthed. Value investors went one way, growth another. Same with momentum and fundamental investors! Later we get more segmentation with small and large cap, passive and active, and on and on. But without Loeb, you cannot understand the crossroads from which all this emerged. And without that, you can't really understand not only Ben Graham or Phil Fisher, but more recently Warren Buffett, Bill Miller, Bill Gross, Peter Lynch, John Bogle, and legions of lesser investors like me.

Markets evolve and are too efficient to make last year's hot discovery this year's silver bullet. But that doesn't change what motivates humanity to get repeatedly brutalized by The Great Humiliator (my name for the market) in the quest for market-like returns. Loeb certainly knew that. So here it is, the world, as it was then, as he saw it and battled for investment survival. Enjoy!

KEN FISHER
Founder and CEO, Fisher Investments
Author, *The Only Three Questions that Count*
and the Wiley Fisher Investment Series
Columnist, *Forbes* Portfolio Strategy

INTRODUCTION

THE PUBLICATION OF THIS UP-TO-DATE AND ENLARGED EDITION of *The Battle for Investment Survival* is due to two factors—the steady demand for the first hardcover edition, which has sold over 200,000 copies, and the highly complimentry comments made by various readers of that edition. The contents of the hardcover book, which was last updated in 1957, are included here, practically without change. Here and there, as in the case of the 1964 tax revision, text changes have been made. Basically, the philosophy of the book has withstood the test of time. Some of the chapters were written in 1935 and checked in 1943 and 1957 and again now in 1965; they are still as valid as when they were written.

This edition, however, contains considerable additional material.

A reader of one of my earlier discussions asked—"Have you ever tried out the ideas outlined in your book?" My reply was to the effect that the ideas were tried out first, and the book written afterward.

An earner who earns more than he can spend is automatically an investor. It doesn't matter in the slightest whether he wants to be or not, or even whether he realizes that he is investing.

Storing present purchasing power for use in the future is investing, no matter in what form it's put away. Some popular and common forms include money itself, government bonds, savings bank deposits, real estate, commodities, securities of all types, diamonds and where and when it's legal, gold.

The real objective of investment is fundamentally to store excess current purchasing power for future use. A man lays brick all day and earns $48. Perhaps in time he saves $48 and invests it for the future. Some day he may want someone else to build a house for him, and he would like to hire a bricklayer at that time to do a day's work for the $48 he saved. That at least is the ideal situation.

In real life, it works a little differently. The value of money fluctuates. In later years, it surely will not cost exactly $48 to hire a
bricklayer for a day. It may cost less, but most likely it will cost
more. Thus, just keeping the $48 will not always do. Since this book
was first written the cost of labor has been constantly rising.

In fact, attempting to offset inflation, the rising cost of living or
the depreciation of the dollar, however it is labeled, has become the
number one investment consideration.

The average individual will pay storage and insurance for putting
away things he wants to keep for the future. But when it comes to
putting away savings he not only does not expect to pay, but also
he wants others to pay him either interest or dividends for the use
of his savings. If he feels as well that there are risks involved of not
getting it all back, then he wants to be paid a profit besides, either
in the form of a higher rate of income or a potential capital gain.
Altogether, of course, he expects too much and aims at too little.

All the above boils down to the necessity of measuring the return
from investments in purchasing power rather than dollars. You must
get back a sufficient number of additional dollars to make up for lost
purchasing power if prices are rising, and a high enough percentage
of your original dollars if prices are falling. I put it this way because
usually there is some profit from investments in times of rising prices
(but rarely enough), and generally there are losses in times of falling
prices, and usually too many.

When I started investing about 1921, it seemed a peaceful enough
occupation. By 1943, I started calling it a "battle," though a lot of
people might have used that term much earlier, during 1929 to 1932.
In 1957 it seemed a "war." The hazards are still increasing.

The person who studies a problem from every angle and defines
the risks, aims, and possibilities correctly before he starts is more
than halfway to his goal.

Believe it or not, some people almost always make money in the
stock market. Admittedly, they are few and far between. It is my
belief that most of those who succeed do so within one of the patterns
described in this book. What success investors eventually have is
governed by their abilities, the stakes they possess, the time they
give to it, the risks they are willing to take, and the market climate

in which they operate. I am certain that, depending upon the degree and the proficiency with which they are applied, the experiences, ideas, guides, formulas, and principles outlined here can do no less than improve the readers' investment results regardless of what they might do.

As we said before, almost everything written in earlier editions for this collection of discussions still is valid. However, I am adding some new ideas which have been tested and found equally valid, and some discussions of the more complex influences that dominate investing today.

Readers of previous editions keep calling attention to what they felt was an inconsistency on the major premise of diversification. There is no inconsistency. Diversification is a necessity for the beginner. On the other hand, the really great fortunes were made by concentration. The greater your experience, the greater your capability for running risks, and the greater your ability to chart your course yourself, the less you need to diversify.

GERALD M. LOEB

Summer, 1965

THE BATTLE FOR
INVESTMENT
SURVIVAL

IT REQUIRES KNOWLEDGE, EXPERIENCE, AND FLAIR

NOTHING IS MORE DIFFICULT, I truly believe, than consistently and fairly profiting in Wall Street. I know of nothing harder to learn. Schools and textbooks supply only a good theoretical background. Individuals, partnerships, and closed corporations have scored great successes for themselves in the handling of money in the stock market, but, as far as I know, none with a record of uniform success is available to the general public.

Into this field the outsider turns for quick and easy profit, or a high income, or a haven of safety. On the average, he gives it less thought than most of his activities, and he is usually careless as to whom he consults or through whom he deals. Frequently he fails to distinguish between results obtained by chance and those secured through knowledge. Often he is "sold" something instead of buying it on his own decision, and often he is the victim of sharp practice.

Knowledge born from actual experience is the answer to why one profits; lack of it is the reason one loses. Knowledge means information and the ability to interpret it marketwise. But, in addition, making money in the market demands a lot of "genius" or "flair." No amount of study or practice can make one successful in the handling of capital if one really is not cut out for it.

The engineering student attends a school and is taught certain rules regarding stresses and strains. In later life these rules always apply. True, there may be several answers to a given problem, and one man may solve it quicker or in a more ingenious way than another, but an answer based on sound principles always holds.

There is no such thing as a final answer to security values. A dozen experts will arrive at 12 different conclusions. It often happens that a few moments later each would alter his verdict if given a chance to reconsider because of a changed condition. Market values are fixed only in part by balance sheets and income statements; much more by the hopes and fears of humanity; by greed, ambition, acts of God, invention, financial stress and strain, weather, discovery, fashion, and numberless other causes impossible to be listed without omission.

Even the price of a stock at a given moment is a potent influence in fixing its subsequent market value. Thus a low figure might frighten holders into selling, deter prospective purchasers, or attract bargainseekers. A high figure has equally varying effects on subsequent quotations.

Where is the institution or individual who can guarantee successful investment? How many can stand on their records? Who can show a worthwhile return over a sufficiently long and varied number of years in a high proportion of investments with purchasing power maintained and reliable liquidating values always growing? There are those who will step forward and claim the distinction, but, as in the case of perpetual motion, something will always be missing.

This, then, is the problem which the "Man on the Street," often far from a success in his own field, thinks he easily can solve. A few minutes in a broker's office, a visit from a bond salesman, a small fee to an "advisory service," and he is buying something, or letting someone sell him something. If he makes a "profit" on his first transaction, he probably thinks himself a smart man or is certain Wall Street is simple. Naturally he wants more. If he loses, he loses so quickly that he is sure he can recover equally fast. He usually knows next to nothing about this broker or dealer or adviser. How long have they been in business? What do their balance sheets look like? What are their records? He has only the sketchiest knowledge, if any at all, of the thousand and one ways they might cause him to lose his money.

Any way one looks at it, nothing is more difficult than succeeding in Wall Street, yet nothing is attempted by such poorly equipped people or is considered as easy.

This being the case, what can we do about it? What is the bright side, if such a gloomy picture has a bright side? What are the virtues of Wall Street? Is the subject worth studying at all?

The principal virtues of Wall Street are its continuous quotations and the comparatively satisfactory liquidity of selected securities. There is no alternative form of investment, such as, for example, real estate, which can give the "Man on the Street" the ease and low cost of purchase and sale, the ready and frequent appraisal, the high liquidity and the protection from fraud possessed by the active security dealt in an auction market.

Therefore, by all means, don't pass up Wall Street; but try to make the best of it; realize its pitfalls; don't expect the impossible.

There are *some* rules that hold, and my first is to buy only something that is quoted daily and can be bought and sold in an auction market daily. The greater the volume of trading and the broader the market in a particular security, the closer to a fair price at a given moment that security is likely to be. Then, too, there is a great value in knowing whether one is making or losing. There is a great value in being able to realize the profit or cut short the loss. There is the greatest protection in all the world in the ability to shift capital quickly and at small cost.

Money has been made in securities that are not regularly quoted. Money has been made in securities that at the start, at any rate, couldn't be resold. But my object is to point out how the greatest risks and pitfalls of the stock market can be eliminated, and, in my opinion, if the average man avoids securities for which there is no ready market, he saves himself from a host of dangers with which he probably cannot cope. It is more difficult for the dealer to charge a false price for an actively quoted security. It is more difficult for him to obtain an abnormal fee or margin of profit. It is more difficult to hide from a client a subsequent loss or at least delay its discovery.

Without in any way minimizing the hazards, I regard the listed markets as the best field for the attempted enhancement or preservation of surplus funds. Therefore, the more one learns about them, the more chance he has to preserve something. It is like anything else in life. Only a few amass fortunes. Only a few become really competent professional men or achieve real success in any line of endeavor. The great majority go about their daily lives performing their daily tasks, including the humblest, in far from an ideal manner.

It remains for each of us to strive to do better, and this applies to investment just as it applies to anything else. The extent to which one realizes one's distance from perfection is the real measure of how successful one may become in Wall Street. It is the realization of the danger that is important: "Fools rush in," and in Wall Street that is fatal.

There is no line of endeavor in the world where real knowledge will pay as rich or as quick a monetary reward as Wall Street.

◆ 2 ◆

SPECULATIVE ATTITUDE ESSENTIAL

PEOPLE EXPECT TOO MUCH OF INVESTMENT. They think, incorrectly, that they must always keep their money "working."

If investment were merely what most people think it is—just buying something for income—fortunes would be extremely easy to establish by simply letting the money compound itself.

Capital compounded at 6% doubles itself in money value in only twelve years, and at 5% in little more than fourteen years. The fantastic results of this process were illustrated by the late Frank A. Vanderlip in a *Saturday Evening Post* story of January, 1933. He pointed out that if the rich Medici family in Italy just six hundred years ago had set aside at 5% compound interest an investment fund equal to $100,000, its 1933 value would be $517,100,000,000,000,000 (five hundred and seventeen quadrillions). The original sum could have been represented by a globe of gold about nine inches in diameter, and the final figure would be 46 million times the existing monetary gold stock of the world.

Investment is far more complicated than just getting money value back with interest or at a profit. When the prices of things one buys are going down, the principal danger of loss is selecting a bad risk or paying too much for it. If we were sure prices would fall, cash itself would become an ideal investment.

But when we fear prices will rise, then the problem becomes not merely increased, but multiplied. Mr. Vanderlip illustrated this point in a dramatic way, too. He showed that if an investor had placed $1,000 in a savings bank in 1900 and had allowed it to accumulate at compound interest, he would have had $2,000 in 1920. However, according to Mr. Vanderlip's calculations, the investor would have had to add from his pocket another $1,000 in order to buy exactly as many goods as he could have purchased during 1900 with the original $1,000 deposit.

That is the greatest threat to successful preservation of capital—the varying purchasing power of money. There are many other threats, such as taxation, regimentation (including rationing), war, new inventions, political changes, and revolutions. The weather and shifts in mass psychology both have very great effect.

No, the hope of the average investor cannot in practice be realized. The preservation of capital should be looked upon as something that normally costs a price. It should not be regarded as merely incidental to a rental or profit.

Indeed, should some super-solvent agency agree to preserve the buying power of capital for a substantial length of time at a stated fee per annum, informed people would embrace the plan enthusiastically if they felt there was any real possibility of the agency staying solvent.

The number of individuals possessed of the necessary flair for combating the obstacles to successful investment and possessed of the necessary drive to cultivate this ability through education, experience, and the right connections is comparable to the proportion similarly successful in other fields requiring a like background. Really top-flight investors are no more frequent, proportionately, than capable Army generals, Navy admirals, doctors, scientists, lawyers, artists, composers, and musicians. Some individuals can invest and speculate sufficiently better than the average to show an overall profit. Many who lose only a portion of their spending power are, in fact, doing better than most.

The purpose of this and subsequent chapters is to help the hard-headed few to make profits, which cannot be done without the acceptance of the foregoing logic as the first step.

A very clear definition of the investor's objective is equally necessary. To achieve success, one must set the investment goal very high. Not only that but the goal must also be a speculative one, for only there lies safety—paradoxical as that many seem. The buyer must not merely seek the repayment at some future time of the dollar capital invested. Nor can he concern himself excessively with income, in whatever form it may be obtained as an incident of ownership while the investment is held.

The program must be aimed at obtaining a sufficient profit to offset the average losses sustained in all investment, the inevitable personal errors of judgment, the effects of currency depreciation and taxation, and the unexpected necessity of having sometimes to close out an investment earlier than originally planned.

Definitions make dry reading, but it is essential that we have a clear conception of the financial terms which are so often loosely used and which are basic to our present subject. In the first place, we are limiting our concern in these discussions to the proper handling of capital in the form of securities or cash.

The problem of preservation of capital is that of storing for future use today's excess spending power, in such a way that it can be reconverted to usable funds at any time without an overall loss.

"Investment" is fundamentally an effort to obtain, in addition, a rental from others for the temporary use of capital.

"Speculation" means using the capital in such a manner that its spending power is not only preserved but also increased, through the realization of profits in the form of dividends, or capital gains or both.

Successful investment is a battle for financial survival.

IS THERE AN IDEAL INVESTMENT?

DISCARDING ALL THEORY I think the average "investor" is looking for a permanent medium to place a given number of dollars where it will return a reasonable income, and the original number of dollars will always be quickly obtainable in case of desire or need. This might be termed the standard or goal of orthodox investing. It is not to be found today, at least as far as I know, because all the possible investment mediums fail in one or more particulars.

Unfortunately, even if such an "ideal" permanent investment medium were to be had, it would fall short in another and most important particular. That other factor is, of course, the ability to get income and principal repaid in units of the same purchasing power as originally invested. There is nothing unreasonable in this desire. Please note, the only demand is to return what is invested plus the rental of profits secured from its use. It is not like buying a "gold clause" bond with a check on a bank and demanding repayment in the actual gold. The layman will usually argue that "a dollar is a dollar," but despite this he will at a later date see the point if the shoe happens to pinch. At least as far as my experience goes, this totally ideal "investment" is as totally non-existent.

It is not hard to see why it should be merely a theoretical formula. Nothing is safe; nothing is sure in any field of life. Specifically the wealth of the world does not increase fast enough to allow payment of compound interest or pyramiding of profits on existing "invested capital." Every so often adjustments are made partly through bankruptcies and other scaling down of obligations and partly through currency depreciation. And it's all as old as the hills.

In my opinion, all this is natural and normal, though I regret the impossible representation of complete safety and security held out by channels dealing in all types of "investments" including not only securities but also to an even greater extent "insurance," "real estate," "savings and loan," etc.

For years the tide has been swinging back and forth, and as the advantage has swung too far towards the debtor class, a cry for "deflation," usually popularly noted in objection to the "high cost of living," has generally grown until something was done about it, and then as the edge went to the creditor, "inflation" or, in other words, general complaint as to commodity prices being too low and money too scarce, dominated the public mind.

Thus it logically follows that in order to attempt even to approximate our definition of what the public really thinks it is getting when it buys a "safe investment," it is necessary to "speculate."

By speculate I mean principally to try to foresee these tides and, from an elementary standpoint, to attempt conservation of purchasing power through purchase or retention of fixed interest and principal obligations (including "cash"—a form of government promise to pay) only during cycles of deflation, and various forms of equity holdings only in cycles of inflation.

Thus it is really necessary at the start to admit and expect that the great majority are not going to be able successfully to invest or speculate, or whatever one calls their handling of their capital, any more than the majority succeed in the first place in securing their proportion of existing wealth or, for that matter, of existing happiness.

Successful preservation of capital must also overcome the increasing handicaps imposed by modern popular and socialistic governments, supposedly to help the masses.

Obviously, our ideas will sound wrong to most people. Any investment policy followed by all naturally defeats itself. Thus the first step for the individual really trying to secure or preserve capital is to detach himself from the crowd.

It is necessary to think in individualistic terms. One has to consider what seems best for one's own preservation. The masses always have, individually, an average of next to nothing per capita, contrasted to the minority of successful individuals. Thus they are always trying to wrest away the possessions of the few for what they believe their own advantage. It is surprising how much they can appropriate without much resistance. But after a while the industrious and the thrifty finally are worn down, and they begin to turn for protection to imagined "antisocial" devices.

In the history of the world we find the record of savings really saved through buying gold, hoarding precious stones, and other forms of "hard wealth" privately secreted. In the future history of America most of us will, in my opinion, learn this lesson too late. Currently this is a personal matter for each individual to decide and execute for himself without consultation.

Curiously, it is those of slight wealth who need this sort of protection rather than those of great means, who can really suffer large depreciation without really feeling the loss. And it is usually the latter who are best fitted to cope with the problem.

As to capital not so hoarded or employed in regular business channels but available for "investment" in the popular sense, the outstanding requirement is the specialized understanding that will discern trends correctly and analyze values essential to the constant shifting of funds necessary to success.

If not able to do this, one must have at least the insight to select honest and capable expert guidance. Such guidance is rare, but it can be found. Yet, rare as it is, even fewer have the psychological ability to recognize it or the confidence to follow it through.

◆ 4 ◆

PITFALLS FOR THE INEXPERIENCED

BEFORE anyone starts to dispute the suggestions to be enlarged on here let us understand that this is directed at the average inexperienced investor or speculator. One must confine one's first efforts at cooking to boiling eggs; one does not begin with Baked Alaska, no matter how fine a dessert the latter may be when properly prepared. Likewise, variously experienced occasional readers of these discussions will recall profits made in types of security ventures outside our field of the active, listed market. There are many ways of making money which we are temporarily eliminating.

Personally, I feel that, first, one must learn by experience the basic principles of successful dealing in securities through trading in active listed leaders, and particularly one must acquire the ability to control personal emotions or fear of loss, or greed for a larger profit, etc., which affect most people's decisions and are very costly. Later, one can desert the chosen field I prescribe (if one must—most will stay in it exclusively) and specialize in some other branch. The idea, however, that an average individual can dabble successfully in a variety of bank and insurance stocks, new issues, obscure counter securities and all the other fashions that come and go, is, of course, too absurd. Yet most people try it about in proportion to their lack of expertness. The less expert, the wider their activities.

The first thing, therefore, for the average venturer into Wall Street to decide is that it is a step in the right direction to restrict purchases and sales to liquid, listed securities.

For one thing, the cost of buying and selling is reduced. This is a big item and consists not only in the spread between the "bid" for a stock and the "offer" but also commission. On brokerage orders, which are the kind that this policy practically dictates, the commissions are visible, fixed and small. The spread between the "bid" and "offer" varies with the liquidity of securities, but is very close in the really active, listed issues.

The cost of buying some new stock issues at net figures is invariably much higher than the brokerage and spread on old ones, and in many cases is exorbitant. The new publicity given by the SEC to this sort of thing frequently reveals some amazing "underwriting" or "distributing" fees. Unless the dealers have been able to secure a property from its original owners at a bargain, the security in order to show the retail buyer a profit, must first cover the inflated offering cost.

There is another source of potential loss and occasionally of potential profit in new offerings, and that is the failure to price the issue right. Here, again, I think the occasional underpricing one runs into is so rare, and when it does occur allotments are so small, that it is best for most to avoid this field altogether. The host of untried ventures, of overpriced issues, of fraudulent promotions that will be automatically cast aside by such a policy of avoidance will repay many times over the few good things one might be allowed to buy in small amounts.

In a way, so-called secondary distributions, special offerings, etc., are also difficult for the inexperienced as compared to liquid active listed issues bought on a commission basis. Secondary distributions are sales made off the exchanges on a net basis by a sales staff working against a block of bonds or stock on an owned outright or "best efforts" basis. Usually, the stock exchange price is used as a basis for confirming the net trade. Occasionally, registration is involved. The stock exchange price can be "stabilized" where SEC permission is granted to facilitate the distribution. This may seem a little technical for the layman, which is exactly the reason why he should be informed about it, or confine his operations to the listed, active leaders which are not ordinarily subject to distribution.

A third way of distributing securities is to place over-the-counter issues at net prices which consist of an "asked" price, plus a commission, all lumped into one.

It must be self-evident that the costs of doing business in this manner and the lack of knowing just what is going on are something to be avoided by the average person. But there is another angle, and that is the almost universal tendency to sell people what the dealer has under option, or can get at a concession, or what is actually owned for his own account, rather than to sell something that fits the client's need. In other words, it is better to buy things than have them sold to you (though, unfortunately, nearly everything is sold to the consumer), and better to deal with someone who is unbiased if you are going to depend on his advice. The Buick salesman is not going to tell you a Chevrolet will fit your needs just as well at a lower figure, and neither is a dealer with a "profit" in one security going to suggest the purchase of some other in which he makes nothing or at best a minor commission.

A very important advantage of the liquid, quoted security is the ability to follow its progress daily. Nothing is a quicker indicator of trouble than special and unusual weakness, and in many over-the-counter issues, or even in the quiet listed ones, trouble will not be discovered until it is too late. In the latter cases, quotes may be at hand in papers or only "offers" given, but, in any event, no running record of sales and sales volume is available to give one a chance to realize something is wrong.

Under our present system dealers and their salesmen will continue to do a big business. Part of their clientele, especially those interested in bonds, will be institutions whose representatives are professionals and can meet them on equal terms and in a legitimate way. Part will be those who have had early success in the handling of funds and have graduated to a broader field. Part will be shrewd professionals or well-posted capitalists who can pick and choose and get real bargains before the price of popularity is added. This, however, is another source of occasional profit I advise leaving to the professional risk-taker.

In every line of modern endeavor the value of specialization is apparent. This holds just as true in the handling of capital. Those who will select and master one medium are far better off than those who must dabble in realty, foreign exchange, commodities, obscure unlisted stocks, foreign bonds, etc.

Cutting out everything except active, seasoned issues, listed on a major stock exchange, obviates hosts of pitfalls.

I know that some will ask how a small and new industry can be financed if everyone follows such a policy? What will happen to the small dealers all over the country, and their staffs? My answer is nothing at all, for the reason that only an infinitesimal following will be won exclusively to the active, listed leaders.

Those who are successful in the listed leaders thereby will learn the general principles of successful investment. Many subsequently will turn to specialize in a sideline. For example, one might study convertible bonds, and really know what he is about. There will always be institutions with staffs equipped to survey new projects and supply capital at a proper cost where success seems reasonable.

Our concern is simply to point out means for the preservation of capital. Only a few will follow these thoughts, and even fewer will succeed with them in practice. If enough were to turn to a policy of "leaders only," that of itself would bring its own correction. The favored stocks might advance beyond all reason and thus check the movement. The less-favored issues might decline or fail to advance and thus create a spread that would send bargain hunters buying. The demand for "leaders" might cause an increase in the supply through mergers, etc. There is no need for anyone to get disturbed over some of the principles laid down in this collection of articles. Therefore, regardless of others, our first rule is to concentrate in active, listed issues.

Above all, avoid the promoter, the "penny share," the new stock with a glamour or romance title and certainly the gratuitous ministrations of the "boiler room" operator and "sucker list" mailings.

HOW TO INVEST FOR CAPITAL APPRECIATION

HAVING DECIDED to invest only in the more active, listed issues for the start at least, the next point is to learn to "invest for appreciation." Every purchase must be considered almost solely on the basis of what it will return in income and appreciation added together and treated as one. Looked at in this light, a thousand dollars invested in a stock with an assured dividend of say $50 a year on the purchase price but not likely to advance more than a point or two in the coming 12 months suggests an expected profit-return of $60 or $70, whereas another issue paying no dividend but likely to double in price would promise a profit-return of $1,000.

It is absolutely futile to try to get results except by buying into anticipated large gains. It is far better to let cash lie idle than to buy just to "keep invested" or for "income." In fact, it is really vital, and just this one point, in my opinion, represents one of the widest differences between the successful professional and the loss-taking amateur. One often is kept out of a dangerous market by this rule. Obviously, the possibilities of decline must also be carefully weighed and the largest positions taken when it seems as if the odds are in one's favor. Actual income needed for living expenses need cause no problem as withdrawals at predetermined percentages can safely be made against one's purchases. At times it may happen that enough "income" exists to cover one's needs. At other times the debit will be against realized or unrealized appreciation. Occasionally it will be against capital. Even so, in my view it is usually much safer than buying for "income."

The only way to begin is to learn by doing. Here lies the greatest handicap of most investors. They have had no experience. And, unfortunately, most of them go for advice to others who either have had no experience or have had enough to induce them to leave markets alone and concentrate on brokerage or advisory or statistical work.

Experience, as I see it, means every sort in every kind of market. Hence the purchase of one issue and its successful or unsuccessful retention over a period of years proves nothing. Years ago, in wondering how one could gain such invaluable market knowledge and yet not pay a prohibitive cost in tuition, I thought of the plan of learning by always maintaining a position not in excess of a hundred shares of an average-priced stock, yet always striving to be long or short the most suitable issue of the moment. This plan takes a minimum of capital. It also results in a minimum of risk, as the beginner is forced to close one commitment before he opens the next. Ordinarily, new investors buy one stock after another, and should the market go down, they lose on the whole position before they realize their inexperience. A purchaser of a single stock under this plan is forced to a decision whether to keep it, take a loss or a profit, or exchange it for another. It is quite different, and many times more valuable in teaching market technique, than the imaginary "paper transactions" in which many tyros indulge. The latter are completely lacking in testing the investors' psychological reactions stemming from such important factors as fear of loss, or greed for more gain. This method also teaches that if there is no one outstanding purchase or sale at the moment, one should strive to be out of the picture entirely.

This means frequent swapping, and I guarantee that in no time at all most people who think these discussions too pessimistic as to the difficulties involved will change their minds. Furthermore, this method tends to stress and teach the paramount importance of timing. It is not enough to buy something cheap if it stays cheap. One must buy it just as it starts to get dearer. One must decide between 100 shares of an average-priced issue, or 50 of a high-priced one, or 200 of a low-priced, or 10 of 10 different issues. In each and every case the advantages and disadvantages will become very clear in a reasonably short time, where no amount of reading would be a satisfactory substitute for experience.

All this, of course, means that one must devote some time every day to the subject of investment. Nothing is more logical, yet nothing more surprising to most people. They must devote months to earn a net savable profit, after living and running expenses and taxes, and then in a few moments often toss a large part of it to the winds because they look on investing very much as buying seats for a theater. One *must* devote time to investment, and, in doing so, one's surplus savings become, instead of a doubtful asset for the future, in many cases a more powerful factor in increasing one's wealth than the original way of gaining one's living.

This initial experience fund should be quite small, preferably not over 10 percent of one's assets; $5,000 is a useful amount, and in no event need it exceed that figure. This period of learning by trial and error is obviously going to take time. In the meanwhile, it is going to take some self-control to let the balance of one's funds lie idle. It may even prove costly if we happen to be in a period of rapidly depreciating purchasing power for money. But it is not as apt to prove so costly as experimenting with one's total funds. A 10 percent ratio would seem to limit or exclude a large number of readers. This will not prove to be the case in practice, because there always will be some venturesome people who will take the risks that are necessary to achieve greater success. Probably in most cases they will feel that at least they have had a chance, which should give them a good deal of satisfaction.

There is the question also whether many of the readers of these memos are going to find the time to trade at all. Naturally it is going to take time daily from one's business. However, as pointed out before, in many cases one will earn far more with the time applied to keeping what he has made or increasing it than by 100 percent devotion to his regular occupation. In any event, if a person is sure he cannot take the time or "interfere" with his regular pursuits (if conserving one's surplus is "interfering"), then he must delegate the whole thing rather than dabble at it. A reading of these chapters should be helpful in making up one's mind whether to handle one's own affairs or turn them over to a professional, and if the latter, what to look for in a professional adviser. Another point is that, after experimenting with trading, many may convince themselves that they are not cut out for it and that they are better off devoting all their time to their own particular business. I think a great deal has been gained if one determines that once and for all, because, in my view, one should devote either a generous amount of time, or no time at all. Halfway measures are impossible.

All this suggests the question—are we learning to trade for the quick turn or to invest for the long pull? We are investing for appreciation, and the length of time one holds a position has nothing to do with it. I lean towards rather short turns for many reasons, unless tax considerations rule it out. To begin with, experience is gained much more rapidly that way.

Short-term investing once mastered has very much more the elements of dependable business than the windfalls or calamities of the long pull. One simply can't continue to buy and sell successfully without being "good." Without a succession of varying trades one can never be sure of one's ability and consequent safety. There is much more peace of mind in frequent turns. One can take a fresh view often. Long worrying declines, without apparent reason until near the bottom, are avoided. There are many other advantages. The majority, perhaps, claim that there is much more peace of mind in the long pull but if my observation of thousands of accounts since 1921 means anything, this is a popular fallacy.

By "short-term," however, I do not mean to imply one must close a trade quickly just because one is thinking of the short term. Trades should never be closed unless a good reason is at hand. But many "long-pull" traders ignore a sign of a change of trend because they feel it is temporary. Often they are right but eventually they are wrong, and usually at great cost. The short-term method requires the closing of the trade for a reason, and if later the situation changes, then one can re-establish the position. It sometimes can be done at a profit, and sometimes only at a loss in which case one has in effect paid for insurance.

Once in a while the long-pull buyer stumbles on some good thing and imagines himself a great speculator. More often than not he later gets a rude awakening, though occasionally he is fortunate enough to retain what he has.

However, the long-pull position has its uses, and in these days taxes often compel it. However, opening the trade must be done on what I might term short-turn principles. There is nothing I am going to write here that applies exclusively to any policy. Some of the best long-pull buys grew out of a continuing series of bullish short-term indications. Some of the really vital last-chance selling points first look like minor temporary tops.

◆ 6 ◆

SPECULATION VERSUS INVESTMENT

How MUCH RETURN can one make in the stock market? Trying to get a stated "income" from dividends, interest or both of 3 percent, 4 percent or 5 percent, or whatever it is, really amuses me because of the simplicity of the point of view displayed. Yet it is, by all odds, the more or less general point of view adopted by the majority—customer and customer's man, bond buyer and salesman, almost anyone in and out of the business.

There is no doubt that the average individual, seeing this point of view accepted without question, moves with the masses and adds his acceptance to the rest. Actually here, as in many other phases of life, the majority is decidedly wrong. In fact, the individual who does his own thinking must learn to question most mass movements of majority point of view, for they are usually wrong.

It is for these reasons, and especially because I am personally completely convinced of the inevitability of loss when attempting to secure a safe income of small return, that I constantly suggest speculation rather than investment as the policy less apt to show a loss and more apt to show a profit.

My feeling is that an *intelligent* program aimed at doubling one's money might at least succeed in retaining one's capital or actually making a good profit with it.

Any aim less than this is doomed to failure.

Of course, a lot depends on how much capital one is seeking to double. It is naturally easier to handle reasonable sums of money than great accumulations of capital. This discussion is not directed at possessors of the latter. As to the former, if one is lucky enough to possess a sum that is unwieldy because of large size, the important thing to do is to employ only that portion of one's capital that one does feel he can "double." It is better to leave the rest sterile than to risk it pointlessly until one feels one is competent enough to increase one's investment in the market.

As an example, I should think most people not trained to Wall Street, but having professional practice or a liberal salary plus several hundred thousand dollars capital, are hardly justified in employing more than $100,000 in the market in an average sort of year. Why risk the rest? If you can make $25,000 to $50,000 in a year in the process of attempting to double $100,000, that is more than enough from any point of view. If one loses, then surely it is better to lose on part of one's capital than on all. If you try to get 6 percent on your several hundred thousand or on that part not employed in speculation, you almost surely will lose, sooner or later.

The amounts cited are merely to lend concreteness to an example. The actual amount is really a personal matter, and the thought here is to stimulate consideration along these lines rather than to lay down a limit of $100,000 as a speculative fund. Some people can safely handle far more. Some people are happy only if they handle more. Others are worried by, or are incompetent to handle, as much as $100,000.

Those that haven't even the $100,000 to start with are in the majority, and here, especially, I advise laying plans to double your money. You can be far from achieving your goal and still make a great deal, but if you start to get a mere income, the slightest miscalculation puts you in the red.

Many of you might worry about the risk inflation can bring to the unused part of your capital. The risk is real. It is undoubtedly less than the risks of market speculation until such time as you really know what you are about.

It may seem strange at the same time to write about losing funds one is trying to save and making 25 percent to 50 percent on funds one is trying to double. Actually a little reflection will show it is not so illogical as it sounds. How many have direct knowledge of individuals who were consistent money-makers while they were actively after profits, but who lost all or a large part of what they had when they decided they had enough?

In a sense there is no direct comparison. Trying to invest for 6 percent is like trying to retire. You are the "absentee" creditor or part owner as the case might be. You sit back and stop thinking, letting the money work by itself. Trying to double your money requires your active presence and a lot of work.

SOUND ACCOUNTING FOR INVESTORS

PERHAPS THE PRIMARY CONSIDERATION in seeking to preserve the purchasing power of that portion of one's capital allotted to securities is to clear up once and for all what I regard as the popular fallacies referring to "income."

In my opinion, the only sound plan is periodically to value the account at the "market" (which would of course automatically include any interest coupons or dividends, etc., collected since the last valuation as well as a reserve for taxes) and pay out to oneself either a predetermined regular fixed percentage, such as $1\frac{1}{2}$ percent of the equity in the account quarterly, or a varying amount dictated by personal requirements. Taking the suggested figure of $1\frac{1}{2}$ percent per quarter as an average standard, this sum probably at times would be covered by the actual "income" of the account, and at other times this rate would not be reached. However, to me this is not even worth bothering to determine. What one does want to watch is whether the periodical valuation of the account shows a gain in excess of this percentage. This gain might occur in several ways. For instance, the account might be fully invested at 6 percent and the capital values remain unchanged. Or the investment "income" might run 3 percent plus a gain of 3 percent on an annual basis in capital values. Or there might be wholly non-dividend-paying securities which have advanced on an annual basis of 6 percent in market quotation.

However, whether it's a gain or loss or unchanged, I see no reason why the 6 percent annual ($1\frac{1}{2}$ percent a quarter) rate on the equity should not logically be paid out. It works in a sort of automatic way to increase the amount paid out as the account prospers and decrease it at other times. Thus, on a $100,000 equity the payment would be of course $6,000. If a year later the equity was $150,000, the payment at that time would rise to $9,000, or if the equity had decreased to $50,000, the payment would run only $3,000. The amount paid out simply would be debited against the account, decreasing the cash, or, in some cases, secured by the sale of a portion of capital assets and rarely by increasing a margin debt.

The advantages of this plan are many. To begin with there is the elimination of the self-deception involved in the old "income" idea. A man buys a 6 percent bond at par. A year later it is selling, for purposes of this example, at 70. He has received his 6 percent income, but actually the transaction stands as funds invested, $1,000; interest received, $60; market value of principal, only $700; net loss, $240. Against this compare simply holding $1,000 if a safe 6 percent investment does not seem available at the time, and paying out of principal $60, leaving $940 cash at the end of a year, or a net loss of only $60. Or compare buying into some attractive speculative situation yielding nothing but advancing say 50 percent in a year. The latter would work out as $1,500 market value at the end of the year less $90 paid out in lieu of "income," leaving a net remainder of $1,410.

Naturally I realize the speculation may have turned out a loss instead of profit. But we have to assume that the account is going to be run intelligently. I don't think any account can in truth be run properly if income is a prime requisite. Running it in the manner suggested here eliminates artificial handicaps and, as will be seen later, opens the path to at least immeasurably greater average chances of success. Incidentally, the method of periodical market valuation here advised is essential to the proper handling of trust accounts, etc. If a trustee keeps securities on a "cost" basis, the tendency is to avoid taking losses where inevitable mistakes occur. But if everything is kept marked to "market," the beneficiary is constantly informed of the true picture and the trustee is not so hesitant to make switches. Accounting of individual investors must be sound in considering results achieved, and I advocate simply figuring the changes in the equity from month to month and setting up round-figures reserves right along against approximate taxes due if the account were liquidated at the valuation figures. This tends to prevent overtrading; it prevents over-estimates of profits; it prevents hesitation about the sale of any issue because of taxes and has many other advantages.

In addition, a running tax reserve on both realized and unrealized profits and losses also has to be kept, and the chief value of this is in figuring tax switches towards the end of the year. This also brings out the smaller net profits after taxes that succeeding trades can net as the realized profits for a given year begin to run up into high tax brackets. As every trade should be considered on the basis of how much one expects to gain against how much one is willing to risk, this is vital information. Thus one would logically take larger positions and higher risks while in the low brackets than after one reaches the higher tax levels.

◆ 8 ◆

WHY COMMITMENTS SHOULD NOT
BE HAPHAZARD

In ACTUALLY ENTERING the security markets it seems fundamental that one should know why a commitment was opened, what one expected to make, how long it was expected to take, and what one was willing to risk. Personally, I cannot see how one can expect to figure the proper size of a position or the time to close it out unless it was first opened with a full understanding of these points.

In my opinion, commitments should not be closed haphazardly or, even worse, allowed to remain open without justification. For example, one might be convinced that a quick move was in prospect for a particular leader. This being the case, the stock is bought for a quick move, and if the move fails to develop in the anticipated direction quickly, the stock should be sold. When it was bought, no thought was given to its value other than as a medium for a quick trade; hence, it should not be held later as an "involuntary investment." On the other hand, one might buy into a situation expecting an increase in the dividend in say two months. In my opinion, trading weakness in such a stock does not call for liquidation unless one is convinced that either the anticipated dividend increase will not occur or that a generally changed speculative picture will alter one's appraisal of what the higher dividend might mean marketwise.

In considering a commitment a clear idea should be had of the levels at which one expects to close it out either at a profit or at a loss. Obviously, if one anticipates making only a very small amount, one's chances of being successful are rather small. Also it is really impracticable to risk less than a point or two which, with commissions and tax, is rather high to set against an expected point or two gain. Obviously one's judgment has to be nearly 100 percent perfect under such conditions. But if it is a trade on which one figures to risk say three points to make a theoretical 30, then one can obviously be very over-optimistic and still do well. Readers are thinking that that kind of trade rarely exists. The fact is it rarely does, which is a good reason for seeking it out and not overdoing things in the interim.

I suggest that at the start the size of commitments in one sense be kept small—that is, the relationship of funds employed to total capital. One should strive for a long profit on a small commitment; in other words, there is much more logic in trying for ten points profit on 100 shares of a particular stock than for one point on 1,000 shares of the same stock. A backlog of cash is a great help in meeting emergencies and in freeing one's judgment so that commitments are opened and closed for financial cause and not affected by need, fear, greed, or other human failings which are fatal to profitable security investment. Of course, the possibility of a "margin call" should never even remotely develop in a well-run account.

Except in special circumstances, such as where young people with insufficient capital feel they are capable of trying to move ahead quickly, I do not and never could see much necessity for margins or other forms of borrowing. If one's security investments are managed efficiently, small relative percentage investments will bring large returns, and the necessity for over-speculation with its many handicaps will not occur. On the other hand, if inefficient trading requires heavy investments for results, eventual losses will wipe out early gains. I am naturally aware of what I previously have written elsewhere about the occasional advantages of borrowing during inflation, etc., but in both cases I am thinking relatively. Thus a given situation might at times call for borrowing, but I feel rather sure that I would always counsel a good deal smaller debit than the popular margin percentages at the time.

In another sense, large commitments, meaning thereby a few relatively large blocks of shares, are preferable to a great many small positions. These few large holdings may total only 30 percent of funds available at the moment, in line with the previous paragraph. However, confining oneself to situations convincing enough to be entered on a relatively large scale is a great help to safety and profit. One must know far more about it to enter the position in the first place, and one will retreat from a mistake much quicker if failure to retreat means an important loss. A large number of small holdings will be purchased with less care and ordinarily allowed to run into a variety of small losses without full realization of the eventual total sum lost. Thus over-diversification acts as a poor protection against lack of knowledge.

9

SOME "DON'TS" IN SECURITY PROGRAMS

READERS SHOULD NOT EXPECT to obtain here an infallible formula for the preservation of capital in spite of the obstacles cited in previous chapters—the changing purchasing power of money, politics, war, public sentiment, and the vicissitudes of individual securities. The contention that investment is a battle for financial survival would disprove itself if the difficulties could be explained away so easily.

The object of these discussions is to influence the investment thinking of readers in the direction of improving the results they may expect to attain. This is an attainable and worthwhile aim.

We have already sketched the fundamental necessity of having a thorough understanding of the difficulties and of keeping the objectives clearly in mind.

The basic practical working policy is never to invest unless the possibilities of the chosen stock seem very great. Investing solely for "income," investing merely "to keep capital employed," and investing simply "to hedge against inflation" are all entirely out of the question.

No security of any kind should under any circumstances be bought or retained, under this policy, unless in the investor's well and deeply considered judgment the profit possibilities are large and greatly outweigh the visible risks. And the latter must be counted with detailed care.

When an investment is made, its prospects must be so good that placing a rather large proportion of one's total funds in such a single situation will not seem excessively risky. At the same time, the potential gain must be so large that only a moderate portion of total capital need be invested to get the desired percentage appreciation on total funds.

Expressing the matter in a different way, this means that once you attain competency, diversification is undesirable. One or two, or at most three or four, securities should be bought. And they should be so well selected, their purchase so expertly timed and their profit possibilities so large that it will never be necessary to risk in any of them a large proportion of available capital.

Under this policy, only the best is bought at the best possible time. Risks are reduced in two ways—first, by the care used in selection, and second, by the maintenance of a large cash reserve. Concentration of investments in a minimum of stocks insures that enough time will be given to the choice of each so that every important detail about them will be known.

This policy involves not only avoiding diversification but also at times holding one's capital uninvested for long periods of time. The bargains which must be sought to raise investment performance out of the average class, in which net losses occur, into the exclusive class of those who make and keep profits are not available except occasionally. It should be recognized also that such opportunities will inevitably be available principally when the majority of buyers of securities refuses, because of fear, to take advantage of low prices. Just as inevitably, the opportunities will not be available when securities are generally popular and eagerly bought. It should be axiomatic that the successful investor will keep his capital idle in times of popular over-investment and over-confidence. He will be sorely tried at times when profits and income are seemingly easy to procure.

Any program which involves complete investment of all capital at all times is not apt to be the most successful one. It should always pay in both dollars and cents and peace of mind not to be overcommitted. Unpredictable news developments can change the complexion of things without warning.

It is true that cash has lost purchasing power in this country but fortunately in our lifetime at a very slow rate compared to the rapid depreciation that can be suffered in a real stock market decline.

Buying on margin does not come into this discussion at all, as it is mainly the concern of traders in the strictest sense of that term.

Another concept essential to success in the battle for investment survival is that the investor must learn to think in terms of ultimate rather than current results. It is impossible to obtain 100 percent of the theoretical gain in each major movement of an individual stock or of stocks as a group. Efforts to do so, inevitably lead to failure of the entire investment program. It is a real achievement if through judicious investment at intermittent times a satisfactory average profit over good years and bad is actually gained.

This whole thesis, which may at first sight seem extremely speculative, will in actual practice prove many times more conservative and safer than the policy followed by most investors.

10

WHAT TO LOOK FOR IN
CORPORATE REPORTS

IT HAS ALWAYS seemed to me that if one is to draw profitable conclusions from the published reports of most listed corporations, rather special points of view are a requisite. A real specialist in a particular industry will, of course, see and apply accounting tests which make themselves evident as the examination proceeds, due to his specialized knowledge, that will usually be quite revealing. If he wisely collaborates with a market specialist, a gainful decision will be the result.

However, most lay investors and the usual sources of counsel are rarely so well-informed. This situation, plus the ordinary public habit of accepting headlines as accurate condensed summaries of corporate results, makes for a widespread lack of knowledge concerning actual corporate positions. More often than not, majority bids and offers persist for years at levels that are wide of what would be paid or sold were the figures understood.

As a simple workable plan of getting a closer appraisal of real results (from this one angle—other influences may seem together of greater weight marketwise and cancel out the bearish accounting impression), I particularly scrutinize companies that cannot show enough cash income to care for plant growth, needed expansion in working capital, dividends, etc., without resort to continual new financing. There are a few exceptions, practically always in the very young and rapidly growing concerns—hardly ever, in my opinion, in the large mature businesses. Such situations imply an unprofitable field, poor management, or unwise overdevelopment.

I think a great many corporations have been kept going only by a combination of the leverage created by heavy borrowing or preferred-stock issues and the constant refunding and injection of fresh capital. Assets are acquired and capitalized with other peoples' money, and to what extent or for how long they will continue to be earning assets is a moot question. Surely no ordinary investor or statistician can decide.

Next, I feel statements of inventory companies should be regarded with caution. I refer to companies which handle large quantities of goods that fluctuate sharply in price. Many such concerns go through all the motions of being in business, advertising, maintaining sales staffs, and all the rest, and never really make an actual trading or manufacturing profit. They make when prices go up and lose when they go down. It would work for a reduction of overhead simply to close up and speculate frankly in their particular commodity. Marketwise, for trading periods, shares of inventory companies might be temporarily most attractive. My point is to know why and what you are buying. There are, however, a few corporations in which inventories play a big part that do keep books conservatively.

High profit margins are frequently an invitation to increased competition, unless the situation is monopolistic for one reason or another. Low fixed assets, especially if combined with ability to do profitable business on small working capital, may be regarded similarly. Asking stockholders to authorize writing down of fixed assets is a sign of injudicious previous expansion. It is usually a black mark against a company. However, here and there legitimate mistakes are made and writedowns are logical. And, of course, marketwise it usually pays to consider trading purchases if such news is expected. Just be sure not to hold so long that recovery breeds further unwise expenditure.

What I look for is a company that regardless of reported profits is somewhere getting enough cash income to take care of the factors mentioned previously, i. e., to amortize debt, increase working capital, maintain or, if profitable, enlarge plant capacity and efficiency, and pay dividends. They exist, and in no small number, as a study of comparative balance sheets will show. I would seek actual trading or manufacturing profits, though in some cases realized inventory gains mean something when they are more than luck and go hand in hand with the ordinary business results.

As I see it, the tendency in this country has been to overreach for new business, and usually at the wrong time. If addition to fixed assets can be made during a depression at bargain levels, it might be a good business risk. However, to expand during a boom is fatal unless the anticipated profits after taxes will amortize the extra capacity in the very briefest time, preferably to the normal average old plant valuation. As an example, a factory producing a million units, valued on the average at a million dollars, with "normal" profits of $100,000 a year, adds capacity for another half-million unit production. Boom times make this addition cost a whole million, or twice average valuation. As I see it, the wrong way is to build the addition and then also to mark up the value of old buildings in the property account to reproduction cost. Right way, build only if the boom permits a profit the first year—net after taxes in addition to "normal" profit—sufficient to write off the extra boom-time cost of $500,000 of the new addition. The latter might have to be shut down a few years later.

The rising cost of facilities with obsolescence limited by the tax laws to a percentage of the original cost may result in a large overstatement of earning power and a shortage of cash in what on the surface appear to be prosperous enterprises. A few conservative, far-seeing managements as a result set up additional depreciation reserves on which tax is paid. This is the exception rather than the rule but should be considered by the investor as part of his own analysis.

"Cash flow," which is the professional term for in-pocket—out-of-pocket bookkeeping is one revealing way of looking at things.

In this connection, an increasing number of companies are including tables in their annual reports showing the source and disposition of all funds received and disbursed during the year. Among such companies are giants like Standard Oil of New Jersey, Gulf Oil Corporation, International Paper, and Sinclair Oil, to mention a few.

International Paper calls its summary "Consolidated Summary of Financial Operations—Detail of Decrease in Net Working Capital." Gulf Oil labels its tabulation as "Employment of Funds." Perhaps the most illuminating of all is that supplied by Standard Oil of New Jersey which is given as a six-year summary of changes in consolidated working capital.

We are reproducing, on this page and the next, two years of the six-year summary for Jersey to illustrate its great value. We will also reproduce the Sinclair table for 1963 as another good example.

The figures of both companies are presented in an exemplary manner in every particular. However, where there is a tendency to obscure or confuse the situation a complete "source and disposition of funds" table simplifies the efforts of the investor to get at the bottom of things. Unfortunately, it is just the company that is trying to create a misleading impression that is certain to leave these figures out of its shareowner reports.

The listing agreements between the New York Stock Exchange and the companies whose shares are granted trading privileges might very well be expanded to cover this point. The same might be said of Securities and Exchange Commission requirements.

STANDARD OIL OF NEW JERSEY
Two-Year Summary of Changes in Consolidated Working Capital

	(Millions of dollars)	
	1963	1962
ADDITIONS		
Net income accruing to Jersey shareholders.....	$1,019	$841
Net income accruing to minority interests.......	47	39
Depreciations, depletion, and retirements.......	584	586
Sales of properties and equipment..............	74	36
Nonrecurring gain on Ethyl investment.........		75
Total additions	$1,724	$1,577
DEDUCTIONS		
Additions to properties and equipment.........	$886	$1,062
Cash dividends to Jersey shareholders	592	538
Cash dividends to minority interests	31	26
Net change in long-term debt..................	15	(13)
Cost of shares reacquired, less proceeds from shares sold...................................	35	(4)
Other—net	69	(3)
Total deductions	$1,628	$1,606
Net increase or (decrease) in working capital....	$96	$(29)

Sinclair Oil — 1963

	(Millions of dollars)
SOURCES OF FUNDS	
Consolidated net income	$178.1
Sale of 4.60% debentures......................	136.9
Disposal of Texas Pacific Coal & Oil stock	76.3
Sale of Capital Assets	8.1
	$399.4
DISPOSITION OF FUNDS	
Capital additions..............................	$149.2
Dividends	29.8
Long-term debt (due after one year)............	46.2
Purchase of Corporation's own stock	1.9
Reduction in carved-out oil payments...........	14.4
U.S. Government and other short term securities	89.6
Other miscellaneous net.......................	5.5
	$336.6
Increase in working capital	62.8
	$399.4

◆ 11 ◆

CONCERNING FINANCIAL INFORMATION, GOOD AND BAD

THE AVERAGE SECURITY BUYER usually decides on a stock commitment because of an impressive analysis of a situation, or as a result of noting a certain convincing price action or because of some form of "information."

There are very few, however, who can discriminate between sources of valuable and sources of misleading information. Purveyors of the latter may be stupid or may have an axe to grind. If the information itself is correct, the vital and difficult market significance is generally not understood. In fact, the latter situation is so nearly universally true, that the wider spread of information fostered by the Securities & Exchange Commission and the New York Stock Exchange will not in most cases make anything more than the most minute difference in attempting to curb supposed advantages of "insiders" and put them on a more nearly equal footing with security buyers and sellers at large. Actually, as I look back upon it, most insiders never knew enough really to profit from their "advance" news unless it was something completely outstanding. Likewise, investors, when they occasionally uncovered something accurate and important, rarely sensed what to do about it marketwise. It always was and always will be the power to understand and the ability to act that turns information into profits.

Incidentally, the Interstate Commerce Commission has required publication of voluminous data on railroads which has not resulted in saving the public generally, much, if any, money. Thus, while getting honest, unbiased information is naturally essential, it is useless without either personal interpretative ability or access to one who has this faculty. For example, I have known directors of a company to vote in secret a surprise dividend and to hold completely divergent opinions as to the ensuing market reception of their action.

Much has been done to curb dishonest information. The findings of the special study of the security markets made by the Securities & Exchange Commission in 1964 may furnish the layman with some cautionary thoughts in certain directions. However, it is in several volumes and requires concentrated reading. Despite all this, it will always be difficult to check the spread of irresponsible suggestions and inaccurate rumors.

It is a lamentable fact that a part of the legitimate facilities of markets is abused by a class of people too indolent to think for themselves, who hope to secure quick and easy profits following someone else's suggestions. In this, as in all else, we get out of things what we put into them, and no more. Hence, the old law of the survival of the fittest tends to eventually eliminate the "free riders." However, there is a difference between this type and the sincere seeker of help in finance, who shows by his demeanor the seriousness of his purpose and his desire to pay for this help, not necessarily in a dollar fee, but by faith in his adviser's integrity, courage to follow his judgment, and loyalty when the inevitable mistakes occur.

In a contact between the latter and a real source of expert opinion or interpretation of information, either secured through special research or through so-called "inside" sources, it should first be realized that, while I feel it possible to find expert advisers who can give good counsel on how to profit in the market, in my opinion it is absolutely impossible to secure equally worthwhile opinions on pre-determined lists of individual securities. It is vital to know the superiority of volunteered opinion as compared with answers to queries. If one stops to think, it is one thing to guide someone to a profit on one's own ground, picking the time and medium. It is entirely another to have at hand worthwhile information or opinion on any and every security requested at any and every time. Therefore, I feel that any source ready instantly to pass on everything and anything should be regarded with skepticism.

A worthwhile source of good information will, in my experience, never continue passing it on to anyone who keeps coming back for further advices, either on accepting losses, averaging or taking profits, pyramiding, etc., unless, of course, the relationship is very close.

Personally, if the tax situation allows it, I think much is to be gained by going for advice armed only with cash and not with a portfolio of old pets or involuntary remnants of former ill-starred commitments.

12

WHAT TO BUY—AND WHEN

WHEN AND UNDER what conditions should an investment actually be made by one who follows the theory of buying only securities which seem to have great potentialities for profit? In the preceding chapters it was pointed out that this system involves remaining completely uninvested for long periods.

For practical reasons one necessarily has to make compromises. The factors that make an ideal investment are never all present at the same time. Even if such an opportunity actually did exist, it would be almost impossible for anyone to recognize its existence. Nevertheless, describing such conditions should be helpful. There are times when a majority of them might occur.

In the first place, the general background should be favorable, which means that popular sentiment should be bearish and the securities market well liquidated. Business conditions should be poor, or the general expectation should be that they will become poor.

The security itself should always be either a common stock, or a bond or preferred stock whose position is thought by the investing public at large to be so weak that it sells at low prices and is given generally low ratings. The company selected should be operating at a deficit, or its earnings should be abnormally low. Or, if earnings are currently satisfactory, the popular expectation must be that they are headed downwards. The stock should be paying no dividends, or the dividend should be lower than normal, or general opinion must lack faith in the continuance of a reasonable dividend.

The price of the stock must reflect a majority view that conditions affecting the company are bad, or soon will be bad, or will continue bad. At the same time, the buyer must hold an opinion contrary to these surface indications, and his opinion must be backed by sound judgment and access to reliable sources of information.

The importance of full consideration of popular sentiment, expectations, and opinion—and their effect on the price of the security—cannot be overstressed. Major buying points often occur without a full scale actual business depression. At such times the fear of a depression exists. Earnings and dividends can be normal, and yet the shares in question may be very attractive if misguided popular fears as to the future drive the price down to a level that might at other times represent a period of deficits. And vice versa, the expectation of favorable conditions to come might cause a speculatively high price to be put on shares when actual results of the company's operations are still considerably below normal.

Thus it is the earnings discounted *in the price* which are the determining factor, and not always the earnings level actually existing at the time of proposed purchase. There is little to be expected marketwise, for instance, in buying the shares of a company with a strong growth trend if the current price places a liberal valuation on that growth for several years to come.

It is important to stick to issues which in past times of bullish enthusiasm have had active markets and which can be expected to have active markets again. However, at the time of purchase they must be low-rated and unpopular, with their prices down and discouragement about their prospects quite general.

At long intervals even the highest grade shares become depressed, and then the opportunities are especially great. That happens only once or twice in a business lifetime. The objective is always buy that which the majority thinks is speculative and sell it when the majority believes the quality has reached investment grade. It is in this policy that both safety and profits exist. As price is the all-important consideration, the type of corporation and its characteristics are of relatively minor consequences.

The complete opposite of the thoughts expressed above is the theory held by people who wish to invest surplus cash as soon as it becomes available—that is, who desire to make investments at regular monthly or quarterly intervals. I never did approve of this point of view. Certainly those who want to follow it should buy the strongest and most stable companies. Companies in the consumer class are much to be favored. The products or services sold should not be great public necessities, as the latter become targets for political interference. Labor costs should be low, and the ability to finance expansion out of earnings should be present. Also, the actual cash income should be larger than the amount reported as earnings.

However, these considerations are not essential for buyers following the policy described in these chapters. In fact, such ideal investments are not often available at a price discount sufficient to make them attractive. More often and more profitably the purchase may be made in a company that still has considerable debt and in which ownership by the management may be small. If one can gauge trends correctly, the very reason for the purchase may be that debt will be reduced, perhaps eventually eliminated, and that management, seeing the improvement ahead, will increase its ownership substantially.

Except in cases of panic or near panic prices, the fact that a stock is widely held by investment trusts is not a good reason for buying, as such stocks are generally of the high-grade kind difficult to buy cheap. Since the aim is rather to buy an issue which is unpopular, the hope is, on the contrary, that while the investment companies do not hold much or any now, they will later, at a higher price, become interested and add it to their portfolios. The distinction of being the stock most frequently listed in published institutional holdings simply means not only that the price is probably high rather than low but also that there is a large number of potential sellers should the situation take a turn for the worse.

Willingness and ability to hold funds uninvested while awaiting real opportunities is a key to success in the battle for investment survival. Market valuations of most securities change in a single period of a very few months by an amount equivalent to many years of dividends or interest coupons. Therefore such changes in value are much more worth while seeking than is straight investment return.

I said at the start of this chapter that the theoretical idea is rarely encountered in practice. Nor is it readily recognized.

I feel that the simple equation of weighing what you think are the possibilities for profit vs. the risks for loss is really the soundest way to go about it.

13

IMPORTANCE OF CORRECT TIMING

As SOON as a security is purchased, the buyer loses the power to avoid a decision. It becomes necessary for him to decide whether to hold or sell. As an inexorable consequence, the percentage of correct conclusions must be lowered. Therefore, intelligent investors expect to make a great many more errors in closing transactions than in opening them.

When nothing but cash is held, no decision need be made at all unless conditions are completely satisfactory. Either a suitable opportunity may be present, so that a purchase can sensibly be made, or the pros and cons may be so balanced that nothing is done.

The worst that can happen if the latter decision is reached is that an opportunity will be missed through caution, which is an inconsequential misadventure. Other opportunities always come in due time, and if one's attitude towards speculation and investment is shaped along the lines described in these chapters, nothing will be lost in either eventual profits or peace of mind.

Another reason why selling at the right time is more difficult than buying is that the development of a frame of mind in which only real bargains are sought carries with it a tendency to lose confidence too early. Periods of overvaluation and public over-confidence are, naturally enough, likely to follow periods of depression, and often do. Likewise, very good general business conditions will normally succeed very bad conditions. In such active periods, stocks will sell at excessive valuations, so that their price advances will often outrun the most optimistic expectations of those who bought very early and very low. The latter will begin to feel uncomfortably unsure of their position as soon as normal valuations are restored, or when the indications of overvaluation are first to be seen.

For these reasons, the background for intelligent liquidation cannot be described simply as a reversal of the factors that make for a real buying opportunity. Such would be more nearly the case if we were discussing the proper time to make short sales. But what we are concerned with here is not initiating a position but unwinding one already held. Scores of stocks are unsatisfactory long holdings without being clear-cut short sales.

Other situations may make it necessary to consider selling. The favorable developments which were expected when the security was bought may fall short of original anticipations. Or the holder may face a loss if he sells.

In this one instance it is possible to state a mechanical rule to be followed. Naturally the exercise of good sense and logic and the possession of accurate information, rather than adherence to any formula or system, constitute the basis of all successful investment. But it is sound policy to get out of long positions which begin to prove themselves wrong by declining in price. This is the one automatic proceeding in handling securities, the only proceeding in which no judgment is needed.

Losses must always be "cut." They must be cut quickly, long before they become of any financial consequence. After the elimination of a stock in this manner, the transaction must be, in a sense, forgotten. It must be left out of future consideration so completely that there is no sentimental bar to reinstating the position at higher level, either very soon or at any later date, if the purchase again seems strongly advisable.

Cutting losses is the one and only *rule* of the markets that can be taught with the assurance that it is always the correct thing to do. As a matter of arithmetic, any grammar school boy can learn the formula. But, as a matter of actual application, it requires a completeness of detachment from human frailties which is very rarely achieved. People like to take profits and don't like to take losses. They also hate to repurchase something at a price higher than they sold it. Human likes and dislikes will wreck any investment program. Only logic, reason, information, and experience can be listened to if failure is to be avoided.

Little of a definite nature can be outlined as the proper procedure when the question is whether or not to take profits. A sound practice is to realize a 100 percent gain with at least part of a large commitment. Such a profit is equivalent to dividends for sixteen years on a straight 6 percent basis, not compounded and without adjustment for taxes. If a doubling of one's investment can be achieved within six months to a year, the investor can then comfortably enter a long period in which cash is held idle (until the next opportunity presents itself) without diminishing final results to anything nearly as poor as the general average—frequently a net loss—which is obtained through continuous full investment.

It is advisable always to keep uninvested reserve funds on hand in order to take advantage of unexpected opportunities. The need for buying power in such cases may in itself be a factor dictating the sale of securities already held.

Perhaps the best way to describe when to sell is to review handling of a commitment from its beginning. Belief that a stock is in a buying range justifies a small initial purchase. If the stock declines, it should be sold at a small and quick loss. But if it advances and the indications which supported the original purchase continue favorable, additional purchases can be made at prices which the buyer still considers abnormally low. But once the price has risen into estimated normal or overvaluation areas, the amount held should be reduced steadily as quotations advance.

This is as near as it is possible to come in describing proper selling policies.

14

STATISTICAL ANALYSIS, MARKET TRENDS, AND PUBLIC PSYCHOLOGY

THERE IS ROOM for much improvement in the average run of statistical analysis attempting to appraise the value of a particular issue. Most of the time the figures considered are not, in my opinion, the useful and vital ones at all, and generally the whole method of approach is academic and theoretical neglecting fundamental trends which are far more important than statistics on individual issues.

In my opinion, the primary factor in securing market profits lies in sensing the general trend. Are we in a deflation or inflation period? If the former, I would hardly bother to analyze most equities. I have known people to go to the expense of securing a thorough field report on a company, complete except for proper consideration of market factors, buying the stock because of the report and later losing a fortune in it at a time when a market study would have suggested that all equities should be avoided. And I have seen individuals make a great deal of money buying, without much study of individual issues, the leading stocks under circumstances that suggested a fall in money and a rise in shares. Thus effort should be concentrated first on deciding the trend and next in seeking out the most responsive stocks.

I certainly feel that it is more feasible to try to follow profitably a trend upwards or downwards than to attempt to determine the price level. I do not think anyone really knows when a particular security is "cheap" or "dear" in the sense that cheapness would occur around a real market bottom and dearness around a real top. For example, shares have a habit of sometimes seeming dear in the early stages of an advance, and later at far higher levels new and unexpected developments often make them seem cheap again. There is no rule about it.

I have seen stocks make bottoms when they seemed so cheap that one actually mistrusted one's intelligence, and I have seen bottoms reached at times that suggested to the majority that the shares in question were actually a good short sale. The reverse is true for bull-market tops. The money that has been lost "feeling" for the bottom or top never has been generally appreciated. The totals, if they could be known, must be staggering. Naturally we are concerned only with factors influencing security prices that are open to successful interpretation. It would be satisfying always to buy on the bottom and sell on the top, but as we do not know how to determine the bottoms and tops and would lose too much trying to guess, then of course it is only logical to turn our attention to those profitable methods we might actually learn to follow.

The most important single factor in shaping security markets is public psychology. This is really another reason why I am not particularly impressed with academic calculations purporting to show what this or that stock should be worth—nowadays involving complicated calculations often worked out on a computer. Personal knowledge of what is ahead in the way of developments in the next six months to a year and a half, and due regard to market factors always count a great deal more. I feel that the psychology which leads people to pay forty times net (to use that yardstick for an example) for a stock under one set of conditions and refuse to buy the same shares under another set of conditions at ten times is such a powerful and vital price-changing factor that it can overshadow actual earnings trends as an influence on stock prices. For instance, increases in earnings are often more than offset marketwise by decreases in the public regard for a stock in the interim. To put it another way, frequently the market might temporarily appraise anticipated earnings at say twenty times estimates, but later the actual net will be capitalized marketwise at a lesser ratio—and vice versa.

The same considerations rule as between different stocks at the same time. Thus we may have a fashion in vending machine or photographic shares which will carry them much higher at a given time in relation to assets, earnings, dividends, and future prospects than other groups. Later, when they are out of fashion, these yardsticks may actually figure out to greater advantage, but the public mind is on something else. Sometimes for years certain popular shares will be persistently overvalued by the public, which continues to pay an unreasonable sum in proportion to the theoretical valuation. And likewise, frequently, theoretic undervaluation will persist for years. It does not help one's account to feel sure one is short theoretically overvalued stocks that are currently rising or long those theoretically undervalued but actually sinking in price.

One should bend every effort to determine what the tendencies of the public are, right or wrong, and profit from them. I find that even the name of a stock, which obviously has nothing to do with theoretical values, is an important factor in securing or losing public favor. I am certain in my own mind that certain bull speculations of 1929 would have been impossible under different names, and likewise an unpopular name will greatly decrease the price the public will pay for actually good value.

In line with these thoughts, such individual research as is done in analyzing stocks should be highly practical and definitely linked to the market. I am personally interested mainly in analysis that sets out to determine primarily whether the sum total of all market factors will tend to lead one to expect higher or lower market prices. I would not make such an obvious statement if I did not daily come across analytical work done without the slightest regard for this real fundamental reason for its existence.

In taking up individual security analysis one naturally is going to attempt to forecast the trend of profits or dividends, but unless this is done in connection with former market appraisals of past earning power and previous yields, under varying conditions, the practical value which can be drawn from the figures is greatly decreased. It means little to estimate earnings of a given company at say $1 a share without a background of past price-earnings ratios under varying conditions, to use as a partial guide in estimating how far the present market might go in discounting this anticipated net. The same is true of yields. It is helpful to calculate the total of the redemption value of prior securities and the market value of the equity for purposes of comparison with such figures as sales.

In short, in my opinion everything of an analytical nature covering specific securities should be persistently linked to past market appraisals and set up for use solely to determine future market possibilities.

PRICE MOVEMENT AND OTHER MARKET ACTION FACTORS

OF ALL THE FACTORS that go to make up a well-rounded opinion on the general market trend and, more especially, the individual stocks selected for a commitment, I would easily rank the actual price movement first.

A basic reason for this is that the going market price, whether tagged as "overvalued" or "undervalued," is what determines your equity. For example, in 1963–64 Syntex Corporation on the American Stock Exchange rose from the equivalent of 20 to over 190. Within a few months it declined to under 50. Regardless of the realism of these highly fluctuating market valuations, anyone short on the way up or long on the way down would have suffered by the change in price just the same.

Thus, full consideration must be given to what investors think something is worth and not only to what its theoretical value might seem to be.

Some people follow the price movement by "watching the tape." Others "follow" charts. Still others will have nothing to do with either, but nevertheless look at the daily stock table and are to a varying degree affected (sometimes unconsciously) by the price and volume changes. I feel that practically all relevant factors, important and otherwise, are registered in the market's behavior and, in addition, the action of the market itself can be expected under most circumstances to stimulate buying or selling in a manner consistent enough to allow reasonably accurate forecasting of news in advance of its actual occurrence. These price and volume changes not only will add the most important confirmation (or vice versa) to market expectations based on analysis or advance information, but also will supply the most vital clues in the shape of calling attention to unfamiliar issues worth checking in other directions.

Security buyers and sellers affected by market action might be classed three ways. First is the "public," frequently spurred into great mass buying or selling movements by the spectacle of changing prices and volume. Before the Securities and Exchange Act of 1934 these movements were sometimes legitimately started and nurtured by professionals. Sometimes this was done illegitimately. More often than not the public itself built up its own picture on the tape as one followed the other into the market, each impressed by the action created by the previous purchasers or sellers. Regardless of initial profits, I doubt if anything other than losses ever accrued to this type of trader or investor in the long run.

In the second class, I would place self-styled accomplished chart or tape readers who are guided exclusively by what they think they see in lines on the charts or symbols on the tape. If they really use only theories based on market action to form their conclusions, my guess is that they also lose in the long run, as few are expert enough to profit from these indications alone.

The successful type is the real expert in this highly specialized form of interpretation who understands the proper weight to give market action factors in relation to others and especially realizes that as the price movement reflects everything, it necessarily reflects not only good buying and selling but also commitments made incompetently, rashly, or frivolously. He goes further than noting whether given market action is "bullish" or "bearish" and realizes the need to attempt consideration of the causes and forces behind the indication and whether it is likely to prove correct. It would be quite simple but a very long process to enumerate myriads of possible commitments which, reflected on the tape, would tend to mislead those who make a fetish of market action with supposedly inflexible rules governing its interpretation and who lack the ability to sift the wheat from the chaff.

Thus, while I feel that market action is almost always entitled to receive the greatest consideration of the various factors that go to make up the final appraisal of a stock's position, one should realize the large possibilities of drawing erroneous conclusions either from inexpertness as regards interpretation of the market movement or neglect of supporting factors such as statistical and economic influences, the technical situation, sponsorship, and company developments not generally known or discounted.

In the consideration of market indications, the most important point is the time element. Outstanding strength or weakness can have precisely opposite meanings at different times in the market cycle. For example, consistent strength and volume in a particular issue, occurring after a long general decline, will usually turn out to be an extremely bullish indication on the individual stock in question. In addition, if later its leadership is gradually followed by other important shares, the signal for a turn in the whole market probably has been given. On the other hand, after an extensive advance which finally spreads to issues neglected all through the bull market, belated individual strength and activity not only are likely to be short-lived but may actually suggest the end of the general recovery, especially if the early leaders begin to show no further response. Obviously, judgment of action should also be in relation to the publicly known and unknown news. What might otherwise be considered weakness may be an indication of strength under certain news conditions, and vice versa. It must be obvious, for example, that heavy volume at slight concessions might be a most bullish indication if it followed really bad news that would ordinarily be expected to upset the market very much. And, vice versa, a merely firm market in response to what should be very stimulating news could be an important bear clue.

Individual movements or activity should be judged only in relation to the movement and activity of the list as a whole. For instance, one should give the greatest consideration to active stocks showing the least decline in a technical reaction or showing the most strength in a rally, provided the time element mentioned above is favorable. Simply an exhibition on average strength or weakness is of no particular significance.

The larger the public participation, the more accurate conclusions are apt to be. I feel it is comparatively easy for a trained observer to figure correctly the mass reaction to a given set of conditions, but in a professional market possibly dominated by a very few individuals or groups, profitable conclusions can rarely be drawn simply by attempting conventional interpretation of market action. However, here, as in everything else connected with the price movement, it is possible for the extremely astute individual to allow for the character of the market and, through shrewdly anticipating the probable failure of the major portion of such thinly participated moves, actually to profit by a reversal of his usual procedure, i. e., selling on bullish indications because of the expectation of failure under the special circumstances, and vice versa.

Confirmation of whatever happens to be the currently popular theory of market action, such as the widely heralded breaking of a generally watched resistance point, is apt to be misleading, especially temporarily. Usually the expert in such matters is only theoretically interested in such events anyway, as he has long before and at much more favorable levels seen signs that such a test was likely, and very possibly he even has a rather good idea of whether it will succeed. It is much safer, if one does want to follow such indications, to wait until a second confirmation is given, even if it involves some additional cost.

When all is said and done, all technical market judgment is based on very much the same theory and varies mainly in the different means used to attempt to obtain a true picture of the actual situation. However, it should be noted that it requires keen judgment to sense the full extent of probable weak buying or selling. For example, after a long decline, the first early public participation is apt to be a bullish sign, sometimes suggesting much more to come. Allowance has to be made for the position of the market, the general outlook, the size of the public purse, and a great many other factors in order not to jump to misleading conclusions. Thus, in the beginnings of the "Coolidge" market, premature selling of stocks developed on the early expansion of brokers' loans above previous highs to totals which based on past experience were dangerous but which actually were later vastly exceeded before the break. While this occurred in the early twenties the same principles apply today.

The buying or selling power of the "public" once on a stampede is almost beyond calculation, and the fact that they are probably doing an eventually costly thing does not in any way decrease the loss in fighting the trend or make up for possible profits in not taking advantage of it.

Theorists may claim that "stocks are too high" or "too low" based on their individual and varying idea of what people should pay for a given situation at a given time. But the real price of stocks is based on the majority appraisal of the moment. If the public's pocketbook is longest and widest open, their appraisal goes for a time anyway. If our theoretical analysts had sufficient funds to buy all the stocks offered under their own estimates of theoretical levels and likewise to sell in quantity above, then they would fix stock prices marketwise. Usually they are not a factor in actual practice except as to the extent they can influence others. The point is that it is incorrect to say that stocks sold too low in 1932 or too high in 1929. They were worth the price, at the time, in both instances—no more, no less. From a practical point of view it is vital to investment success to banish such ideas and give the proper market valuation to the desire and ability, or lack of desire and ability, on the part of people to bid or offer stocks.

Readers of this book are apt to feel that it includes more of an account of what may be misleading marketwise than a formula of certain profits. The answer, in my opinion, is that instead of considering the purchase and sale of securities as something that can be done quickly in an offhand manner, one must realize that investment actually is the most inexact sort of science. This is especially true because of the important part psychology plays in shaping prices. My rule for profitable investment is predicated on full recognition of the difficulties involved. Instead of rushing in on some flimsy basis or for that matter on some important, well-planned and carefully checked, and seemingly conclusive single line of thought, my advice is to question its correctness by testing the conclusion from all the other available angles and then form a composite opinion.

◆ 16 ◆

FURTHER TECHNICAL OBSERVATIONS

IT IS AN UNSATISFACTORY PROCEEDING to try to give, in these brief discussions, the principles behind successful selection of the right stocks to buy in an upswing (or to sell in a bear market).

The real point in the practical application of these theories is the flair for knowing when to believe the indications and when not to believe them; the intuition that tells one correctly what each of two diametrically opposed reasonings of the same situation may suggest. Experience, of course, is essential in determining whether one can develop the ability to make these paradoxical decisions correctly.

To illustrate: During a reaction in a bull market, nine times out of ten the active issue which declines the least will be the one that advances the most in the next surge to new high ground. On the other hand, once a market has really turned down into a primary bear swing, issues which seem to show more strength than the average are frequently only postponing an inevitable decline. They are "out of line with the market" just as sometimes issues which lag in a rally are "behind the market," and sometimes issues which lag are showing that they lack some of the fuel which makes a bull-market leader. Which is which?

It is this kind of judgment that must be applied to the rules, and that is the reason why no hard-and-fast formula for success is possible.

There are a few general observations, however, that I suggest should be helpful when applied to a background of reading and practical testing.

I am inclined to favor doing one's major forecasting from the tape or, to put it another way, from the price movement. This to me is elemental and necessary to success. Thus, once convinced the market is headed up, I should tend to follow the strongest of the active issues—those reacting the least in weakness and rallying the most in strength. They must be *active* to minimize the danger of reaching false conclusions from unimportant indications. Preferable are those issues which are more active when they are moving up than when they are reactionary, except sometimes just at the bottom, when a bit of weakness on the decline acts as a "shake-out" and prepares the stock for a more vigorous advance. Here again judgment rather than rules applies.

It is possible, for example, for a stock to get *too* active on the advance and thus make a top that might be termed a "blow-off" or "climax," just the reverse of the "shake-out" mentioned above. Here, again, the utter impossibility of doing anything with over-the-counter issues or issues traded on the smaller Exchanges, or even dull issues on the big board, should be evident. There is nothing to watch; nothing to judge; nothing to indicate. No fair-weather signals; no foul.

Thus one is really endeavoring to buy the issues that in a sense are hard to buy and easy to sell. This means, when buying, shares which are just a little stronger than one might expect compared with the general run of active issues. However, I am talking about the action of shares in the early stages of a market or during a temporary recession in a clearly up market or just at the point when a market is emerging from a weak spell.

The strength I speak of must be just noticeable to an experienced trader. The type of strength that shouts so anyone can hear is sometimes bullish but perhaps more often a warning signal. The best all-inclusive ironclad description I can give is that if the stock acts in a way to "look" good to the uninformed public, then the strength is a sign of danger; if it tends to create a desire among the poorly equipped to take profits or sell short or await a reaction, then the stock is usually worth following. Even this statement needs qualification. Uninformed buying, per se, is not always a sign of the top. It is in fact frequently the sign of a wild advance. The timing element again becomes paramount.

The real bear signal occurs when the uninformed buying has spent itself—an easy sentence, but one of the most difficult points to determine accurately in this wide world. A helpful sign is to watch the effectiveness of the buying. If stocks advance proportionately, that is normal. If stocks mark time despite the public accumulation, watch out. If stocks decline while such buying proceeds, real trouble is probably not far off.

I cannot overstress the importance of thinking more of the time something occurs rather than of just the occurrence itself; of comparing the action of one issue with others rather than just following an isolated move; of watching the effect of the news on prices rather than bothering too much about the news itself; of looking into both demand and supply as against the usual practice of thinking about only one side of the market at a time.

We all use a great many phrases and expressions quite loosely, especially those referring to good or bad buying. One might think sometimes, when listening to Wall Street talk, that all the orders filled that day were buys or sells as the case might be. "Nobody" had any stocks in 1932. "Everybody" had them in 1929. Obviously, there are misstatements here. Or in the more modern sense the buying climax occurred where the Dow was above 760 in 1961, and the selling climax when it was below 530 in 1962. All the stocks are always owned by someone. The question is, by what class? And, of course, every selling order executed must be matched by a buying order, and vice versa. Again, who is on each side? In this connection, I think it helpful to separate market orders from limited orders. The former are much more significant.

In speaking of shares that are hard to buy and easy to sell as being desirable under certain conditions, I am taking it for granted that they can be bought in quantity and that the reason we class them as hard to buy is that one must pay relatively just a little more for them than for other active issues at the moment. I certainly don't mean issues impossible to buy: To illustrate: Issue A, typical of the market as a whole, is down to 45, from 50, while issue B, also actively traded, is selling at 47, also down from 50. Issue B is in demand at 47, but plenty of the stock is for sale at a fraction up; in fact, there is a great deal for sale until perhaps it goes above 50 again. This is my "hard to buy—easy to sell" stock. Issue C is down to 43 from 50—a weak sister. Issue D, down from 50 and now quoted 47 bid for 1,000, 100 offered at $49\frac{1}{2}$, is out as far as I am concerned because practically no stock is available near the bid.

Some readers have no doubt heard of the expression "up-book" or "downbook," referring to the specialist's book of orders on the floor. These "books" used to be sometimes available but now are kept privately under new rules. However, it is interesting to consider them because I think the same principles which they taught still hold true, even if today one can get only a general idea of whether buying or selling orders predominate, and that from general observations and unprohibited sources such as the experience of some of the typical commission houses.

By "upbook" is meant a listing of open limited buy and sell orders on the specialist's book that suggest that the stock in question is going up, and by "downbook" the inference is that the stock is more likely to go down. Most laymen think that when there are a lot of buy orders on the specialist's books and few sells, his stock is well supported and more apt to go up than down, and vice versa.

As a matter of actual practice, in most cases exactly the reverse is true. The reason for this is that the market must ordinarily move against the largest limited orders. You cannot buy what's not for sale, nor sell when there is no bid. As in everything else, there are, of course, exceptions, but on the average the above holds good. Inexpert efforts to improve markets in stocks on the part of corporation officials or large stockholders invariably revolve around bringing "buy" orders into their markets when it is "sells" they really need. In fact, a close spread between the bid and the offer is the important need. In making markets you want to sell stock to many people so that they become interested in buying more or telling their friends to buy, and thus the beginning of a broad natural market is laid.

When you buy a stock you expect to resell it higher; hence you definitely want one that is likely to be easy to resell and that has a natural market Certainly you do not want an issue whose price partly depends on the creation of an artificial demand; nor do you want the stock of a company if it must pay for spreading bullish information about shares around the Street, through a misguided hiring of the wrong type of stockholder relations counsel.

All these subterfuges are practically nonexistent in permanently active issues. They are seen more in the less active or very particularly the *temporarily* active issues, which latter must be especially avoided. Thus, I repeat, in a bull market paying up a bit for an active leader that seems "hard to buy" or looks as if it has a little start on the rest of the leaders usually pays well. It is better to chase the limited than to wait for the next local.

The most important factor in attempting to read tape or chart or price movement "indications" is the *time* element. To say a stock is a buy if it makes a new high or crosses a resistance level is pure drivel if nothing is said about the *time* this is accomplished. In brief, the earlier in a cycle the indication, the more important. If it is late enough, it means nothing. Thus a bullish indication for General Motors after a long general decline, weeks before the averages give their indication, would probably be a most important bull tip. But if after months of bull market some laggard finally is dragged through its old top, then I would guess more often than not that it is meaningless as a buy signal, though it might be important as a bear point.

Thus what is vital is a comparison of the action of one stock with others as regards relative strength and weakness, relative activity and dullness, and relative time of accomplishment. The achievement of certain fundamental action in an individual issue is significant only when compared with the action of other issues.

Outside of the tape, ordinary sense in appraising the prospects for the leaders will be all that is actually needed to select the "right stock." The tape largely will do it for you.

While we are on the subject, I might add that the most consistently reliable danger signal in a stock is a sharp advance and complete retracement of the gain on great activity after a long series of advances in a market which one would ordinarily regard with suspicion anyhow. For instance, if a stock goes back and forth in a trading range, that, of course, is normal. But if it gets away for a straight gain, it should hold 50 percent to 99 percent of it. There is rarely a second chance to get aboard once a stock is started, and if it comes back and gives one the second chance, it is usually better to pass it up. That stock is no longer hard to buy.

Curiously, it might be easy to sell, as in the early stages of real breaks an enormous amount of public buying usually is done on a scale down.

In fact, the smart trader pyramids on new highs; the uninformed one "averages." There is something about new highs that makes them look unfamiliar and dangerous to the tyro. The first time an issue sells at 20, 25, 30, 35, 40, 45, 50, 55, it looks very risky. But after 55 then 49 looks safe and secure. Thus most "distribution" is done "on the way down."

Some people lay considerable stress on the volume appearing on tape or on after-the-close reports as to who bought or sold. This again is an expert's job. Ten thousand shares of "xyz" at 50 might mean a lot of different things. Some traders or some institutions who are pretty smart and have plenty of money may simply have wanted to buy the stock. In the past some floor trader might have bought some of it. Some in and out trader in a brokerage office may have bought it for relatively quick resale at a profit or a loss.

Let me digress here to say that at this point some market regulators feel some of these transactions should be curtailed. This, of course, is an example of the "one-side-of-the-market-only-thinking" which I have already discussd. The 10,000 shares for sale at 50 might very well have been an accumulation of small sell orders from all over the country. These small sellers under such circumstances might receive the advantage of disposing of their stock at a favorable price otherwise unable to obtain. The professional buyer may later suffer a loss. There are always two points of view.

It is not generally realized that someone anxious to buy much more than 10,000 can, if he knows his job, buy the 10,000 without much fuss and possibly with much less than 10,000 appearing on the tape by "stopping" on the floor as much stock as possible. "Stopped stock" is not printed on the tape. This, of course, has nothing to do with a "stop-loss" order to buy or sell.

Then, of course, there is the matter of brokers' names. If J. J. Smith is president of J. J. Smith Motors and J. J. Smith, Jr., is a member of the New York Stock Exchange, J. J. Smith can have his son give an order to another floor broker to buy or sell in case he wants to keep from making things too evident. The cost to his son of "clearing" the transaction through another broker is only a fraction of the total commission. And, of course, a floor trader can, if he wants to pay the price, hand a buy order in J. J. Smith Motors to young J. J. Smith,

Jr., for the effect. I mention these isolated unrelated possibilities to attempt to show the many sides of the stock market and why it is not as simple as it looks.

This sort of information has come to be in very scarce supply in modern times. Very few floor brokers today take the trouble to report what's going on to their people off the floor after the market is closed for the day.

From an entirely different angle, i.e., getting orders executed promptly after one decides what to do, there are some people who are so intent on securing every fair advantage that they even allot a certain type of order by the floor location of the posts where the stocks in which they are interested are traded and by their proximity to certain brokers' phones. It takes time to walk across the big room of the Stock Exchange. One can save considerably by having such technical details just right if one is really active.

There is a difference in how an order is executed. I know one trader who has one order phone for fast service and one for slow. Orders put over the first are filled at once, regardless. Orders on the second are waited out even at the risk of losing one's market.

MORE ON TECHNICAL POSITION OF MARKET—ITS INTERPRETATION AND SIGNIFICANCE

TECHNICAL POSITION of the stock market is one of the major factors logically part of the decision whether to buy, sell, or wait. It is a consideration that is important from the longest-pull investment point of view and not simply a short-term trading indication.

Most of the really valuable technical information is not readily available. It can be obtained, however, from a keen broker, and would necessarily mainly represent his judgment rather than any quotable numerical facts.

One speaks of a "weak" technical position or an "overbought" condition of the market and, vice versa, a "strong" position and "oversold" condition. Obviously every share traded is at all times owned by someone so that this refers to the quality of the ownership. Accurate appraisal of the situation is worth dollars and cents to the investor and is accomplished by accurate and inspired interpretation of a variety of indications.

For example, a knowledge of the position of the odd-lot houses is of great technical value. They ordinarily fill brokers' orders by taking a limited position, counting on buyers and sellers eventually largely automatically canceling out one and another's commitments. Thus a flood of small public odd-lot selling orders would tend temporarily to cause the odd-lot dealers to become long of stocks. This is generally an excellent short-run bullish indication. It should be noted that its basis lies in the belief that a preponderance of small orders to sell suggests at least a temporary selling climax, and vice versa.

Information about certain phases of the odd-lot orders is now published in the financial pages of many daily newspapers and therefore is easy to tabulate, chart and study. Years ago, there was an old fashioned idea that an odd-lot dealer (or floor specialist, for that matter) could simply go contrary or "copper" the public's orders. Many factors have made this theory no longer valid. Stocks which have been bought as odd-lots often become split and their sales, in many cases, then become roundlot transactions. Personally, I do not feel that the small investor has become any smarter but that the day of final reckoning has been postponed.

From a practical money-making point of view, the odd-lot houses sometimes go along with their customers and sometimes stay neutral and occasionally take the opposite track. Their function is to fill their orders most economically, and their positions are a necessary incidental to this end.

As far as we are concerned, our interest lies solely in the value of these published odd-lot transactions as a help in judging the quality of the buying or the selling, and drawing a useful inference as to the general technical position. This will go a long way towards giving the investor, gifted with the knowledge of odd-lot interpretation, a feeling as to the degree of risk in the stock market and its probable trend.

In my opinion, the technical clues the published odd-lot figures offer, are invaluable, and rank close to the very top of the possible technical factors in usefulness. Technical market forecasts based on market action itself generally are not completely dependable until after the market has turned and traveled a considerable distance in the new direction. The people who follow market action do not get their information until the market has moved up considerably from the bottom, if it's a bullish signal, or down considerably from the top if it's a bearish one.

People who depend more on the buying or selling quality information given by the odd-lot figures are in a far better position to know of a coming trend before it actually starts. For example, action students wait for a breakout of the Averages from a trading range before knowing whether it is to be up or down, and even then it may prove a false start. But correct odd-lot quality of buying or selling interpretation can come closer to predicting beforehand which way the move is likely to be, i.e., whether the trading in the range was "accumulation" or "distribution." I say "closer to predicting" because there is no such thing as certain prediction. The odd-lot transactions may, for example, reveal six weeks of poor buying in a trading range, and yet the breakout could be up and not down, through the simple fact of the poor buying increasing in volume and intensity. However, the odd-lot figures would even in such a case correctly reveal the risk. When it comes to odd-lot positions in individual stocks only a few figures are made public and these only at monthly intervals. Good floor brokers, however, can often ferret out what is currently going on.

Profitable use of the odd-lot figures takes an enormous amount of data and knowledge possessed by very few and difficult for most to acquire.

This, in a way, gets back to my feeling partly expressed in other discussions that it is next to impossible to know what is "cheap" and what is "dear" in stock prices though trends are more open to intelligent forecast. Likewise, here I find difficulty in judging just from size alone how much a weak long or short interest is really positively indicative of a change in market direction. Obviously the danger point varies with outside considerations. They must be given full weight, but, in addition, a very useful gauge is the response or lack of response of the market itself to rapid changes in the type of stock ownership.

Thus if the public sells stocks and they decline, or if brokers' loans decrease and stocks drop, it would seem a natural enough trend. However, it is when these tendencies persist and the market break halts that the strong suggestion of a turn is given. In brief, it is ineffective weak buying or selling or poor quality expansion or contraction of holdings that is the real danger signal. The buying or selling power of the "public" once on a stampede is almost beyond calculation, and the fact that they are probably doing an eventually costly thing does not in any way decrease the loss in fighting the trend or make up for possible profits failing to take advantage of it.

Another interesting and useful short-run indication of the technical position is secured from a general knowledge of approximate ratio of limited orders entered on one side of the market as compared with the other. Curiously, stocks generally move in the direction of the heavy book, which is to say they tend to decline on a combination of heavy limited buying orders entered on a scale down and a much smaller number and amount of limited sell orders entered on a scale up, and reciprocally. The reasons for such action, which is contrary to one's first expectation, seem to me to lie in the obvious necessity of stock being available for sale to make important buying possible and likewise plenty of bids are necessary to permit heavy selling.

One of the considerations in deciding to buy a stock, for instance, is the ability to do so quickly, in quantity, and without affecting the price too much. If only a small amount is offered at rising limits, that of itself may easily prove to be the deciding factor that turns intending purchasers into another issue. Some thought about this aspect of the situation explains why stocks under certain conditions advance during the execution of an important selling order and frequently decline because of the existence of large buying power at a given level. Many inexperienced (marketwise) corporation executives formerly approved plans to attempt to support their stocks, and actually unwittingly supplied the means that permit heavy liquidation which otherwise might not occur. Per contra, insiders who wish to popularize and broaden the market for their shares, as well as hoping to see a higher market valuation, frequently fail to see why they are called upon to sell some of their shares to help the prices. Their idea of stimulating higher levels is, in this case incorrectly, to buy.

A final aspect of the technical position is consideration of the type of stock ownership for the purpose of adding to a long-range investment appraisal. Changes in stockholders' lists are sometimes used in the attempt. It is very difficult to make a rule about it but, personally, for initial long-pull purchase, I prefer a company with the nearest thing to ownership management, very few stockholders, and those holding large blocks, other things being equal.

It would naturally not apply in an unfavorable situation with the large blocks closely held only because of inability to dispose of them. Assuming a rise in price, slow distribution would occur probably at first by a shift on part of some of the large holdings to brokers' hands. Final investment distribution is likely by a further shift into many odd lots bought for cash with resulting gigantic stockholders' lists. It is interesting to note in this connection that *Fortune* once described American Woolen Co. as one of the "great corporate losers in United States industry" and also as a "typical widows' and orphans' stock." This is only one of many. Very likely the shares would at about the time of greatest numerical expansion of stockholders begin to receive high ratings as one of the "most popular" issues with institutional buyers as well.

Frequently when the latter stage is reached, absentee ownership and mercenary management are reflected in declining real earning power. By that I mean that the management would probably own only the minimum number of qualifying shares and would receive their principal compensation from salaries rather than sharing in the risks and profits through large holdings of stock. However, this decline in status often is not fully evident at once as the concern moves along on momentum and lives off its fat. Market declines are slow at first due to the reputation of the company and the very widespread and well-intrenched ownership, but none the less inevitable. As in everything else, there are exceptions, but in selecting the best market medium this angle of thought is worth more attention than it currently receives.

18

ADVANTAGES OF SWITCHING STOCKS

A CRITIC helps us by observing that he feels there is less peace of mind in the short than in the long turn, to say nothing of its being more difficult. He visualizes holding something comfortably for appreciation as against worrying (as he puts it) about getting in or out.

Of course, one always thinks of holding the one stock that is outstanding in any given cycle. But in practice very few can single out just this one stock and the right time to own it. Furthermore, the big stock of one cycle is rarely the choice issue of the next. Most people hold issues that are passé or immature in a bull market and see their favorite doing nothing while others surge ahead. There is nothing so comfortable about that. And, of course, it is the common experience to worry when long of shares through a prolonged bear cycle.

I see peace of mind in the short turn because I feel the realization of something is a relief compared with the threat. You can buy a stock and it can tantalize you with a slow, long-drawn-out decline. Once you sell and take your loss, it's spilt milk and not worth crying over.

The short turn tends to get one in the right stocks in a practical way because it is based on movement and current prices, and not on expectations that might be poorly conceived. Short-turn trading, properly done, is certainly the safest form of speculation that exists.

It is necessary to redefine "short-turn trading." Years ago it might have meant hours or days or weeks. Today in an investment rather than a tax sense it means six months to a year and a half.

The right way to do it is to pyramid. I have a buying power of 1,000 shares. I think Studebaker is going up. I buy 100 shares. It doesn't go up when it should, or worse, goes down. I sell it out. The loss can be charged to insurance, or experience, or as necessary cost of getting started right. Next, I buy 100 Chrysler. It begins to advance as I anticipated. So I buy 200 more. It still does well, so I buy another lot. And so on. First thing you know, if it's good I am long a big line of the right stock with a small initial risk. I lost only on 100 shares in Studebaker; I risked only 100 in Chrysler. To a degree, the risk in the stock I bought on the way up was mainly the risk of my paper profits; it was not like entirely risking capital as in the initial purchase. Of course, there are other dangers. There are times one gets whipsawed. Unexpected catastrophic overnight news can make trouble. It is surprising, however, how rarely it does. If these principles were always practiced, one would always be long the right quantity of the right stock, because the measure of what stock to buy and how much of it to buy is the action of the market itself.

I spoke of buying in opening a trade, so now I will speak of selling in closing it. Actually, one might have sold first and bought later. However, the principles are the same. It is, of course, enormously more difficult to close a trade properly than to open it. When you open a trade it's voluntary. When you consider closing one it's a decision you are forced to make—hold or close—even though you find it hard to know what to do. You can always stay out, but once in, you must know whether to stay in or get out.

My best reason for selling a stock is because it stops going up, or worse, starts going down. Of course, it's vastly more complicated than that. One could write a book on the subject, but learning by doing will teach you more than reading the book. Obviously, one is going to sell stocks many times and see the same stocks go higher. There is no rule against buying them back. It is much safer to buy and sell a stock a dozen times starting at 40 and ending at 100 than just to buy and pay 40. If the stock starts to go down and you are long at 40, you won't worry enough to sell. But if you bought your last lot at 100, you will jump pretty quick. And if you pyramid instead of averaging, you won't get back in, or at least you won't stay in for long if it happens to go into a real decline. But the owner at 40 might very well average at 60 after seeing the stock at 100.

So often what seems at first just another minor reaction later proves to have begun the major decline from the top. Years ago I recall buying a certain stock at 8 or 9. I bought some more at 12 and 17, and various other prices on an ascending scale. One day about delivery time the stock at 25 looked as if it were going through the roof. I bought some more. Between 2:15 P.M. and the close the whole market was boiling. But this stock was turned over in huge volume to close about the same. Next morning I sold out. I fully expected to buy back in a few days. The stock never acted well again, as it happened, and in time passed off the board into receivership.

Some very great fortunes have been made by holding some favorite stock through thick and thin. But that is not the question. How many have been made through chance and how many through judgment? I think most of them by chance, coupled with certain other qualifications, definitely rarely by judgment. It is rare enough to find those that made the fortunes. It is even rarer to find them with the ability to switch when their company has reached its zenith. The practical question for the everyday man is,—will he make more profit switching around, as I suggest, or putting everything into long-pull hopes? The answer is certainly in favor of switching. In fact, he has a real chance of finding himself in the leader of the day through my method and next to no chance through following more orthodox lines.

I might add that whenever somebody tells you that he doubled or quadrupled his money in a given stock you ask him how long it took. Doubling your money in six months is wonderful. Doubling your money in twelve years is only at the rate of 6 percent annually.

19

"FAST MOVERS" OR "SLOW MOVERS"?

ONE OFTEN HEARS about the "safety" in trading for cash or the advisability of confining commitments to "safe" stocks. Personally, I have long regarded these thoughts as fallacious in actual practice.

By a "safe" stock one generally means an issue that is fairly slow and steady in its movements, or an issue which is selling relatively low and apparently not at a vulnerable level. As to a position in a "safe" stock, it is likely to be most exasperating during a rising market when other shares are scoring rapid advances; and during a period of decline when one is long, then the slow action of the safe stock will lull one into a sense of false security. The issue which is safe because it is low and cheap is ordinarily a poor mover, usually creeping or backing and filling without getting much of anywhere while the sensational trading moves are practically all in shares which have broken out of the accumulation stage.

My feeling is that if one is trading for rapid profits, one must concentrate in those mediums that will give one the action one seeks. The safety should come not from the selection of a slow mover or a cheap issue or, worse yet, a group of such shares, but by concentration in the one outstanding, fast-trading leader that is jumping in the right direction. There is more safety and more profit in so timing one's buying in the latter type of issue that when one gets a report on the purchase the bid is then already in excess of what one has paid. I have seen moves of this sort which carried an amazing distance without a full-point setback.

One cannot afford to be wrong in such a fast-moving issue, and one is sure to be much more certain about one's opinion before one acts to get in than in the case of a slow issue, and likewise much more watchful to get out quickly if the stock doesn't act as anticipated or reverses its action. Here, as I view it, is real safety. Here also is a chance to build a backlog of profit which is partly a safety fund against future errors.

In the same way, a sizable position in an issue, even on margin if that is what the individual's situation calls for, is relatively safer than the imagined security of having something paid for and locked up. One is more careful establishing the margin position, and one watches it more carefully. In short, know you are right and go ahead. If in doubt, stay out.

This discussion rather leads into the question of "high-priced" vs. "low-priced" stocks. Frequently the highest pershare prices represent the lowest total valuation for a company when price is multiplied by shares outstanding and compared with total earning power and other figures. I generally favor issues selling at high prices per share. They are more apt to be in the rapid-mover stage. They are likely to have a better-grade following. Most people think very largely in terms of "points" and "shares," and, unless financially unable to do so, are just as apt to buy "1,000" of a high-priced issue as "1,000" of a cheaper share. They are also just as likely to try for "five points" in one as the other.

Actually one should regard one's possible profits more on a percentage basis than on a point basis, and one should measure the force of an advance the same way. It is, therefore, quite useful to have a logarithmic chart just as a reminder. A move to 10, from 5, is five points, true enough, but certainly no one would think a move to 130, from 125, meant the same thing. Yet traders will not see anything dangerous in the doubling of a low-priced share to 10, from 5, though they will avoid, fear, and, occasionally, even sell short a stock that moves to 175, from 125, or 50 points, when an issue in that class actually would have to rise to 250 to double. A "log" chart, of course, shows such movements in proper scale and tends to temper the judgment.

Occasionally, once in a good many years, normally high-priced stocks can be bought for low prices, such as in 1932, 1938, 1946, 1957, 1962, for example. This is so obviously advantageous, if one has the cash at the time and the foresight, that it needs no discussion and is, in fact, not what we have in mind at all.

Sometimes one can buy low-priced stocks of companies that also have small capitalizations, and realize some very amazing profits. However, it should be realized that the possibilities of selecting one of the few that make good, and selecting it at the right time, are quite slight.

Low-priced shares with huge capitalizations are usually quite undesirable.

◆ 20 ◆

DETECTING "GOOD" BUYING
OR "GOOD" SELLING

IN MY OPINION, far and away the most important thing to master in Wall Street is the tape. It is possible to see only the tape, and nothing else, and make a lot of money. It is a safety valve and automatic check on everything you do if you understand how to read it.

My strong belief in this point of view is another compelling reason for my early insistence on active listed leaders. The best means for judging the rest is simply not at hand. Dealing in outside stocks or bonds without benefit of an active quoted auction market is like firing a steam boiler without a safety valve, or running a train with the signal system out of order. I marvel at the courage of those who do it, but on reflection realize they don't know their danger. I am talking from experience. I have seen the ups and downs of thousands of accounts.

The way to learn to read the tape is to try it. Try it, one stock at a time, with small positions. A very few will have the advantage of knowing someone who understands it. Most of the books and courses (excepting a very few) are theoretical. In a speech before a group of students I tried to bring this subject more up to date. This discussion, "More on Tape Reading," can be found on page 267 in the Postscript of this edition.

One must realize that tape reading and chart reading and all the systems based on using the market's own current action as a forecast of its future are today pretty widespread. I mean by that, practically everyone has a smattering knowledge of them. Of course, what everyone knows isn't worth knowing.

The appearance of each transaction on the tape adds, as it properly should, its mite to determining the market price. One person sees a transaction and thinks it's put there for a reason, so he ignores it or does the opposite of what he feels its appearance is intended to suggest. Another perhaps also thinks he recognizes its character, but feels, coming as it did, that the buying is strong and worth following in its current stages anyway. And a third never heard of a transaction occurring for any reason except that someone wanted to buy or sell. He draws still another conclusion. How different is the result than in other lines where things are concealed instead of being brought out into the open.

In any event, the first thing to learn about tape reading is the ability to see the difference between indications recorded on good buying or selling and those which are the result of light-waisted action. This is not an easy thing to do, but is nevertheless essential. Anything one does on the tape is revealing to one who can read it. In the pre-1934 days before it became illegal, so-called "Manipulation," that is, trying to make buyers and sellers react in a common way, was revealing. The good manipulator knew that the very impression he painted on the tape to draw some buying power would generate a certain amount of selling from those who could really understand what they saw.

There are times when one will see "poor buying." But if it is just the start, one might want to follow right along as it sometimes takes months to fill all the outside buy orders once the public gets the bit in its teeth. On the other hand, at the point where every last elevator boy is in stocks, then additional desultory "poor buying" would be a bad thing to follow indeed.

My main point is to develop a realistic attitude; 99.99 percent and more of those who try to deal in Wall Street think they are right and the tape is wrong. But it's the tape that is watched by both the margin clerk and the tax collector. Stocks that are high and going higher are a good buy. Stocks that are "cheap" and growing cheaper don't interest me from a buying angle.

Statistics, mentioned above, are useful at times and have their place. Sometimes stocks are deadlocked. Statistics are useful in helping to suggest (along with other things) which way they may break out of that sidewise zone. However, I class the tape first and indispensable, and, second, accurate information from brokers and banks on the kinds and amount of buyers, sellers, loans, etc. Then come statistics and all the rest.

Back in 1929 I had the "privilege" of seeing a very extensive report on a listed corporation. I think it was reputed to have cost $10,000. It was bound in leather. The people who had this compiled bought a lot of the stock analyzed and lost a fortune doing it. Why? Because they stressed individual statistics instead of the tape and because they made several other common mistakes such as forgetting the importance of correct "timing."

At a time like 1929 no real tape reader would have committed an error like this. I actually bought a client 10,000 Radio at 110 as I recall it. I thought it was going straight up. It didn't and we were out at 109.

I saw the top in 1929 and sold stocks in time. It came about, as well as I can recall, something like this. All stocks, of course, did not reach their best prices simultaneously. The issues we traded in not only changed during the year but also narrowed in number. Thus, as this stock and that began to "act" badly, I was switching into those that still acted well. This of itself would eventually result in getting us out altogether. But there were other signs. Ordinary statistics were of no use. Steel common looked cheap enough above 250 on earnings of above $25 a share. The vogue those days was investment trusts. One house had a special reputation along that line. I forget, but I think it was their third issue. If any new issue (or old one for that matter) should have been a success, this was it. But shortly after the offering it was supported by a "syndicate bid." Well, if ever there was a sign of a market that was overbought here it was. If people couldn't or wouldn't buy that, what could or would they buy? Of course, that wasn't all. There were brokers trying to keep clients from buying more stocks because they couldn't finance them. It was things like this, that told the top of the market. And after the top, the tape told the tale of 1930 and 1931 when the oracles were saying all the way down that everything was OK again.

You don't have to go back to 1929 for examples.

◆ 21 ◆

QUALITIES OF THE GOOD INVESTOR OR
INVESTMENT ADVISER

IN THE PRECEDING CHAPTERS I tried to show briefly the non-existence of any really ideal medium of permanent investment. My conclusion was that those with surplus current purchasing power who wished to preserve it safely for later use and receive a rental in the meantime had little chance of genuine success. Intelligent hoarding and well-planned speculation were suggested as more promising alternatives.

Hoarding is unpopular, and not as yet understood in this country. It is not always a solution. The thought behind it is that spending a portion of a "hard" hoard periodically as needed will leave the remainder of the hoard worth more than say the depreciated purchasing-power value of a bond plus interest in an inflation period, or the result of investment mistakes during deflation.

The other alternative of "well-planned speculation" is possibly even more unsatisfactory, because safe investment is usually sought for either truly surplus funds by those active in ordinary professions, businesses, or trades, or for protection and income by retired or incapable absentee investors, all of whom either do not want or are not able to keep the close vigil necessary for a well-planned speculation policy.

Nothing, in my opinion, has ever been devised to solve this problem in a wholesale way—nothing probably ever will be. I said before that the only hope I see for a very small minority of this class lies in either developing the ability themselves or obtaining honest and capable expert guidance. This expert help might come from a friend or it might come from professional sources. My feeling is that it is rather definitely not to be found anywhere on a wholesale scale available to anyone willing to pay the price. I would say that it is more a question of genius than merely a surplus of statistical or economic facilities, or a heavily-staffed organization. I think it is also rarely found in a public figure, temporarily followed by the crowd because of a big success. And if by some infinitesimal chance it is found, it usually is not available, as truly successful speculators or speculative managers know that their success is greatly affected by the amount of capital they employ. Furthermore, their success makes any monetary remuneration offered by intending clients unimportant.

I will attempt to list what I feel are some of the qualifications to seek. It is obvious that absolute 100% scrupulous honesty, combined with a real code of ethics, is the first requirement. I have already said it required genius. It takes a flexible mind—not a man with one dominating idea who is forging ahead when the times are in step with him and totally helpless when they change. It takes someone who really appreciates the risks, as over-confidence is usually fatal. The man who made a hundred times what conditions normally suggest as feasible in one great deal is ordinarily a poor adviser or manager. He probably made it rushing in where wiser men would not go, or through a lucky circumstance of a single-track mind operating for the time being in a single-direction situation, or maybe he was just "sharp." In any event, this type rarely repeats. A man's mind must be unbiased and unfettered. If he has some necessary goal, it will warp his judgment, as profits can be made safely only when the opportunity is available and not just because they happen to be desired or needed. If he has some dominating outside interest which results in a bias either as to what is to be done or the frequency of doing it, there can be no really successful result. It certainly takes someone who is constantly "on the ball." The market has to be his first love day and night, as it were.

As the search seems so hopeless, the reader might well ask, Why bring it up? The answer, of course, is that while the nearest approach to the ideal is in fact next to hopeless, I do think that much can be done by the thoughtful investor in either training himself to speculation or securing guidance that will greatly improve his results as compared with the average. He may gain only by *losing less*, but even that is obviously worth striving for.

22

GAINING PROFITS BY TAKING LOSSES

ACCEPTING LOSSES is the most important single investment device to insure safety of capital. It is also the action that most people know the least about and that they are least liable to execute. I've been studying investments, giving investment advice, and actually investing since 1921. I haven't found the real key yet and don't ever expect to, as no one has found it before me, but I have learned a great many things. The most important single thing I learned is that accepting losses promptly is the first key to success.

I've seen thousands and thousands of accounts and thousands and thousands of portfolios. One of the most frequent examples is a diversified portfolio. Some of the securities owned are shown at a profit and some are shown at about the current market and a few are shown at losses. Those which occasionally show substantial losses constitute the important problem. Only too often an investor is prone to say that the losses are only on paper. He looks at the dividends and the capital gains and forgets that some capital losses are inevitable, must always be expected, and when present must always be deducted from gains to get an exact picture of what the account has actually accomplished.

It is a great mistake to think that what goes down must come back up. I could cite any number of cases where poor stocks have been held year after year, going from bad to worse, with any number of opportunities in better ones passed up. Classic examples of course are issues such as New York Central and Western Union if bought prior to 1929. There are far worse examples for both of these companies are still in existence and their stocks are recovering and have resumed their dividends. In the old days, people used to talk about Interborough Rapid Transit bonds and New Haven stock, and later on they began to talk about Kreuger & Toll. These are examples of dead issues that are known to everyone. There are dozens and dozens of small disasters that escape public notice but their effect on portfolios is just the same.

Another typical kind of loss is present in numberless trading accounts. Whenever the owners get a small profit, it is taken. Whenever they sustain a paper loss, the stock is held in the hope that it will come back, and eventually the account is entirely frozen.

The third type of typical "loss" isn't a loss at all in a sense. If an account is kept adjusted to the market, stocks which, after rising, start to fall back have to be marked down again. Here we have a case of diminishing profits rather than losses, but it raises the same question: "What to do about it?"

If there is anything I detest, it's a mechanistic formula for anything. People should use their heads and go by logic and reason, not by hard and fast rules. What I am offering here is strictly speaking not a formula but more or less a guide, an alarm bell to get people to stop and think and say, "What shall I do next?" I am tempted to make it a real formula and say, "By all means, sell something."

In the first place, in all cases where actual losses are involved, I'm inclined to say that when a new investment has shrunk by 10 percent, it is time to stop, look and listen. I think it usually ought to be sold out and the loss taken. If you make an investment of $10,000 and the market value shrinks to $9,000 I'm almost inclined to say, dogmatically, sell it out and try again.

You might even buy the same stock back later, but you'll find that you'll have quite a different kind of thinking, much more unbiased once you have sold it out. Probably, you won't buy it back, or you will find that you can buy something else. The big problem is to look at investments completely coldly, allowing no sentiment to play any part. Nine times out of ten it is better to sell a stock which is down because it is then so much easier to do your thinking unprejudiced by your position.

There are a great many readers of this chapter who own particular investments which have individually shrunk many times the 10 percent. What should be done in such cases? Supposing a stock that was bought has shrunk so that it's worth 50 percent or 25 percent or 33 percent of the original cost. Again, I have to violate my rule and come forth with a sort of formula. My feeling would be to sell part of it out. I don't know whether it should be $\frac{1}{4}$ of the commitment or $\frac{1}{3}$ of it or even $\frac{1}{2}$ of it, but sell a part of it out and the next time the market looks in a buying position, consider whether you want to buy that part back. You probably will find that you don't want to.

On the other hand, the next time you have some reason to be bearish on the market or to be in a selling mood, take another bite out of that issue and sell another $\frac{1}{4}$ or $\frac{1}{3}$; or if you sold $\frac{1}{2}$ in the first place, sell the rest of it out. That way, you'll have free capital to put where it will do you some good.

What about a stock that goes up and shows a big paper profit? This chapter is not concerned with trying to find the top. It's only concerned with taking "losses" to prevent profits from shrinking too much. I recommend somewhat the same system as in the case of losses. If the stock shrinks 10 percent from its top quotation, think of selling out a piece of it. After that, every time that for some reason you feel in a selling mood, sell another piece. Sometimes, it might be that you think the market is having a rally which is a failure. Another time it might be that you think the particular stock is not acting as well as the average. Another time, the market may actually be weak when you may have expected it to be strong and that in itself is a reason to sell a piece.

Of course, I realize there are many people who have commitments so small they will wonder whether there's any use selling a part. In general, these remarks apply to 500-share positions, say, and up. I think the odd-lot trader, or whoever trades in 100 shares or something like that, had better sell the whole lot at once. But still the odd-lot trader or investor can apply the principle if he has a portfolio of stocks, by selling out some and keeping others. If you do this, be sure to sell the weakest lot, not the one that shows the best profit.

In fact, I'll come up with another formula. I think almost regardless of the account, I'd sell 10 percent of it every year. I say 10 percent, but maybe it ought to be 20 percent or more. What I mean is that I would always try to keep an account fresh and growing and in the live issues of the day and not in a lot of frozen back numbers. About the best way to do it is to sell a portion every year, more or less automatically. If reasons don't develop for doing this, then just sell for the sake of selling.

Quite a lot of people hesitate to take profits because of the tax they have to pay. That is another good reason to chip away at a position, especially if it has a big profit which starts to shrink. I'd rather break a tax liability up by paying some of it each year than let it grow and have some enormous tax situation that plagues one in later years.

It is better for a lot of reasons to have a more or less level tax bill. A great many people lost the benefit of the forgiveness tax in 1942 because they had taken no profits that year. They had plenty of paper profits but they held off realizing on any of them. If they had taken a portion of them as advocated here, they would have had a level annual tax and would have had some real benefits from the forgiveness tax.

It is quite possible that in the future the taxes you paid in the past will play an important part in determining what you will pay. I'm quite sure that even though we can't foresee what or why or how this will work out, if you have had a more or less uniform tax bill every year, it will be to your advantage. It will be much better than having had a great big tax one year and no tax the next. Of course, we can't always arrange those things, but in a great many accounts it can be done.

I know that people who will watch their losses and cut them short and I know that people who will watch their profits and when they tend to diminish, begin to take some of them, will fare the best in the long run. It over-shadows almost any other investment principle I know.

It is also a good idea to take losses from a tax standpoint. Generally six months or less, while losses are still short-term, is a key time to check.

There is nothing more difficult to practice than accepting losses. This is especially important because there are bound to be times when you sell something and it turns right around and goes up.

There is only one way to look at it and that is to think of the costs of selling at the wrong time as comparable to an insurance premium.

23

YOU CAN'T FORECAST, BUT YOU CAN MAKE MONEY

THE DIFFERENCE between the investor who year in and year out procures for himself a final net profit, and the one who is usually in the red, is not entirely a question of superior selection of stocks or superior timing. Rather, it is also a case of knowing how to capitalize successes and curtail failures.

I made my first venture into securities some time before 1920 and I have devoted the better part of most of my business hours since then looking for the key to profitable investing. I once read about a meeting of economists who agreed that if their forecasts were $33\frac{1}{3}$ percent correct, that was considered a high mark in their profession.

Well, of course, I know you cannot invest in securities successfully with odds like that against you if you place dependence solely upon judgment as to the right securities to own and the right time or price to buy them. Then, too, I read somewhere about the man who described an economist as resembling "a professor of anatomy who was still a virgin." I think both of these observations can be applied with equal force to security analysts, generally speaking.

My own experience bears out these views. First of all, I quickly found out you had to learn by doing. That is why I sowed my security wild oats so early. And that is why, after many years of practical experience in hiring and handling and using "research staff" men, when I was called upon to school my brother at it, I adopted a practical method. Of course, I had him read every worthwhile book on the subject (which takes only a few nights for a fast reader) and of course I took him on the rounds of the financial press, the advisory services, banks and corporation meetings and brokerage research departments, and suggested he read the leading financial journals.

However, the important part of my teaching was when I set up a $10,000 fund for him and told him to buy everything he thought worth buying and see what he could do. There was only one proviso; he could buy only one situation at a time and he had to close out his position at a profit or loss in each one before embarking on the next. Of course, he was expected to keep the account active and turning over. I could imagine no better way to learn the true facts of finance. And I was certainly proved right! Experience teaches you how little you know, even under the best circumstances.

As an example of what I mean, when some of the 1949 forecasts came to my desk I took out some of the forecasts for 1948. Right on top of the pile was an important one listing radio issues as among the most undesirable holding for the year. In fact that was the view generally more or less held in January, 1948. Yet, as it worked out, the "undesirable" radio issues of January, 1948 turned out to be the popular television issues of December of the same year. They were the same stocks and they sold much higher.

How did these expensive research staffs, with their "field research," miss out so badly? They did miss out badly, because I could go on citing such examples indefinitely. Was it partly that "$33\frac{1}{3}$" passing grade in economics also applied to market forecasting? Or were some of these staffs more occupied with research than in making investments of their own?

Much more likely, their findings are entirely all right, but they, and all of us, fail to realize that they are undertaking the impossible. Dwight W. Morrow once said, when asked when he would know that the deflation of the "thirties" was over: "I will tell you six months after it has happened." Now that is the real truth. My own forecasts don't suffer from any lack of practice or experience and yet fall far short of what would be an acceptable standard of accuracy in scientific lines. This is especially true of long range forecasting, yet I manage to reach the opposite shore time and time again. Why?

A lot of hunting for the answer turned it up, and it proved quite simple. My flair was not in picking out more winners than the next fellow, nor in knowing more often the right time to buy them, but rather in recognizing my good from my bad.

In the preceding chapter I told about cutting losses short and I will dismiss that, therefore, with a sentence here. It's a basic part of successful investing. The other basic part is following up profits. By that, I mean having a greater amount of the stock which proves to be your best selection and giving it the time to advance more. Or, if it's a case of market timing, it amounts to the same thing, namely, having more stocks when you are right than when you are wrong.

Of course, when you begin a campaign you don't know what you'll find. Usually, if you want the odds as much in your favor as can be, a buying position combines an idea you have about it being the right time and price to buy, combined with an idea as to which are the best issues. You will soon begin to find out whether you are right or wrong on the trend. If you seem to be wrong, quit as cheaply as you can, of course. If you seem to be right, you will want to enlarge your position. And when you do that, you will also sense that the issues you bought are not all acting in the same way. Here is where you will start to discard the ones you begin to find less attractive and concentrate on those you find doing the best for you. Usually, if handled right, you end up perhaps altogether in one issue.

In my practical experience, the way to successful investment lies much more in learning how to utilize your best thoughts and minimize your worst rather than in being better at selection or better at timing than the average.

◆ 24 ◆

STRATEGY FOR PROFITS

DELIBERATE, planned speculation is, in my opinion, the best and safest method to improve one's chances of preserving the purchasing power of capital or maintaining its constant convertibility into cash without loss. Those who imagine they are interested only in "income" are knowingly or unknowingly not alive to the facts. They run the risk that at some future date their capital will have shrunk in excess of total income received in the interim.

There is only one intelligent approach to the employment or protection of capital, and that is to use it for profit. "Profit" is the net increase in the market value of invested capital at the current bid price, adding to it the dividends or interest received. If market depreciation exceeds income, then a net loss results and no profit or income is realized at all.

The majority of people have been taught to believe in the sanctity of assured income and somehow brought to think that if they watched fluctuations in the values of their investments, they were "speculators." The fact that dividends have been paid for many years back is in itself no guaranty that they may not be reduced or discontinued in the future with consequent decreasing or vanishing of income, plus capital losses realized or unrealized. Nevertheless, many unlisted issues are held by people who find comfort in vain assumption that because they do not see their holdings change in price daily the securities do not fluctuate in value. Of course, this view is entirely fallacious, as witness the declines which occurred between 1929 and 1939 in values of private real estate mortgages, mortgage bonds, and other unquotable or rarely-quoted types of investment.

The tables herewith list a selection of the better-known and more active New York Stock Exchange issues, showing the range in round figures between the highest and lowest prices for 1964 in comparison with the dividends paid, and the costs of dealing in $10,000 worth of

TABLE I — ANNUAL PRICE SPREAD VS. DIVIDENDS

Stock	1964 Range	Point Spread	1964 Dividend
Texas Gulf Sulphur...........	65–21	44	$0.40
Chrysler	68–38	30	1.00*
Radio Corp...................	39–30	9	.60*
Amer. Tel. & Tel..............	75–65	10	1.95
DuPont	294–226	68	7.25†
Xerox........................	132–70	62	0.40
General Motors	103–77	26	4.45
Pan Amer. World Air	38–27	11	0.60
Ford	62–49	13	2.00
Westinghouse Elec.	47–29	18	1.20
U.S. Steel	65–51	14	2.00
Pennsylvania R.R.............	43–25	18	1.25
Brunswick Corp.	12–8	4	nil

* *Plus stock.*
† *Plus 36/100 share of General Motors.*

any particular issue. The purpose is to stress the relative importance of fluctuations (capital gains and losses) as against dividends or interest (income). The costs of dealing shown in Table II at various price levels are far lower than under any other method of buying securities. Moreover, they emphasize how little consideration need be given them in deciding when to buy and sell.

The strategy of successful investment or speculation turns, first, on the ability to submit results to honest periodic appraisal. If money is being lost, the realization that it is being lost is worth a good many dollars and cents in deciding future policies.

This chapter is directed at the average owner of capital whose ordinary day-to-day living is made in other lines. In my opinion, success for this class of untrained security buyer will come more easily if he begins by adhering to six principles:

(1) Employ a broker to fill orders and help obtain information and make decisions.

(2) Buy only leading, listed and active securities that are quoted daily in the better newspapers.

TABLE II—COST OF BUYING AND SELLING

Stock	Close 12/31/64	Cost to buy $10,000 worth of each issue (a)	Cost of "round trip" (b)
Texas Gulf Sulphur......	$51\frac{1}{8}$	$85.00	$181.59
Chrysler	61	81.09	172.54
DuPont.................	$240\frac{1}{4}$	104.46	224.76
Amer. Tel. & Tel.........	$68\frac{1}{4}$	78.19	166.33
Radio Corp..............	$33\frac{7}{8}$	46.89	99.56
Xerox..................	$98\frac{5}{8}$	48.86	105.88
General Motors.........	$97\frac{7}{8}$	54.79	117.79
Pan Amer. World Air ...	$28\frac{1}{2}$	117.92	235.60
Ford....................	$54\frac{3}{8}$	83.84	178.94
Westinghouse Elec.......	$42\frac{1}{2}$	99.18	211.64
U. S. Steel..............	51	84.93	181.52
Pennsylvania R.R........	$38\frac{5}{8}$	102.93	220.19
Brunswick Corp.........	9	173.21	372.12

(a) Includes New York Stock Exchange commission.
(b) Includes full New York Stock Exchange buying and selling commissions, federal and New York State taxes and registration fee.

(3) Consider the fluctuations in price and not just the dividend rate.
(4) Don't over-diversify.
(5) Don't always be 100 percent invested.
(6) Cut losses.

A good Stock Exchange broker is carefully regulated by both the Exchange of which he is a member and the Securities and Exchange Commission in Washington. Many, if not most, brokers today also act as dealers and at times receive special compensation. A broker in the dictionary sense of the word has no securities to sell. In fact, the security buyer, in paying him a set and publicized commission, makes him his agent, and thus the representative of his own interests. His advice and information is unbiased, not only as between the merits of various issues but also as to whether the time is right to buy or sell or act at all. The commission charged for buying or selling is low enough to allow switching, taking of profits or cutting of losses if future conditions justify. There are those who might accuse a broker of stimulating unwise trading to make commissions. Unfortunately, this is occasionally true. However, if you are careful to select a fully qualified man he will necessarily be a man of integrity. You can make it clear to him that, for the purposes outlined here, you want him to act solely as a broker and as your agent and trustee, as it were.

The dealer, or the broker, acting as a dealer or for special compensation, is primarily a salesman who, as an expected part of his business, represents the attractive features of what he happens to have on his shelves to sell. The relationship between dealer and security buyer is exactly the same as between any seller and buyer in any line. Good dealers are a necessary part of our business system, and have a vital function in supplying new capital to industry. Their logical clients are professionals who understand the advantages they offer.

For non-professionals, the benefits of confining purchases to active, widely-known, listed securities are manifold. The spread between the offering price at which they can be bought and the bid price at which they can be sold in the auction market is as narrow as can be found in the security business. The price paid or received can be checked at the time on the Stock Exchange ticker tape, and later in the newspapers. Banks are always immediately willing to lend the largest amounts of money at the lowest rates on active, listed collateral.

The day-to-day price path of such a security, when carefully followed in relation to the market as a whole, to other securities in the same general group, and to the news, furnishes an invaluable clue to the state of affairs in the company, and occasionally provides a danger signal. Published prices are at all times a correct guide for appraisal of investment funds. The maximum of information is ordinarily available on such shares. The business of large, well-known companies is safer.

Thus the two principles of employing a broker and confining purchases to active, leading, listed issues provide automatic advantages which make a very sizable difference year in and year out in increasing profits or reducing losses.

The third to sixth principles now remain as the intangibles where only judgment rather than precise rules can apply.

It should be obvious that all the really choice issues are very well known. Hence, the average investor must put his emphasis on timing. Everybody knows General Motors Corp. is a good company. Few know when to buy it and sell it. Being a good company has not prevented its earnings, dividends, and price from registering many wide ups and downs. I think the hazards of trying to buy and sell unquestionably good companies at the right times are infinitely smaller than specializing solely in company analyses or attempting to unearth new and untried ventures that will grow into popularity and solid success. It is best to concentrate one's efforts, and to select a broker who concentrates his efforts, on market timing.

If timing is right, one stock—the leader if it can be recognized—is all that is necessary to buy. Or perhaps a very few stocks of different degrees of risk, say two or three. The practice of diversification among dozens of issues is sheer folly for medium or even fairly large securities accounts. The cost of buying and selling is higher if diversification forces odd-lot buying. No mixed list can do as well as the prime leaders. Selection of too many issues is often a form of hedging against ignorance. Some people imagine falsely that it is safer. One can know a great deal about a very few issues, but it is impossible to have a thorough knowledge of all the ones which go into a diversified list. The chance for errors in judgment is thus increased by diversification, and certainly keeping posted on a broad list after it is purchased is much more difficult than keeping posted on a few very select shares.

Aim at a real profit. Reject everything that does not promise to advance generously in price. Keep cash if enough issues with such promise cannot be found or if the investment per issue becomes unwieldy. Shares purchased for a big profit may be sold long before the original goal is achieved, but the better ones will do far more than gain 4 percent to 8 percent if intelligence is applied to the handling of the account. Issues that just seem to pay a dividend or look amply priced can usually go down as fast or faster than those that hold the greatest promise for advance. Thus, keep uninvested unless and until a particularly opportune time presents itself. This policy is commonly called "speculative." In fact, it is speculation recognized as such and undertaken only when the odds are in one's favor. To buy something expecting it to double in price and see it decline calls for a far greater error in judgment than "investing" funds the day received in something one hopes will pay a steady income, and seeing that cut or pass its dividend.

Nevertheless, mistakes will be made. And when they are, there is no cheaper insurance than accepting a loss quickly. That is the tactic of retreat rather than capitulation. I think it would be very difficult for an investor losing, say, 5 percent to 10 percent each time on a succession of ventures, to continue to lose time and time again without checking his errors or stopping altogether. On the other hand, a buyer who holds regardless of unfavorable news or action can become involuntarily locked in his "investment" for years, and often no amount of future waiting can extract him from his predicament. It is important to regard the situation with an open mind, unbiased by a bad stale position, and it is important to be able to act each time convictions are very strong. Unless losses are cut, such an attitude and such action are impossible.

These rules also apply to bonds and preferred stocks. My own bond buying suggestions are confined to just three types:

(1) U. S. Government issues with stated repurchase prices.

(2) Very high-grade, very short-term issues.

(3) Active bonds selling at speculative (low) prices due to investment selling where either the general timing of the situation or individual prospects strongly suggest a turn for the better.

If there is any doubt that bond fluctuations are not more important than bond coupons, just check prices over the past years for former high-grade issues bearing low coupons, and note the large number which have sold or are selling thirty, forty and fifty points below par. Such bonds are down sometimes because of loss of quality, but more often because interest rates have gone up. There are always many high-grade, high-priced bonds and preferreds that can decline in price in years to come through a recurrence of either or both of these reasons.

25

THE EVER-LIQUID ACCOUNT

THERE IS A PHILOSOPHY of handling investments that perhaps is quickest described by dubbing it "The Ever-Liquid Account."

The name is completely descriptive. Handled in this way, one's funds are *always* liquid. Briefly, in its operation, an ever-liquid account is normally kept fully uninvested; i.e., in cash or equivalent only. "Equivalent" means any kind of really liquid short-term security or commercial paper. Book values and market values are always kept identical. Income is real income; i.e., interest, dividends, capital gains realized and realizable, less capital losses taken or unrealized in the account, which is always marked to the market. Investment and speculation are merged.

My experience with this philosophy of investment is that it gives some people great peace of mind. It seems to prove more profitable In deflationary periods and less so otherwise. I do think that it has a place in certain types of investor thinking. By the nature of the world, everything is today less safe and sure. This method recognizes that fact and does not tend to lull people into false security. In fact, in *apparently* bringing diminishing current returns, it may actually be protecting against large capital losses to be suffered in the future by the always "fully invested" class.

Income and appreciation are obtained in the ever-liquid account by entering the stock market as a buyer when a situation and trend seem clearly enough established so that a paper profit is present immediately after making the purchase. In order to keep the account truly ever-liquid, one must use a mental or an actual stop on all commitments amounting to some predetermined percentage of the amount invested. There are those who have used 3 percent and others up to 10 percent. Of course one does not make a purchase unless one feels rather sure that the trend is sufficiently well established to minimize the possibility of being stopped out. Yet it will happen occasionally anyway.

The decision of what and when to buy is made on a personal basis using various yardsticks best understood by individual investors. More or less, I use all of the accepted sources of information, including a general understanding of economics, statistical research, etc., together with material gathered through personal contact with corporation executives and observation of the character of buying and selling orders, etc. However, the stock finally selected must of necessity be a very liquid active market leader or give extremely strong promise of shortly entering that class; and in order to buy and hold it or increase one's line of it, it must be advancing in price. To that extent, technical factors are vital but otherwise they are only incidental.

This investment philosophy leads into concentrated purchases of single issues rather than diversification, because one of the primary elements in the situation is that one must know and be convinced of the rightness of what one is doing. Diversification as to issue and type of investment is only hedging—a method of averaging errors or covering up lack of judgment.

This ever-liquid method also rarely calls for attempts to buy at the bottom, as bottoms and tops are actually impossible to judge ordinarily, while trends after they are established and under way can be profitably recognized.

It is a method that leans towards pyramiding; i.e., towards following up gains and retreating before losses. Such an account, properly handled, bends but never breaks. "Averaging down" is, of course, completely against its theory.

In normal markets, by which I mean active markets with broad varied participation and not unusually subject to unpredictable news developments, the belief that it is the right time to buy a certain leader will be so positive in the competent operator's mind that he will not hesitate to take a rather large position at once in one selected leading issue. This position will be much larger than if it were a segment of a diversified list, but, on the other hand, it will tend to employ a far more conservative percentage of one's capital than would ordinarily be spread about the board by orthodox speculation or investments. There might be times when an investor would use 20–25 percent of the account in such a single issue, though this percentage would not apply in special cases where the amount of capital is very large or very small. There naturally must be a relationship between the amount of capital, the breadth of the market in a particular stock, and the tax bracket of the owner of the account.

If the market advances as expected, more of the same stock will probably be purchased. If the markets are narrow and highly dependent on news, little or nothing will be done. What is done will be on an ever-smaller scale as far as the initial commitment in any particular issue is concerned. If the shares go down, the loss will be small. If they go up, more can be bought. The theory calls for such large profits, if successful on the small amounts employed, that the account can get a satisfactory average return with a large part of its capital seemingly sterile. And there is always a generous reserve to try again in case of losses.

It offers complete protection against holding investments that seem very sure on the basis of all the known facts and yet decline marketwise. After a small decline, the ever-liquid method forces liquidation regardless of other facts. The fact of the market decline itself is the ruling fact of the situation. More often than not, many months and many points lower the real causes of the decline become evident to the "transfer it into your own name and lock it up" class of buyer.

At times, of course, a stock will decline for temporary reasons, and then start on a real advance. There is no rule against repurchase lower or higher as far as the ever-liquid account is concerned. In fact, repurchases at higher than the original or first liquidation price tend, in my experience, to return profits rather more than the average buy. The reason for this phenomenon is that the market, in getting stronger when the general expectation suggests it will get weaker, is, in fact, giving an A-1 buying suggestion to those who will see it and are not afraid to follow it. However, the ever-liquid account, having taken a loss and being out of the market, is in a preferred position because its owner goes back into the same stock only if conditions justify. He is not just locked in and hoping. In the interval of time, another issue may, on the revival of an uptrend, seem far more attractive. There is a lot of meat in these last two sentences.

This procedure puts a premium on ability. It is not easy. Lack of knowledge shows up quickly. Luck plays no part in it. The accounting reflects the real situation, and one is never kidding oneself with a taxable income from gains on a few coupons clipped, dividends received, and profits taken while actually there exists a far greater unrealized loss in issues still held and "too low to sell."

The ever-liquid account is the acid test of successful investment or speculation. There are many other ways of making money in the security markets of course, but none that I know is so little dependent on luck or chance or where the results are more accurately reflected from an accounting standpoint.

I may as well anticipate someone saying "inflation." The fact is that liquidity and mobility are the great allies of safety against change. Intelligent capital is like a rabbit darting here and there to cover. Fixed investments, like real estate anchored to the ground, are far too inflexible for real protection against any hazard whether it is a tax hazard or a war hazard or a political or style hazard or what have you?

Hence, the "Ever-Liquid Account."

26

A REALISTIC APPRAISAL OF BONDS

HIGH-GRADE SHORT-TERM BONDS if of unimpeachable quality, are the practical equivalent of cash. Under certain conditions where investors have large sums deliberately awaiting declines in equity prices, such senior issues are desirable temporary holdings. No difficulty should be found in selecting only the first quality. Paper of this kind should be certain to be paid, otherwise it really comes into another category; hence, seeking slightly higher than current average yields is to be avoided and is almost the only danger, other than the obvious one of holding excess cash or equivalent in an inflation period.

A discussion of bonds in general hardly belongs in this book with its emphasis on the superiority of attempting to achieve capital gains over income. In fact, most bonds of this type are more sought after by institutions with fixed money obligations than by individuals.

To touch on the subject, high-grade long-term bonds are desirable only if bought on a favorable yield basis and at a time when the purchasing power of their interest coupons and the capital invested in them, when repaid or realized through sale in the market, shows a true return. By that I mean to avoid buying such bonds when basic yields are thought to be due for a rise because such increases will cause wide declines in price without any change in the character of the security behind the bond. For example, a 3 percent 20-year bond will sell at 100 if on a 3 percent basis, but will decline $13\frac{5}{8}$ percent in value to $86\frac{3}{8}$ if yields for similar securities increase to a 4 percent basis. To illustrate the second precaution, there is little point to receiving say 4 percent on capital if, when it is returned plus interest less taxes, the cost of living has risen to such an extent that the total of interest and repaid principal in currency will buy only as much or less than the principal itself at the time of the bond purchase.

Medium and low-grade bonds, long and short-term, can be judged more like stocks. It is better to look at them frankly for their appreciation possibilities. They can rarely be bought and sold in really large amounts, and are thus mostly interesting to small investors. When selected by an expert they are actually safer than many popular high-grade issues appraised conventionally. Thus I would rather buy a so-called "B" rated bond in a company on the upgrade than an "AAA" in a receding trend. That is another reason why selection of high-grade issues must be finicky. If they are at a quality ceiling, they can go up only if the trend of interest rates and purchasing power of money is judged correctly, but they can go down not only when these factors are misjudged but also if the quality rating is mistaken.

As a mathematical basis for appraisal, great care should be taken to avoid acceptance of loosely-worded statements as to the number of times interest charges of the particular issues in question are covered. This should be figured on an overall basis, including all prior charges, if any; and also total charges should be figured to help gain an accurate impression of the entire situation. As in the case of stocks, actual cash income should be set against estimated cash requirements including, on the one hand, cash received but allocated to depreciation, etc., and, on the other sinking-fund requirements, etc. Comparison of par, redemption or liquidation value of the issue under consideration and prior liens and comparison with the market value of junior liens and stock equities is usually illuminating.

The table on rates of interest compared with depreciation of money given further in the book is of paramount importance in relation to bonds.

In these times of fear of inflation and consequently fear of cash, bank accounts, and fixed capital and interest obligations, such as bonds, there is one point that certainly is worth mentioning here. It came to light, as far as I am concerned, not in any study of bonds at all, but in studying currency depreciation. Apparently, in times of extreme stress, there is more safety in a prime promise to pay than in a greenback. In Germany, for instance, during the 1920–1923 period, when marks were inflated by the trillion, many bonds fared better. Revaluation and restatement laws helped a great deal. In the case of ordinary, commercial bonds, there were even samples where conscientious directors felt it unfair to pay off their bond holders completely with fiat money. There is no guarantee that what happened in the past will happen again in the future or that what happened in one place will happen in another, but the subject is worth thinking about. The owner of a prime industrial bond, like the German General Electric, came through the hyper-inflation panic with as much as 15 percent of his capital saved, depending on when he bought them, how long he held them and when he sold them. The general idea that he was wiped out completely is erroneous.

As mentioned elsewhere, devoting thought to the social and political aspects and occasionally the ethical aspects of such matters should pay off.

The really popular bonds with the investing public in more recent years are the convertible issues and bonds with warrants to buy stock attached.

Timing Convertible Bond Purchases

If you ask a bond man what special interest the individual investor has in the bond market nowadays he will come back and tell you that it is primarily in convertibles. If you press him still further he will tell you that from time to time the private security buyer will speculate on very thin margin in long-term U.S. Government bonds.

It was not always so. When I first began writing financial columns in 1921, buying bonds for income was the favorite personal investment. Today interest in bonds comes mainly from institutions. There are some wealthy private investors who buy tax-exempts. Occasion-
ally when investors turn bearish on stocks some will temporarily turn to high-yielding bonds for income and to short-terms in the hope of greater price stability. U.S. Government bonds are of course the most widely held in the world.

Convertibles are popular because they seem under certain con-
ditions to combine a degree of bond dollar safety with a chance of profit. You can buy them on much more liberal credit terms than stocks. The actual figures vary but banks will tend to ask only

20 percent margin on a good active convertible that is not already selling at a high premium. It would take 70 percent margin under current rules to buy an active stock.

If you look at the New York Stock Exchange bond quotations you will see such bonds as National Airlines convertible 6's of 1976 quoted above 440; Macy convertible 5's of 1977 selling above 300; and General Telephone convertible $4\frac{1}{2}$'s of 1977 selling at 225. These bonds originally sold close to 100. These illustrate the profits that might have been made by careful selection, pricing and timing. You will also find some convertibles with high interest-rate coupons selling at discounts from par. This reflects their basically speculative nature.

The market price of a convertible bond is a combination of estimated true current investment value plus a premium for the current value of the conversion privilege, if any. This premium varies with the estimated opportunity to make a profit, the length of time the privilege runs and other factors.

The greatest care must be taken in buying convertibles, especially if you buy them on credit. The most common mistake is to look too closely into the size of the premium or the closeness of the conversion price on the bond to the current market for the stock into which it can be converted. I would suggest you look first into the stock for which it can be exchanged. If you are to make a profit, this must go up. You must start by being fundamentally bullish on the equity. Only then can you look into the mathematical factors governing the price of the convertible bond.

There are investors who will get their banks to finance purchases of government bonds on a 5 percent margin. For example, $5,000 on these terms will buy $100,000 market value of governments. Each one-point advance would amount to $1,000 less commissions. The greatest fluctuation here is in the lowcoupon, long-maturity type of issue, such as the $31\frac{1}{2}$ percent due in 1990. These sold above 106 in 1958 and below 85 in 1959. Recently the long-term government bond market has been in a narrow range. In 1964 the low for these bonds was a fraction under 88 and the high a fraction above 90. There are those who feel wider swings are ahead.

You will find posting yourself on the bond market can be rewarding. However, if you turn to it because of the more liberal credit terms, be cautious for a purchase can be more speculative than in stocks.

See Chapter 32, Investment and Taxation, about tax-exempt bonds.

27

MERITS OF MINING SHARES

MINING SHARES are in a special category. They are almost always quoted at better-than-average yields. This is due to the accepted practice of considering the dividend only partially true income and the remainder a return of capital. This is logical enough as obviously extraction of ore from a mine must inevitably be a step toward depletion.

Curiously, in actual practice there seems more justification for extending such accounting methods to the ordinary run of enterprises rather than emphasizing it in the mining field. I think if one went to the trouble of reviewing the figures, one would find the better mines lived much longer than many corporations. One is very much more apt to extend an ore body than to find new sources of profit to bolster a perishing industry.

It also seems to me that appraisals of prospects through examination by competent and honest mining engineers are much more certain of accuracy than similar efforts aimed at evaluating concerns engaged in other lines. Obviously, only very large investors can afford such technical assistance if rendered privately, but the same holds true of costly industrial investigation. The small security-buyer has to turn to sources for information that can afford to employ such professional services, either because of a large volume of business if a broker, or through division of the cost among their clientele if a statistical agency or investment-counsellor.

In addition to mines of recognized investment merit and known minimum life, there are, of course, many pure speculations. The dangers in this field are so enormous that the average small security-buyer had better not even attempt to participate in the extraordinarily generous profits to be had by those few that know the technique. Words like "uranium," "rare earths," etc., seem to be magic to those unsuspecting who are often fleeced. There are good uranium mines just like there are good and bad in other endeavors, but it seems as if extraordinary vigilance is needed in this field.

Of course, fundamental to any mining investment are factors outside of the ore body. These include factors relating to a given mine, such as cost of production, and factors relating to mines in general, such as the metal or mineral price, taxation and politics.

The cost of production varies with each ore body and the depth to which it is mined as well as to existing labor conditions. National as well as local tax policies are important.

Politics enters into prices at times. Gold and silver have both been artificially controlled in price and the price of uranium is fixed by the government. Devices such as stockpiling often alter a price ordinarily fixed by supply and demand. Often wartime controls are a factor. Politics also enters into subsidies for increasing production, such as was seen in aluminum.

Despite these influences in normal times in most cases metal and mineral prices are usually affected by supply and demand.

Despite all these complexities, mining shares nevertheless have great interest and great value for those in a position to get the right information and evaluate it correctly. As in oil, many fortunes have been built from mining. After all, the important tax on a discovery is limited to the approximate 25 percent capital gains rate.

There is one relatively conservative method of investing in mines and that is through a mining investment and finance company. The outstanding one in this country is Newmont. There are some with the most excellent management, records, and reputation abroad. These companies have their own engineering and prospecting staffs and develop new mines in the field. Original expenses are paid out of pocket; successful prospects are financed and later capitalized, and, in part, distributed to the public. I feel the best ones are more attractive (and also more speculative) than general investment trusts, partly for the reason already expressed, that appraisal of mines is more certain than appraisal of industrial or rail prospects. Furthermore, their specialization is likely to be an additional advantage. The frequency of granting options in mining finance is often the source of really huge and unexpected profits, very often all out of proportion to risks.

A final word about gold shares. They long received prime ratings in Throgmorton Street. Over a period of many years, they came nearest to the perfect means of preserving current purchasing power for future use, i.e., hoarding of metallic gold where it is legal.

Gold companies are relieved of any effort to find markets for their product in contrast with the usual extensive and costly sales departments of ordinary business concerns. Furthermore, the price of gold has broadly increased for centuries.

Gold shares are devaluation hedges. The desire for gold is the most universal and deeply rooted commercial instinct of the human race.

Ordinarily, the chief threat to the quality mines is excessive taxation. Labor is occasionally a bearish factor. Competent advice will eliminate serious danger of any but occasional and unimportant losses due to depletion of ore reserves. Gold can for a time lose purchasing power, but to me demonetization is unthinkable.

As with other mines, the income return tends to be high and the fact that a return of capital is included is an advantage that is sometimes overlooked at first sight. Perpetual investments always eventually vanish, and the automatic amortization in the case of gold mines tends to release funds for expenditure in one's lifetime rather than to the tax collectors. They provide cash for constant reinvestment. This of itself is an important safeguard of capital.

Nevertheless, for a long while, chiefly because of political regulation but partly because gold like everything else moves in cycles, the times have been against them. They provide a perfect example of the importance of timing in all matters of investment. There can be little doubt but that eventually the price of gold will increase again. In fact, it could under certain conditions double overnight. This would be cold comfort to the investor who bought too soon and suffered patiently for many years.

28

DIVERSIFICATION OF INVESTMENTS

THIS IS A CHAPTER for the experienced and the professional. The beginner needs diversification until he learns the ropes.

For those who are accomplished I think most accounts have entirely too much diversification of the wrong sort and not enough of the right. I can see no point at all to a distribution of so much percent in oils, so much in motors, so much in rails, etc., nor do I see the point of dividing a fund from a quality angle of so much in "governments," and so on down the list to that so called very awful, speculative, non-dividend-paying common stock. Some geographical diversification might be justified for large funds.

This sort of thing might be necessary when capital reaches an unwieldy total, or it might be necessary where no intelligent supervision is likely. Otherwise, it is an admission of not knowing what to do and an effort to strike an average.

The intelligent and safe way to handle capital is to concentrate. If things are not clear, do nothing. When something comes up, follow it *to the limit*, subject to the method of procedure that follows. If it's not worth following to the limit, it is not worth following at all. My thought, of course, is always start with a large cash reserve; next, begin in one issue in a small way. If it does not develop, close out and get back to cash. But if it does do what is expected of it, expand your position in this one issue on a scale up. After, but not before, it has safely drawn away from your highest purchase price, then you might consider a second issue.

The greatest safety lies in putting all your eggs in one basket and watching the basket. You simply cannot afford to be careless or wrong. Hence, you act with much more deliberation. Of course, no thinking person will buy more of something than the market will take if he wants to sell, and, here again, the practical test will force one into the listed leaders where one belongs. A smart trader isn't going to put all his capital into poor collateral, either.

In the old days when broker's loans were at fantastic heights, the banks used to get a quick idea of the finances of the brokers by the makeup of their loans. If the collateral was all bundles of big active leaders, the bank's opinion was high. But if it was a mixture of new, untried specialties, then the expression was: "So and so is getting to the bottom of his box." Why buy securities that your broker will try to hide in the bottom of his box if his finances permit? Diversification is a balm to many who don't mind taking a chance on something a little sour in a mixed list, figuring on the better ones to pull it out and make a good average.

So buy only staples in securities; the kind that are "not included in this sale." I am thinking now of men's clothing in which all sorts of fancy ties, suitings and shirtings are sold at abnormal mark-ups early in the season and for what they are really worth at the close. But certain solid colored ties, white shirts, plain blue and gray suits, conservatively cut, are practically always excluded from the sale. Securities are not so different, and it is important to deal only in those that always, because of their nature or distribution, have a certain amount of residual interest. Be careful that in "diversifying" you are not supplying the bid for varying groups of narrow market issues that are the style for the moment because there is a special profit in trying to make them so.

Of course, we always have to remember that "one man's meat is another man's poison." The greatest safety for the capable I might say lies in putting all one's eggs in one basket and watching the basket. The beginner and those who simply find their investment efforts unsuccessful must resort to orthodox diversification.

I always feel that the less active a stock and the further distant the market, the more potential profit I need to see in it to make it worth buying. If one thinks he sees a potential profit of 100 percent in an active New York Stock Exchange leader, certainly one would have to expect more to go to a regional exchange or over-the-counter or to a foreign market. This is a fundamental and logical principle.

Another angle of diversification nowadays is the fear of atom bombing and what it might do to property. Investors have looked to geographical diversification because of these fears whereas in more normal times, purely profit motives made for concentration. It is purely a personal matter whether an investor feels that efforts at safety from bombing are more important than trying to get the maximum out of investing.

There is a further diversification which I've never seen mentioned and which is important to consider. This is diversification as between the position of varying companies in their business cycle or as between their shares in their market price cycle. This is a very important consideration because dividing one's funds between three or four different situations which happen all to be in the same sector of their cycle can often be discouraging or dangerous. After all, the final determinant of investment success or failure is market price. For example, industries which are in the final stages of a boom with rapidly increasing earnings dividends and possibly split-ups, often offer shares high in price but apparently rapidly going higher. There is a sound justification for an investor who knows what he is doing to buy into such a situation, especially for short-term gains, but it would be quite dangerous for him to put all of his funds in three or four such situations. Taken the other way, naturally we all seek deflated and cheap bargains, but very often shares like this will lie on the bottom much longer than we anticipate and if every share we own is in this same category, we may do very badly in a relatively good market.

29

TRAVEL AS AN EDUCATION
FOR INVESTORS

ONCE I WATCHED a news-weekly film of fleeing refugees. Their homes were burning in the background. Their businesses, connections, and savings, also, were probably lost forever.

I can recall very vividly the great San Francisco earthquake of 1906. I remember the refugees fleeing that natural calamity. Many lost all they had. Few carried earthquake insurance. Many had fire policies with a "falling building" clause invalidating them. Even the land shifted in value. Good locations became poor. Poor ones became good.

Once I visited Moscow and saw what inflation and confiscation can do to a people. On the dock where we landed was a "Torgsin" store. Offered for sale were the former personal effects of old aristocracy—furs, jewelry, furniture, art objects, all for sale for the account of the State. Driving through the streets of Leningrad, I saw whole city blocks of houses getting a coat of whitewash. The State owned all the houses, so they got the same general treatment as the street-cleaning department would give our streets.

About 1932, I motored through some of the old "ghost" mining towns of the West. Blocks and blocks of once busy streets were boarded up and deserted, values vanished for the moment at least.

Just about this time, someone wants to know whether common stocks are a hedge against war, or what is the best hedge against inflation? No one asks about hedges against quakes or fires or floods or shifts in values due to economic changes, though it would be just as logical. And I think of Russia and Germany and Spain, and of how all the popular "hedges" must have been useless.

If there is an effective hedge against calamity, it is a combination of geographic diversification, retention of capital in mobile form, and the keeping in personal touch with active business, both at home and in other centers.

One must keep personally active, alert, and in the swim. Retired businessmen, in my opinion, haven't much chance. One must not tie up all one's assets in one's home town or in a form that is not liquid and subject to easy shifts. There are far too many people who have a small business in their home city, their own house in the same city, and if they own any securities, some shares perhaps in the local utility company. In addition, their friends and business connections are all within a radius of 10 to 15 miles.

My real thought is that one's greatest assets are his mental competence to do something useful and his connections. Therefore, establish some emergency connections away from home. Establish a fund or funds away from home as well, both as a "calamity hoard" and as an aid to keeping your foreign interests alive.

For example, I think a trip to London is an education if the person making it knows how to get the most out of it. Meet the right people. When you come home, keep up your contacts.

It is growing very popular to combine business and pleasure for the real benefits that accrue as well as for the tax deduction. In order to get the deduction the business done must be real. I mention this because travel does not necessarily have to be all personal expense. The analysts societies nowadays fly a group of their members to Europe and Japan.

Many years ago, a very clever investor told me that time began at Greenwich and moved westward and so did everything else—ideas included. The social conditions affecting investment and living in England today are undoubtedly the most accurate foretaste one could get of the conditions with which we will have to cope in a very few years. Forewarned is forearmed and a visit to London to talk to bankers, brokers, and solicitors and observe what has happened to them and what they are doing about it to minimize the situation certainly should pay the larger American investor very well.

One can travel a bit around the U.S.A. and do a little diversification against calamity as well as discover some good investments just on their own merits.

Texas is perhaps the best place to visit in the U.S.A. along with Washington, D.C., and always, first of all, New York City. The leaders of Texas are aggressive and looking for capital gains and know all about finding oil, be it in Texas or elsewhere. Washington is the source of information concerning the governmental decisions that affect every investment. New York City is still the center and clearinghouse of everything from everywhere.

One ought to be able to move to several parts of this country and the world, and have enough friends to be happy and get a helping hand to start, and have ready at hand enough funds for a grubstake. Ask yourself how many widely separated places you could go to and make a successful new start in life.

Travel is a wonderful education and education is a wonderful hedge these days to those who can capitalize on it. One gets all the advantages listed above—a real vacation, a better knowledge of how to enjoy life, and an advantage over one's provincial competitors at home.

30

GENERAL THOUGHTS ON SPECULATION

THERE ARE THOSE who read these articles and will bring up the following questions: How is the inexperienced man going to speculate successfully? How will he get the time? What will employers say to employees who neglect their work to watch the market? What about those who cannot possibly learn a technique? What's to be done? What are the answers?

In the first place, I think that if any reader of these chapters is convinced—really convinced—he cannot master the market, a great deal has been accomplished, because the great majority will fail in the market, and it's worth dollars and cents to them to know it.

In an earlier chapter I pointed out that there are not nearly enough good investments or speculations to go around. Hence, on an actuarial basis, when one ventures into *any* kind of investment or speculation, the odds are against one. It is not like going downtown in the subway or taking a motor-car ride or even having one's appendix taken out. In all these activities, one normally and correctly expects to arrive at one's destination or recover one's health. This is not true when attempting to store up capital. One is destined to lose in two ways: First, invisibly to the average man, through currency depreciation over the years, or to put it another way, through higher prices for the things one buys; next, through depreciation or a direct drop in prices of "security" you buy. Thus one should attack the problem with the thought that one must excel; one must be the exception to the rule to succeed.

Wherever it is at all possible, I advise trying it personally. This means one must be youthful, as old hands don't learn new tricks. One must have a stake to try. One can decide to spend one's money for a lot of things. One person can drink or smoke his surplus. Another might lose it in the market with the advantage that he might find himself losing something for "tuition" and gaining later lifelong advantage and security. As to the time required, it's of course possible, by working hard, to do a full day's work at one's regular job and still do a lot in the market. Most of the world works, ambling along, doing an hour's work in two.

One might very easily advance the argument that employers don't want employees "fiddling" with the market. In the case of banks, insurance companies, brokers, dealers, and others handling money and securities, the reasons are obvious and valid. In industrial, professional, and other lines I don't know that it's exactly a fair attitude, and I think it's important enough to pick a job someplace where the management is open-minded.

Nothing ventured, nothing gained. I have heard some people say they "never borrowed a penny." I have heard others tell me they borrowed to create a spur to force them ahead. It was usually the latter who won, provided the borrowing was done young and done for business reasons, for expansion and not to bolster up a failing situation.

As in anything else, there are various degrees of competency. Thus, for instance, there may be some who feel they cannot attempt the full program outlined here, and still they might feel able to judge when the common-stock tide was running in and when it was running out. Perhaps this might logically be done with proper assistance. If so, I suggest trying it, buying the best investment trusts which seem true cross-sections of the stock market. Buy those with the best and most honest management and those where all efforts are devoted to making money for the stockholders of the trust. More or less complete freedom for the management is desirable. Then there are the so-called closed end trusts which have a set capitalization and are quoted in the market, sometimes at discounts and sometimes at premiums from asset value. I ordinarily favor these over the open end trusts or mutual funds. The latter can expand or contract their capitalization as the merchandising organizations sponsoring them find new stockholders or as the present stockholders demand mand redemptions. The main idea is to buy when one feels a bull market is in progress; sell and hold cash when one thinks the trend is bearish. Don't expect the trust to do the switching for you.

For those with substantial funds who do not feel capable of even this, I rather favor the investment management department of a bank. One probably can find large established investment-counsel concerns with well rounded staffs that are perhaps more liberal and modern in their viewpoint. There are smaller concerns that revolve around one personality. Sometimes this individual is a genius, and during his lifetime his management is invaluable. However, the situation should be reappraised in the event of his death, and this type of firm should never be mentioned in a will.

Thus we get back to our primary argument all the way through this book that a great deal of personal judgment is necessary if one is to succeed. If it's not a case of judging stocks, then it's judging men. However, when the minimum of judgment is likely to be used, I favor the bank above the average counselor. He will be more orthodox, and if one can't be 100 percent unorthodox and win all along the line, then by all means go the whole hog the other direction and don't experiment in between. Select a New York City trust company, preferably one with a few large accounts rather than a host of small ones.

Finally, I am asked, what about the power of attorney? What about trying to get a broker to run one's account? What about an investment counselor of the individualistic type rather than the big counsel concern? Here we get back to the psychology of selecting the right man, to say nothing of having him willing to take the account. And your contribution must be to put him so completely at ease that he will do what he thinks best without fearing your possible unfavorable reaction. Personally, I think there are a few who will succeed with this. I think the odds are too much against one really to advocate trying very hard along such lines.

I have tried to write out frank conclusions from my own observation and experience, derived from attempting to invest as a private client up to 1921 and since then as a professional, who has handled an enormous number of shares. I think I have stepped on other people's toes; but no more than on my own. Most of what is said here comes from practical experience. Still I realize that quite unconsciously what seems easy and natural and logical to me might seem utterly impossible to others, and likewise that people of different natures and abilities might succeed far better than I can ever hope to, following entirely different policies. One can decide to travel by foot, on the back of an animal, in an animal-drawn conveyance, on a bicycle, train or motor, on a ship or a plane, and still arrive at the same destination. Hence, I am altogether open minded on the whole subject.

The most important thing I have learned over the last 40 years in Wall Street is to realize how little everyone knows and how little I know; luckily I learned that lesson in 1922 and 1923 and not in the period from 1929 to 1932, when it would have been costly. One of the shrewdest speculators I know once remarked that if some supernatural power could guarantee him for the rest of his life maintenance of the purchasing power of *one quarter* of the quoted value of his cash and securities today, he would quickly hand over the other three-quarters in payment. But he sadly concluded it couldn't be done. This is the realistic way people who think straight look at our situation today—not in terms of "6 percent and safety." It is an advantage to be old and have lived life; our children face uncertain times.

The most important things any reader of these chapters can learn are likewise that investment and speculation are difficult, not easy; uncertain, not clear-cut; treacherous, not logical. Here, more than anywhere in the world, is the land of illusion. Things are not what they seem. Two and two don't always make four. "Stocks were made to sell." *Caveat emptor*—"Let the buyer beware."

31

INVESTMENT AND SPENDING

THE PURPOSE OF INVESTMENT is to have funds available at a later date for spending. There are two aspects of the subject of spending which relate directly to investment policies. The first has to do with changes in the cost and availability of the things we wish to buy. The second is concerned with the proper division of available funds between immediate or future spending, or, to put it another way, between investment and spending.

Each of us saves for security in old age and to spend, and principally to spend during our own lifetime. Leaving something for future generations is all right in its way, but a big part of an inheritance is cut down by taxes and thus goes to the government. In these uncertain times, it doesn't pay to over-provide for the future—taxation, social legislation, war, rationing, etc. all work to destroy some of the value of what has been put aside. For successful people these days, it is enough to leave real property to future generations, going businesses or homes, but a really large investment accumulation had better be principally dissipated in the lifetime of the person who built it up.

I recall a shrewd friend of mine, now deceased, who in the days of his life and in the terms of his own abilities felt that a working capital of $250,000 was all he would ever need. Each good year, therefore, he spent everything he made, even though it meant going considerably above his own idea of his average standard of living. If he had a bad year, he dipped into capital to secure funds to maintain his standard of living. This man spent a lot of money, but his ability to make money was very great, and taxes those days were lower. The story is given here to illustrate the principle, not to suggest any specific figure.

It should be remembered that the depreciation of a currency is measured not only by indices of purchasing power alone, but also by the way the cost or availability of things is altered by sales taxes and rationing. The buyer of a motor car in England in 1913 paid no "purchase" tax, as they call it, or at most a trivial one. The buyer, a few years later, not only paid a purchase tax equal to the cost of the vehicle but also had to wait some years for delivery if indeed he could procure a car at all. People in Japan today who have the money to install telephones cannot get them. They have to go into the black market and pay high to buy someone else's listing. Higher sales taxes and the unavailability of products and services thus often work to depreciate the value of savings in the same way as rising prices.

The tendency of most people who have the knack of making money is to keep making more and more. If a dollar were always a dollar, it would be easy to work out a forecast of retirement needs and often avoid over-spending or over-saving. However, we all are plagued by the fear that the cost of living may rise faster than our retirement and emergency provisions. This fear is real, as many annuitants, pensioners and endowment policy holders know too well.

I remember visiting the Temple of Angkor Wat near Siem Reap in Indo-China, and chatting with the French manager of the hotel in that hot, humid spot. He told me that for years he had been working there in self-chosen exile from his native France, to accumulate a quantity of francs that would enable him to return home and retire modestly. Needless to say, by the time he reached his goal, devaluation of the franc had wiped out most of the value of his savings. All his sacrifices were in vain. He might just as well have lived at home and spent moderately as he went along, enjoying his life from day to day instead of waiting for his ship which never came in.

The human capacity for enjoyment decreases at a fast rate, both by age and quantitatively. A cup of coffee means a great deal to a cold, thirsty man. The multi-millionaire gags at drinking more than two or three cups. Also, the man of 30 will enjoy a world cruise more than when he is 65. Usually, however, the pocketbook is longer at 65 and of course time is more available. The man at 65 might enjoy a rocking chair or his petunias.

My philosophy in these matters leans to denial early in life to build a competence, later to maintain it at a productive level, and to spend any excess rather than let it build up geometrically. In the end, it only may lose its value, or go to the inheritance tax collector.

As to the question of a proper division of available funds between immediate and future spending, there can be no doubt that the amount to spend at various periods of a lifetime often becomes an investment decision, though not always recognized as such. At the start, when one first goes to work, the amount of saving and spending is almost certain to be regulated by individual economic factors. There is no point of discussing what to do, or not to do, until earnings grow sufficiently to offer a choice. Earnings at first are likely to be close to the subsistence level, or below. Even so, in many cases, an element of choice does exist. For example, there frequently is parental assistance, or inheritance.

These choices should be seen clearly and appraised objectively. Interested as I am in investment and the earliest possible creation of a fund with which to begin, I naturally counsel conservatism in spending during youth. However, in reality, all of us have first an investment in ourselves as earning individuals, and next an investment in our savings or inheritances. So when I counsel a frugal course, I mean mainly as to diversions. Money invested in one's self, be it for education, appearance, contacts or good health, is another matter. It is, of course, obvious that alliances which on the one hand build monetary overhead and responsibilities, and on the other steal time, logically play no part in any well-thought-out and aggressive program of advancement and savings, or, to put it more bluntly, marrying before one's ship comes in.

Spending casts a shadow to the end of a spender's life. The cost of a luxury expenditure to a successful investor may be very high. For example, if an article costs $1,000 at age 30, and this capital otherwise could be used for profitable speculative investment, the real cost of the article if bought keeps growing with the years. The object itself gradually depreciates to a zero value. On the other hand, one thousand dollars successfully invested becomes $2,000, then $2,000 becomes $4,000 and so on. This is what I mean by spending casting a shadow to the end of one's life.

The creation of a fund for investment can be accelerated by using other people's money as capital as much as possible. For instance, it is the utmost folly for a young man to divert capital into buying a home while he still needs a fund for investment and before he has reached his financial goals unless he has abandoned them as unattainable as far as his mentality is concerned. Let the landlord get his rental out of his house capital if he can but you get the use and profit out of your money. Of course, where the government furnishes most of the capital for a home on long term amortizing loans the buyer can have both his capital fund and his home. In fact, as his investment aims are very high and the government interest rate very low and as the amortization plus general social policies practically prohibit foreclosure, a veteran for example offered such a deal often has a good thing. However, the mathematics of the situation must in each case be carefully figured to make certain the advantages over renting are real.

All of this is designed merely to help readers lay out their investment and spending plans. Each of us has to decide between spending and saving, just as we must choose between working and playing. The tendency in early years is to over-spend and in later years to under-spend. The average younger man will do better to think more of the future. The older and more successful man will do better to think of the present. Successful individuals who have found the key to profits sometimes seem to get on a treadmill of grinding out more and more profits, forgetting that as they get older, the span of life and the capacity to enjoy it keeps diminishing.

32

INVESTMENT AND TAXATION

THE REVENUE ACT OF 1964 marks the first significant reduction in Federal income taxes in many years. Nevertheless, the high rate of Federal taxation imposed today, makes a knowledge of tax principles essential to investors, large or small. No estimate of possible profit, or risk of possible loss—no expectation of net income return—means anything without a correct application of tax influences.

Under conditions existing in this country, the tax situation and the inflation situation are very much intertwined. The investor who wishes to successfully hedge against inflation must consider realistic earnings and balance sheet values, net, after taxes. It is well known, for instance, that current corporate depreciation rates are insufficient to take care of replacement values. This is because amortization is permitted only on the basis of costs and where these assets were acquired or constructed years ago, cost figures in present day dollars are most unrealistic. The effect is to force overstatement of pre-tax earnings. This increases the corporate tax bill, and it also decreases the ability of corporations to protect their common stockholders against inflationary influences.

It is most essential that the relative importance of tax factors versus investment factors be most carefully weighed at all times. The investor must be sure that the attractiveness of an investment is not destroyed by a poor tax shelter. There is little merit to an otherwise good inflation hedge, if vulnerable to taxation. He must also be careful not to overstress tax advantages and buy otherwise poor investments as a result.

Wholly Tax-Exempt Bonds

The study of taxation as applied to investment therefore becomes a very broad one. It divides itself naturally into two parts, concerning the tax shelter or lack of it in the corporation itself, and the tax situation as it applies to the personal tax of the investor. It begins with the type of security involved. Foremost in this category are the tax-exempt bonds outstanding and still being issued by the various states of the Union, counties, municipalities and tax districts, etc. These bonds are "tax exempt"—the owner does not pay any Federal income tax on the interest received. They fluctuate with changes in money rates and the credit conditions of their various issuers.

Unsuccessful efforts are made periodically to overcome their tax-exempt status.

Despite their tax-exemption, these securities are not as desirable as they might appear at first glance. With rising taxes, they have become so much in demand that they sell at high prices and at low income yields. Buyers ordinarily figure their tax bracket and compare yields from taxable income with tax-exempt yields.

Thus, a person with a taxable net income of about $50,000 a year, filing a separate return, would, at 1964 rates, be approximately in somewhat more than an over-all 40 percent bracket and pay a tax in excess of $20,000 a year. He would have to secure a 2¾ percent taxable income to leave him with the same amount net as a 1½ percent return on a tax-exempt bond. The same individual would be close to the 60 percent bracket as regards the last few dollars of his income and would have to secure almost 3¾ percent of taxable income to leave him with the same amount net as a 1½ percent return on a tax-exempt bond if he were figuring "off the top" as it were. If it's a question of a prime taxable bond versus a prime tax-exempt, the mathematical conclusions will be correct.

If it's a question of investment policy, however, then all the characteristics of any type of security under consideration must be taken into account. Net income from interest coupons after taxes then becomes only one of several factors, and in my opinion, not in any sense the determining factor.

Tax-exempt bonds, like prime taxable money-rate bonds in general, have no inflation-hedging characteristics of any kind. Therefore, many wealthy investors, in times when they feel the purchasing power of the dollar is decreasing, prefer common stocks for capital gain possibilities that might offset this loss, even though their net income from dividends, after taxes in high brackets, leaves less net income than does an equivalent investment in tax-exempts.

Tax-Sheltered Stocks

There is another category of temporary and partially tax-exempt income. It can sometimes be procured from the stocks of companies with large tax credit cany-overs, resulting from previous losses. In some cases, following a recovery in earnings or profits, such situations allow the payment of so-called "tax free" dividends for quite a time, or totaling quite an amount. I say "so-called," because actually these dividends are usually free from ordinary income taxes, but not from capital gain taxes. As the latter are smaller, the advantage varies with the tax bracket of the buyer, but often is considerable. There are also certain mining companies paying out more in dividends than current earnings whose annual payments are rated partly income subject to tax, and partly a return of capital and hence not subject to tax.

Stock Selection

The tax advantages of mining and oil stocks are very important. Under present laws, they are allowed as much as $27\frac{1}{2}$ percent of their earnings tax-free in order to give an incentive to discover and develop additional resources. This amount is charged as depletion because obviously material removed from the ground is gone as a productive asset forever. They are also allowed to deduct costs of drilling dry holes or unsuccessful exploration. Put another way, this means that companies of this type not only have considerable tax shelter but are also in a position to utilize their earnings in a way calculated to build up property values. Shrewd investors prefer capital gains to dividends.

To a lesser extent, investment in ordinary growth companies, where dividends are low and reinvestment or plowing back of earnings is made into research for new products or the development of increased production, is advantageous.

It is important to consider the investment price paid for such purchases. Very often, the advantages of owning such stocks are so well known that the premium in the market becomes excessive.

Regulated Investment Companies

Individuals who hold stock in certain types of so-called "regulated investment companies," paying out 90 percent or more of their dividends and profits, are allowed to treat the capital gain portion of such dividends just as if it were a personal capital gain. Thus, assuming that the trust's management is capable, this is a method of securing larger dividends, and avoiding the ordinary bracket taxes on a portion of them.

Small Business Investment Corporations

The small business investment corporations, or "SBICs" as they are termed, are granted special tax privileges. If you own stocks in such companies at a loss you can take the loss and write the entire amount off against your ordinary income.

Advantageous Tax Base

In times of excess profits taxation, investors should look for tax shelter in companies possessing satisfactory invested capital or average earnings tax bases so as to assure maximum excess profits credit. Companies with heavy recent losses that can be carried forward are often interesting, but the investment consideration of an improved future outlook is more important than the mere tax shelter.

Capital Gain Taxes

However, in general, income from securities is fully taxable at ordinary income tax rates which rise on an ascending scale to astronomical percentages.

Special lower capital gains taxes on profits from purchases and sales ordinarily apply only if a security is held for a specified length of time. These taxes generally tax only a portion of the gain, and generally have a maximum percentage rate which is not exceeded no matter how large the total profit of any one individual.

Because the tax on capital gains is lower than the tax on ordinary dividend and interest income, large investors favor companies with maximum growth potentialities. They favor management that can profitably "plow back" into the business the highest percentage of earnings and pay out as income as little as possible—sometimes nothing at all. In the long run, income-paying ability has a definite market value and companies with safe dividends are valued higher as a consequence. Smaller investors buy such shares for yield. For the investor in the high tax bracket, buying a young, non-dividend paying share for ultimate profit and holding it for sale until matured and established as a steady dividend payer, is far more profitable than owning a steady income share which returns a high annual gross yield.

There are often cases where a share that returns a high dividend also has maximum capital gain potentialities. This develops when investors incorrectly question the safety of a high yield, or when a company becomes so strong that its trade dominance permits re-investment of earnings and good dividends as well. In such cases, the low bracket investor buys for income and gain—the high bracket investor ignores the fact that most of his apparent income is taxed away, and concentrates on the capital gain prospects. The net income from dividends after taxes may often be under that of a tax-exempt bond, but if the profit potentialities are there, that is the determining factor.

For some years, in the United States, the required holding period for receiving the benefit of the long-term capital gains rate has been six months, the portion of the gain taxed 50 percent, and the top tax rate under these circumstances was 50 percent of the one-half of the gain. This has meant that an individual reporting what is termed a "long term" capital gain has had in most circumstances a top tax of 25 percent. This is very important to those in both high and low tax brackets; in the first instance there is usually a definite tax ceiling and in the second only half of the gains are taxed.

As a result intelligent investing policies should be geared to the tax laws. The law at the time of investing or closing a transaction should be closely studied. It is changed frequently. As written in 1965 it is necessary to think of taxes all during the year and not just in the last few days of December. Short-term losses, which means less than six months, are particularly valuable if they can be evenly matched with short-term profits. Profits are usually taxed lower if held over six months. Note that the law provides that losses can be deducted right up to the last trading day of the year. Profits, however, have to be established usually four trading days previous to the end of the year. If you delayed overlong in establishing your profit you can tell your broker to sell your stock "for cash." This will hold up to the last day for profits but is normally done at a slight discount.

There are those who attempt to postpone registering profits for tax purposes by short sales against the box. I strongly advise investors not to make any transaction except the normal simple ones without consulting competent tax counsel.

It would seem profitable for anyone, regardless of his probable tax bracket, to attempt short-term trading in the early part of a new calendar or tax year if market conditions are favorable. This policy, when successful, tends to build up a profit much more valuable as a future tax cushion than for its own sake. Later, commitments originally entered into for long-term capital gains, may turn out badly and the loss be offset by the earlier trading profit.

Furthermore, consideration should be given to accepting a certain average amount of capital gains each year, if one's position and the market happen to favor large paper profits rather than permitting them to accumulate. The trend of tax legislation has tended (most of the time) toward higher rates. This is true despite the reduction in 1964. Unfortunately, it probably will not be long before rates start rising again. Paper profits can go as well as come. Tax legislation has been known to be enacted so as to operate retroactively and while no one can foresee the nature of such future laws an average position with a consistent yearly tax is most likely to be helpful.

The Logic of Taking Taxable Profits

One of the great fallacies of investor tax policy is to reason incorrectly that one cannot afford to take a profit because of the size of the tax. In most cases, investors feel that unless the market price of the shares in question promised to drop enough to equal the full amount of the tax, the gain has been accepted in vain.

The fact is that every paper gain is only the amount of the gain less the potential tax. Thus, if a stock is bought at $100 a share and advances to $140, the owner at no time has a 40-point gain. He has a 40-point gain less his tax, whatever it might be. Assuming it to be 25 percent, his real gain is only 30 points, whether he turns it into cash or otherwise.

Should taxes increase, his gain would be reduced. Should the market break, his gain might vanish.

Possible Drawbacks

Considering the advantages, the possible drawbacks against accepting some gains regularly, if available, are small. In the case of very old people, for example, a capital gains tax is entirely avoided in the event of death as a result of the law which provides for valuation at the prices prevailing at the time of death. The personal estate tax in this event would be greater. The future tax advantage resulting from the new and higher scale of valuations would, however, pass to the inheriting party or parties instead of to the real owner of the securities.

Then, too, the laws governing loan values often work to decrease the amount that can be borrowed on a repurchase after taking a profit.

True, in a sense, the owner of a stock with an unrealized gain, and an unpaid potential tax, has the use of the money he eventually will pay as tax, interest free, as long as he doesn't sell his stock and turn his paper gain into a real one. Thus, after a profit is taken and a tax is paid, unless the stock sold declines the full amount of the tax, a lesser number of shares only can be repurchased with the proceeds. This is a more imaginary than real disadvantage and actually sometimes an advantage, because it usually occurs when stock prices are relatively high. Of course, should the stock sold decline more than the tax paid, and should the investor then desire to repurchase, he can repurchase more shares than he originally owned; so it works both ways. The law at present allows the sale and immediate repurchase of the same stock where a profit is involved, but demands a 30-day waiting period in case of a loss. Losses are not deductible where the same stock was repurchased inside of thirty days.

It can be seen from this discussion that examples in a complicated situation of this kind can be very misleading or misunderstood. The important facts, however, are that the tax must be paid sooner or later and that most people make the mistake of not selling because they feel that in some mysterious way they are avoiding the tax. The person who operates on investment principles always will come out better.

Deducting Losses

To touch on another angle of the tax laws, the method and amount of deducting losses is of great importance. The rules change. Currently, most stock losses are first deducted from other stock profits. If there is an excess, the first $1,000 can be taken off ordinary income. The balance of the loss, under the present law, can be carried over indefinitely. Long-term losses carried over must first be deducted from future long-term profits and short-term from short-term. The excess can be deducted at $1,000 a year from ordinary income. The losses are carried forward until they are used up in one manner or another. In the event that the investment position of stocks held at a gain is favorable it is of course possible to take the profit and repurchase them immediately. The effect here would be to secure the tax benefit of matching the profit and loss and through the repurchase increasing the tax base.

Tax Dodges Good and Bad

Every now and then, supposedly shrewd investors devise some tax dodge that seems legally to play hob with the spirit of the law. I am against this sort of thing. Sometimes it will be sustained but such loopholes usually are closed in time. However, there are certain practices which seem both legitimate and logical. Buying bonds that are in default of interest but are about to pay off, and selling them for capital gains on the advances which discount the interest payment, is one.

It is vital for the investor to realize that a correct understanding of the tax factors is almost as important in most cases, and more important in some cases, than a correct understanding of the investment factors. Knowledge of one without the other is sure to detract from the results.

Miscellaneous Tax Angles

There are many variations in achieving the best tax policy and the laws are changing frequently. Tax experts and current tax manuals are essential.

Current tax laws add a new element in making it essential to consider the effect of spacing between years. Taxes are frequently saved by taking losses in a different year than profits. The system of clubbing varying capital transactions creates new complications.

The 1964 law includes an averaging provision that is occasionally of value in saving taxes where a large short-term windfall profit has been achieved.

You should understand the deductibility of state transfer taxes and how you can take a tax deduction for interest paid on a margin account.

In buying investment trust stocks, it is important to compare the cost of their investments with their current market value. Liquidating values ordinarily make no allowance for taxes on unrealized profits. Consequently, it is quite easy to actually buy one's self a tax liability, as it were. This is particularly true of mutual funds which never sell at a discount and always sell at liquidating values without allowance for taxes on unrealized gains plus merchandising loads.

Holders of stocks in high tax brackets, where unusually large dividends are about to be paid, often can profit by selling before the stock goes ex-dividend and thus having the dividend treated as a capital gain rather than as ordinary income. This is particularly true where some large unpaid arrears are paid off.

Charitable Contributions

The law currently allows the deduction of charitable contributions to certain public charities to the extent of 30 percent of adjusted gross income. Not over 20 percent can be given to approved private foundations. For high-tax-bracket individuals this means a comparatively large sum can be given away with a relatively small net loss in income due to tax saving.

Contributions can be made in the form of securities bought at a low price. The gift is calculated at the market price but no capital gains tax has to be paid.

Charitable contributions can be carried forward five years. Thus, if a contribution made in one year totals 40 percent of your income, 30 percent can be deducted in that year and 10 percent in the following year.

Capital Gains Not Income

The capital gains tax itself is unsound. It has caused great damage and promises still more. It is the cause of fallacious thinking on the part of the majority of the American investors. Imaginary capital gains are regarded as real income, and personal expenditures are foolishly overdone on such false premises. The tax has caused market rises to go to extreme and dangerous lengths. Tax receipts have varied unnecessarily because of its application.

I have seen people who thought they had made $10,000 in the stock market—because the Government called it "income" they treated it as such, and unknowingly spent part of their capital.

Anyone whose invested stock capital appreciates slower than dollars are depreciating, measured in stock averages, usually at some point and some time continuously, pays "income" tax for the privilege of losing purchasing power.

Even if one makes a real profit by any standard in the market, it is not "income" and should not be taxed as such nor regarded as a source of funds for current expenditure. In most cases, it is distinctly "non-recurring."

Investment Principles

To what extent, if at all, should one retain stocks which would otherwise be sold, so as to diminish the tax?

Personally, I usually sell when I am so inclined, regardless of tax-and give tax—reduction consideration from other angles rather than refrain from profit realization.

From the point of view of the average investor, I don't concede the possibility of buying at the bottom and selling at the top. Instead, I think most people will have the fewest stocks at the bottom, and a rather larger-than-normal line at the top. Thus, in actual practice, a much smaller actual decline than the preceding advance will wipe out all profits, because the average trader's real losses occur on more shares than the number on which his paper gains were established. This is what happened in 1929, and what will happen again in time, only with greater violence.

Two other great advantages of accepting profits without tax delay are: First, that the profits are real, and the method of obtaining them is more a regular business practice and less a matter of chance. No one can take profits consistently over a period of years in the stock market without real knowledge; yet, many occasionally stumble into profitable commitments. Usually, the gainer thinks he has found a new source of wealth, much to his eventual cost. Secondly, as each transaction is closed and a new one initiated, the price of the new purchase is the only price taken into consideration in calculating risks or taking short losses, etc. Many people who bought stock in the middle stages of a bull market felt no fear around the top because of their seemingly low average, which in a subsequent decline actually proved high. Purchases and sales through such a rising period would probably have resulted in some eventual buys at very excessive figures. Realization of the great danger involved would cause a prudent trader in the latter situation to buy less and sell at once if the market turned sour.

Short-term commitments are naturally made in the issues that seem the most attractive. Long-term positions, held past their best time for tax reasons, frequently result in ownership of shares which have lost their market leadership to another group.

For the competent trader and investor, consideration should be given to the rate of return received on capital, regardless of the market outlook. For example, if $100,000 grows to $150,000 in six months and the market looks higher, but is obviously vulnerable to the unexpected, I think taking profits for the big returns they bring and paying the tax is the proper procedure. Most people, especially investors try to get a certain percentage return, and actually secure a minus yield when properly calculated over the years. Speculators risk less and have a better chance of getting something, in my opinion.

As an alternative plan for those who are so greedy, they cannot, without mental pain, watch shares they have sold climb higher, I suggest initial overbuying of a combination trading and long-pull line. This has several advantages. One is more careful entering into the larger commitment. The whole line is sold if the stock works out badly. The trading line is sold if a profit occurs and the profit is applied to marking down the price of the long-pull line.

A third and more scientific policy is to earmark funds for long-pull and for trading. The long-pull purchases must be selected with a view to holding, for tax reasons, through all sorts of vicissitudes; hence, seeking the very highest managerial ability becomes a factor that outweighs any other.

Deductible Expenses

All expenses reasonably incurred in the process of attempting to acquire income are presently deductible tax-wise from your gross income. This includes the state taxes on the broker's bill. It includes professional help, such as investment or tax counselors, statistical and advisory services, etc. In the case of large incomes which have been built up because of trips and other costly contacts, these expenses can also be deducted. The cost of this book is deductible but check it when you make out your return.

Conclusion

The good of the whole nation would be served by repeal of the capital gains tax. The political climate being what it is, this seems unlikely. Modifications easing the burden might develop in the coming years. One of the most constructive developments, and a very logical and fair one, would be to postpone payment of the tax until securities were liquidated into cash. Exchanges would be permitted without tax. They are permitted now in certain real estate transactions. In the meantime, the good of the individual will be advanced, in my opinion, if he disregards it and sells when selling is indicated and pays the tax bill when incurred. All careful traders constantly set up a reserve for this tax anyway, so that if one gets in the habit of thinking of paper profits, less current tax, it is not so difficult to trade freely and not run the risk of missing one's market.

33

INVESTMENT AND INFLATION

THE CHANGING purchasing power of money, coupled with the rise and fall of prices and costs, are the most basic and far reaching causes for fluctuations in the earning power and value of security investments and security market prices.

"Inflation" means an increase in the supply of money or credit so that prices for goods go up. Increasing commodity prices and increasing costs of living however can also be caused by increasing demand for goods and services or shortages in supply.

"Deflation" means a decrease in the supply of money or credit so that prices for goods go down. Decreasing commodity prices and decreasing costs of living however can also be caused by decreasing demand for goods and services or surpluses in supply.

In addition to many other contributing causes of inflation or deflation, a very great factor is the psychological. The fact that people think prices are going to advance or decline, very much contributes to their movement, and the very momentum of the trend itself tends to perpetuate itself.

The effects of inflation or deflation are first a great shifting of wealth. The total real wealth of a nation cannot be measured in either dollars or prices, but more in unit production and consumption. Judged quantitatively, inflation in its early stages tends to stimulate both production and consumption, and to create a general feeling of prosperity and well being. However, judged individually, there is of course a redistribution of wealth as between the debtor and the creditor, rich and poor, entrepreneur and wage earner, speculator and investor. Once inflation really takes hold, and results in real currency depreciation, then, for the majority, only complete financial ruin and extreme emotional uncertainty follow.

The control of inflation is rarely attempted at its roots, where control is possible, but practically always is instead incorrectly directed at its effects, where such efforts invariably fail. If it runs far enough, it brings its own cure, only by that time the patient is dead.

Deflation, on the other hand, is less disastrous in its final effect on the individual, though generally associated with "hard times." It is also far easier to check and turn, mainly because the methods adopted have general and hence political popularity.

People, by and large, most of the time, cannot, or refuse to recognize either inflation or deflation, but mainly count their wealth as well as their income, gains, and losses in dollars. Thus, the average man almost always feels better, with a larger number of dollars, even though they buy less, than a lesser number of dollars, with a factually larger actual purchasing power or value. Human nature being what it is, no change in this attitude is ever likely, hence the very long pull value of money tends to decrease, and the very long pull value of things tends to increase. Human propensities to propagate and to spend, rather than save, also add fuel to the fire. In general, the very long pull trend favors the forces of inflation over those of deflation and by and large over the very long pull the owner of equities is better off than the owner of bonds. This is an extreme oversimplification of the subject, because the swings up and down cover long periods of time and changes in value, and as a matter of practical everyday success in life, some measure of reasonably correct forecasting is necessary.

Furthermore, statements made as to what to do about it, or commenting on the past effects of similar movements, are apt at best to be highly invalid, because what is true at one stage of inflation or deflation is not true at the next. Or for that matter, what is true in past inflation does not always prove true again. Different inflations spring from different causes. The soil in which they grow varies. The degree to which they run differs. The key to safety under one condition win never fit succeeding situations.

Deflation

Taking up the subject of deflation, first of course cash is the easy and perfect hedge if one can recognize the trend in its beginnings. There is no tax problem involved in a deflationary period, because monetary values are decreasing, even if sometimes real values are not. All security markets stocks and bonds together naturally decline. Stocks decline because both earnings and balance sheet values are reduced by the rising value of money, and also because of liquidation induced by the greater need for money resulting. Bonds decline, because in most cases interest coverage and security behind the principal decrease, but also for reasons of holders seeking or requiring increased liquidity. It is true interest rates decrease, and this tends to bolster very prime credit risks, but in a period of this sort prime credit is rare. An important investment principle to bear in mind is that in times of deflation stock prices invariably drop much more in market value per annum than any dividends the securities in question can conceivably pay. Thus, keeping liquid (in cash) and living off capital actually results in a smaller annual net shrinkage in capital value than attempting to secure so-called "income" for this purpose. Also, eventual profits and often real fortunes are built by buying at the turning points of great depressions. However, unless cash is on hand to buy bargains these opportunities cannot be utilized. In short, hedging against deflation is simplicity itself and involves nothing further than being long of cash. The difficulty comes in recognizing the oncoming depression before security values are already deflated, and in having the proper objective mental attitude that permits keeping cash "idle" and "living off capital." Of course, these two phrases, used in this way, are classically the language of the uninformed, and basically completely fallacious. Cash is far from "idle" if what we wish to buy with it is constantly decreasing in price. Nor are we "living off capital" if the major part of our capital is constantly acquiring more value.

A very potent type of deflation is a collapse in the price of a single commodity. This affects securities where the link is obvious. Thus, copper stocks are affected by the price of copper and sugar stocks by the price of sugar, etc. In recent times this is almost the only type of deflation in which we seem to come in contact. It must be guarded against because owning the wrong securities even in inflationary times can result in big losses.

Inflation

It is when you reach the subject of investment policy under inflationary conditions that the real complexity of the situation begins to unfold. True, at the start, "inflation" is nothing more actually than "recovery" or a "turn for the better," etc. Under such circumstances, the ownership of good equities will result in equally good income and profit. Everything will be low and moving higher. Corporation profits naturally respond to increased demand for goods. Slightly rising prices make for inventory profits and satisfactory profit margins. Costs are still lagging. Social legislation is apt to be at a minimum or favorable. The entire investment climate is good.

The step from one stage to another can hardly be definitely tagged, but the next degree might be called the high-cost-of-living period. Here, inflation begins to pinch in places and its rate accelerates. A great deal depends now on the force behind the movement, but generally, if inflation is to go beyond this point a major cause such as preparation for war, or war itself, or the aftermath of war is likely. War of necessity unites a nation behind the party in power and speeds social reform. The supply of money and credit is increased and the supply of goods and services decreased. Production is to the greatest extent possible for destruction rather than consumption. Efforts are made to "control" the situation through taxation including excess profit taxes and more and higher excise taxes, through rationing and in some cases even capital levies. Investment policy now is much less assured. Equities still seem the best, but a great deal of question develops as to the length of tune the inflationary trend will persist, and the extent to which its force has been discounted marketwise. Fear also begins to be expressed as to the deflationary effects of taxation, profit squeezes, etc.

The situation may turn here or it may go into what might be termed hyper-inflation or super-inflation or uncontrolled-inflation or what have you. This of course is the utterly wild type which practically demands printing press money. Values change so rapidly it is hard to know what anything is worth. Business management is extremely difficult. Stocks go up but nowhere near as fast as money goes down. Eventually, the mental strain on the population and the incapacity of the majority to keep up with the situation causes so much ruin that a "stabilization" and revaluation is forced. Under such conditions of course cash and fixed obligations in general are usually wiped out.

Common stocks under such conditions have on the whole fared better, but nothing to the extent indicated by popular and uninformed general comment. The general theory that a common share is a share in a piece of corporate property and hence if it is a given fraction at the start of an inflation it is still in the same fraction at the end is in itself erroneous. The need for working capital under inflation and other considerations are often so great that new equity financing naturally follows and results in a great equity dilution. Or, if this is shrewdly avoided by the management then the necessity of attempting to convert "paper" corporate profits into more factory or more resources is not always understood or if understood is not always feasible. In terms of market prices stocks at times are inflated beyond values by fear buying, and at others lag behind values by lack of liquid funds to buy, so great is the need for money. Interest rates of course would become astronomical, unless artificially checked, because the effort would be to fix a rate high enough to keep up and somewhat surpass currency depreciation in the borrowing period. The average buyer, buying a list of average stocks, at average times and prices along with the crowd will not do well.

It is impossible to express the situation in any mathematical way as to how much a person might salvage because of the myriad variations of the situation. However, as an eye opener to those who without study blindly think that stocks protect against inflation, I have seen figures showing stock losses in inflation on a gold basis running as much as 97 percent of pre-inflation capital.

My conclusion as to practical inflation hedging in the U.S.A. is that little can actually be learned from a study of inflations which occurred in other countries in years gone by. Primarily, the causes and extent vary, but even more importantly the legislation and controls and tax policies which go with it keep changing. I would say they are modernized as the years go by or to put it another way the loopholes of past inflations through which clever people salvaged their wealth are watched and plugged in future ones.

I think in the final analysis such policies are fixed by political expediency, and I would always examine from a social angle any special "scheme" to circumvent losing with the rest. Political expediency was responsible for our default in going off the gold standard. It was responsible for otherwise completely unfair mortgage moratoriums. It was responsible for equally unfair rent ceilings. If the majority of the voters prefer their bonds and insurance policies paid off at par in dollars of reduced purchasing power to being paid off at a discount in hard dollars, or best of all living within our means and thus being able to pay them off at par in hard cash, then it's such living beyond our national means and fooling ourselves with paper dollars that will prevail.

The paternalistic policy of creating government agencics to set up an insurance fund and "guarantee" against loss is often a contributory inflationary factor. Land prices, labor and home construction costs, for example, are boosted by insuring certain savings and loan investments up to $10,000 per account.

However, the very rapidly increasing productive capacity of U.S.A. factories is a deflationary factor of very major importance, and deserves fully as much attention in evaluating the situation as the purely monetary factors. It is likely that more will be lost to the American investor in the years to come from the tax factor than through currency depreciation, hence the two subjects should be studied together.

It is unlikely in an exporting country like, ours of such great natural resources and productive capacity, that unbridled inflation will ever rule as far as we can now see ahead. I think given time and especially given another world war, a 25-cent dollar, a 10-cent one or worse can happen. But the inflations of the Russian and German type—I think in Germany the mark went to 40 trillion to the dollar—seem completely unlikely here.

Investment policy under such conditions calls for major attention to determining whether the dollar is appreciating or depreciating, and the extent to which stock market prices under-discount, discount, or over-discount the situation. All through these articles, the theme of "purchasing power values" has dominated, even when inflation was not on every tongue as it is today.

Success in investment under varying dollar values thus comes down to success in investing. The two are one and the same thing and the investor who thinks he is buying special "inflation hedges" is more apt to get into trouble than keep out of it. Stocks are only good inflation hedges if bought at the right time and at the right price. And the same rule applies regardless of what the power behind a rise might be. Practically all upward business cycles occur with prices rising, so that whether tagged inflation or not the impetus is usually the same. The only special advice I can give is that the better the quality the better the chance to survive if the road grows really rough. The best inflation hedges lie among the best managed companies with the best long-pull outlook for consistent profits and growth. The special debt ridden issue that is going to be bailed out by inflation—the marginal producer which is going to benefit from the stimulated demand—the company with a "tax shelter" built up through inefficiency—the high cost natural resource share—all this kind of inflation hedge offers only trading, in and out, possibilities. In the long run, they are bound to fail. The danger in buying them lies in the danger that when one is ready to switch to the real companies, the latter wifl seem too high, or the tax penalty will appear too great.

In these times when the revolt of the masses leads more and more to the leveling of the classes, a great bulwark against loss through inflation, social legislation or taxation is to consume as you earn. Buy the fruits of others' labors with the fruits of your own—at the same rates. It's a great time and age for hand holding and paternalism, and I don't advocate completely becoming a ward of the state by no saving at all, but I do think it should be kept within bounds, the thinking of the world being what it is today.

POSTSCRIPT

POSTSCRIPT

The Battle for Investment Survival ends on page 136. This Postscript, consisting of miscellaneous individual articles, lectures, newspaper columns from my NANA-syndicated weekly series, etc., prepared at various times but all currently valid, is added because it is felt that it is a real addition to the book and that they stand better on their own feet than integrated into the previous text.

CASE HISTORY EXAMPLES: These nine "Case History Examples" seem particularly pertinent because sometimes illustrations of this sort supplement a text and bring out some of the points in a most vivid and understandable manner.

The chart on page 140 covers the principal swings of the Dow-Jones Industrial Average from 1929 to 1952, a period which adequately illustrates the points I wish to make.

Similar examples illustrating the same points can be picked for the period 1952–64. However, we have reproduced the case history examples exactly as in prior editions, and have added two recent ones.

The statistics have been largely drawn from *The Value Line Investment Survey*, one of the most useful reference books on leading stocks. Incidentally, this service has the advantage of being loose-leaf and continually kept up to date. The figures have been rounded out and are not intended to be precise. They are, however, correctly indicative of the general situation.

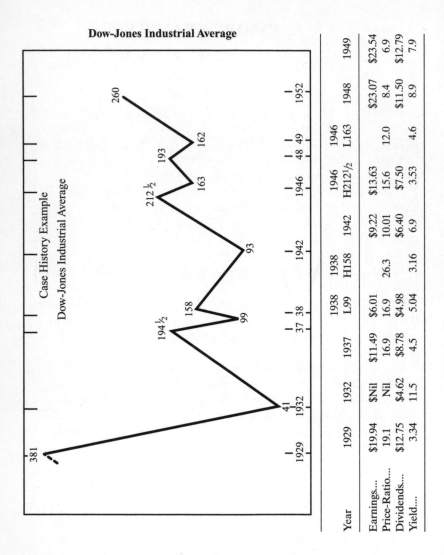

Dow-Jones Industrial Average

Case History Example
Dow-Jones Industrial Average

Year	1929	1932	1937	1938 L99	1938 H158	1942	1946 H212½	1946 L163	1948	1949
Earnings....	$19.94	$Nil	$11.49	$6.01		$9.22	$13.63		$23.07	$23.54
Price-Ratio....	19.1	Nil	16.9	16.9	26.3	10.01	15.6	12.0	8.4	6.9
Dividends....	$12.75	$4.62	$8.78	$4.98		$6.40	$7.50		$11.50	$12.79
Yield....	3.34	11.5	4.5	5.04	3.16	6.9	3.53	4.6	8.9	7.9

34

CASE HISTORY EXAMPLES

A BEARISH STOCK IN A BULL MARKET

Transitron Electronic Corporation

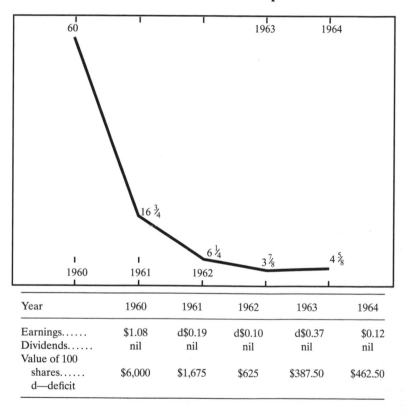

Year	1960	1961	1962	1963	1964
Earnings......	$1.08	d$0.19	d$0.10	d$0.37	$0.12
Dividends......	nil	nil	nil	nil	nil
Value of 100 shares......	$6,000	$1,675	$625	$387.50	$462.50
d—deficit					

TRANSITRON is just one of many examples that could be chosen to show that under modern conditions you do not need a wide open break in the general market such as occurred between 1929 and 1932 to suffer enormous percentage losses. The $6,000 figure chosen for the table represents the purchase of 100 shares at the highest price for 1960. The other figures represent the value of this stock at the lows for the following years.

Over the same period the Standard & Poor's average of 425 industrials was higher in 1964 than in 1960. The same company's average of seven leading electronics companies did not do as well as the general average, ending up 1964 something under its 1960 and 1961 highs, but of course showing nothing like the depreciation in Transitron.

The rise in Chrysler and the decline in American Motors (see page 143) is a striking example of how two stocks in the same industry can move in opposite directions. Many similar illustrations could be given both of industry groups moving in opposite directions and as illustrated here issues within the same group moving in opposite directions.

The advance in Chrysler reflected a change in management which greatly increased the sale of its cars and its earnings and dividend. On the other hand, American Motors, which had prospered mightily in the 1957–59 period, due to its success with compact cars, saw the demand shift and was adversely affected.

The value of 100 shares of Chrysler at the average price of 1959 was approximately $1,450. At the 1964 top the value was $6,500 and at the average for the year was about $5,000. One hundred shares of American Motors bought at the 1959 top would have cost $3,200 (average for the year was $20). By 1964 the average value was only about $1,500.

Years ago the stock market moved almost as a unit Public ownership was restricted to a limited number of basic industries. The economy tended to move up or down.

Modern stock markets are different. There are times when credit conditions, interest rates and other over-all factors at least temporarily affect all stocks. But most of the time individual influences now play a very powerful part. One service lists its companies under

STOCKS IN THE SAME INDUSTRY MAY MOVE IN
OPPOSITE DIRECTIONS

Chrysler—American Motors

Year	1959	1960	1961	1962	1963	1964
Chrysler						
Earnings......	$	$1.02	$0.44	$1.89	$4.33	$5.46
Dividends......	.24	.36	.24	.24	.42	.96
Val. of 100 shares.	1450	1300	1150	1350	3250	5000
Amer. Mtrs.						
Earnings......	3.32	2.63	1.28	1.83	1.99	1.38
Dividends	.39	1.13	1.18	.80	1.00	1.15
Val. of 100 shares.	2000	2350	1850	1500	1950	1500

(The above figures are approximate. In some years the earnings vary because of
internal or other adjustments. In some years the dividends are supplemented by stock
dividends. Price and earnings are adjusted for two splits in the case of Chrysler Corp.)

more than 125 industry headings beginning with "Abrasive Man-ufacturers" and ending with "Utility—Telephone." They also list other companies under "Miscellaneous."

Not only are prosperity and adversity far from uniform but the popularity stock-marketwise of various groups that make for tem-porary overvaluation or neglect is constantly changing.

The record shows how important individual analysis has become to investment success.

DuPont is generally regarded as probably the best known growth stock and typical of the best type of equity investment as opposed to U.S.A. government bonds which are the best type of defensive investment. The chart and tabulations on page 145 like all in this series are general and approximate, intended more to reflect the sit-uation than to be a precise statistical record. In this period, DuPont's best year in earnings was 1950 with $6.59 a share, and its best year in dividends was 1950 with $5.35 paid. The actual high price for DuPont was established in 1951. In general, the earnings of DuPont reflect the prosperity of the country or perhaps something better than the prosperity of the country because of the favorable field in which DuPont operates and its superlative management. Likewise, the fluctuations in the price of the stock reflect about the best that can be expected from a representative equity.

The record shows how much can be lost even in the best stock if bought at the wrong time and price. Shares of DuPont which cost $5,800 at the top in 1929 were worth just a shade over $2,000 a couple of months later and only $550 at the bottom in 1932. Another way of looking at the matter is that a buyer at the top in 1929 had to wait till 1949, or 20 years later, before recovering his investment. The record since 1937 is far more stable, but even so, on two occasions, the stock dropped almost half its peak values.

It might be argued that anyone who bought a good stock like DuPont merely had to hang on to come out all right. In real life, this is a different matter than in theory. The stock may recover after a period of years, but in practice emergencies come up and one has to sell. Also, the atmosphere around the bottom of declines is always a pessimistic one and, human nature being what it is, a person buying a stock at the wrong time is very apt to double his error and sell it at the wrong time.

HOW MUCH CAN BE LOST EVEN IF THE BEST STOCK IS
BOUGHT AT THE WRONG TIME AND PRICE

DuPont

(Adjusted to Present Capitalization)

Year	1929	1932	1936	1938	1939	1942	1946	1948	1952
Earnings	$1.77	$0.45	$1.89	$0.94	$1.92	$1.27	$2.36	$3.28	*$4.60
Dividends	$1.48	$0.69	$1.53	$0.81	$1.75	$1.06	$1.75	$2.44	*$3.55
Value of 100 shrs.	$5,800	$550.	$4,400	$2.300	$4,700	$2,600	$5,600	$4,100	$8,275

*Estimated.

Investment in equities, even the very best ones, must therefore be done with a great deal of understanding in order to be successful.

Douglas is a good example of how growth in a new industry can be profitable marketwise. In 1929, it sold at 23 and of course broke to very low levels in 1932 along with the rest of the market, but by 1935 it had recovered its 1929 level. Earnings in 1935 exceeded 1929 but it was really 1940 before they reflected their war

HOW GROWTH IN A NEW INDUSTRY CAN BE
PROFITABLE MARKETWISE
Douglas Aircraft

(Adjusted to Present Capitalization)

Year	1929	1932	1936	1937	1940	1943	1946	1947	1952
Earnings	$0.67	$0.10	$0.87	$0.95	$9.03	$4.96	$1.82	$ Nil	*$5.25
Dividends	$ Nil	$0.44	$ Nil	$ Nil	$2.50	$2.50	$3.75	$1.25	*$3.50
Value of 100 shrs.	$2,300	$250,	$4,100	$1,300	$4,700	$2,200	$5,450	$2,300	$5,500

*Estimated.

growth at $9.03. It's interesting to note too that in 1941, earnings went to $15.15 but all through the year 1941, the stock ranged lower than during 1940, despite the very much higher earnings. By 1943, the market low was reached but earnings were still $4.96 a share. The lowest earnings on the cycle were in 1947 when Douglas lost money.

HOW LOSSES CAN OCCUR EVEN IN A SOLID ISSUE WITH
A GROWTH TREND, IF TIMING IS BAD AND EXCESSIVE
PREMIUMS ARE PAID FOR POPULARITY

International Nickel

(Adjusted to Present Capitalization)

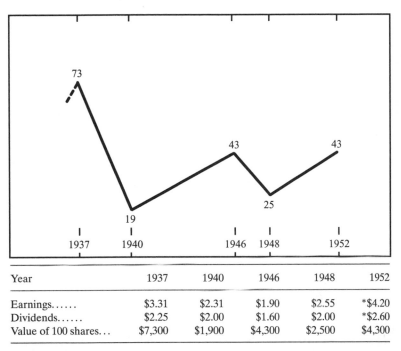

Year	1937	1940	1946	1948	1952
Earnings......	$3.31	$2.31	$1.90	$2.55	*$4.20
Dividends......	$2.25	$2.00	$1.60	$2.00	*$2.60
Value of 100 shares...	$7,300	$1,900	$4,300	$2,500	$4,300

*Estimated.

   The record here shows the importance of growth when not over-discounted in the market. It also shows that the highest prices for Douglas were reached at the time when war expectations were the highest and not at the time when earnings reached their peak. The Douglas 1947 low fairly well coincided with the low year in earnings for that period, and also with general market discouragement.

An investor in International Nickel in 1937 bought a good stock at the wrong time and at the wrong price. (1) The general stock market declined and naturally pulled International Nickel down with it. However, the general market, measured by the Dow-Jones Industrials, was back to the 1937 level by early 1946, at which time Nickel had only recovered to 43. In 1952, Nickel had after 15 years failed to come back to its 1937 high, though many stocks and the

A FORMER BLUE CHIP GONE BAD

N. Y. Central

(Adjusted to Present Capitalization)

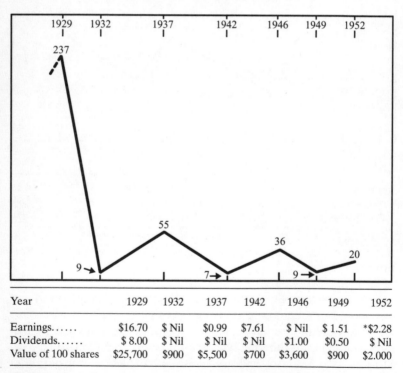

Year	1929	1932	1937	1942	1946	1949	1952
Earnings......	$16.70	$ Nil	$0.99	$7.61	$ Nil	$ 1.51	*$2.28
Dividends......	$ 8.00	$ Nil	$ Nil	$ Nil	$1.00	$0.50	$ Nil
Value of 100 shares	$25,700	$900	$5,500	$700	$3,600	$900	$2.000

*Estimated.

Dow-Jones Industrials were much above 1937. One of the principal reasons is that Nickel was the fashion in 1937. At that time, people bought Nickel to hedge against war and to hedge against inflation and because it could be sold in several different markets for Canadian dollars or pounds or francs. This over-enthusiasm resulted in bidding the stock up to a terrific premium. (2) Earnings declined. During the war years, the government dictated prices and of course taxes were higher. (3) The dividends declined. (4) In 1937, Nickel in the enthusiasm of that day, sold at 22 times earnings and to yield about $3^1/_4$ percent. In 1952 it sold at a price earnings ratio of about 10 times earnings and to yield $6^1/_4$ percent. In other words, even though earnings and dividends were higher in 1952 than they were in 1937, Nickel sold lower, partly because of the elimination of the over-enthusiasm for the shares and partly because earnings in general sold for less in 1952 than they did in 1937 and higher yields were demanded.

The record shows how losses can occur even in solid issues with a growth trend, if timing is bad and excessive premiums are paid for popularity.

An investor in N.Y. Central in 1929 suffered from almost every conceivable cause of market losses. (1) The market and hence N.Y. Central was over-valued. In the 1929–32 decline the market and Central went from over to under-valuation. (2) The railroads lost markets to other transportation. (3) Population gains in the east started to fall to a slower pace than in west and south. (4) Earnings collapsed. (5) Dividends were passed. The record shows how costly bad timing could be and the rallies from 9 to 55 and 7 to 36 illustrate that even in a stock where the long pull tide has been out, great percentage gains can be made by correct timing.

Prior to 1929 New York Central was considered a premier blue chip investment stock with a safe dividend.

Technicolor is a good example of how romance can be overdone. In 1930, when the stock sold at $86^1/_2$, it represented little more than a tremendous capitalization of the idea of color movies. It sold at 61 times its 1930 earnings. A calculation at the time, based on Technicolor capturing 100 percent of the film market, at 1930 tax rates,

ROMANCE OVERDONE
Technicolor

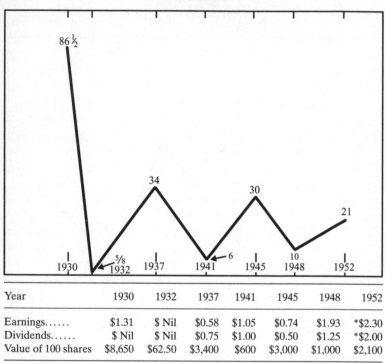

Year	1930	1932	1937	1941	1945	1948	1952
Earnings......	$1.31	$ Nil	$0.58	$1.05	$0.74	$1.93	*$2.30
Dividends......	$ Nil	$ Nil	$0.75	$1.00	$0.50	$1.25	*$2.00
Value of 100 shares	$8,650	$62.50	$3,400	$600	$3,000	$1,000	$2,100

*Estimated.

promised little over $8 per share as an optimum net. A specialty situation of this kind, earning $8, would probably normally sell around 7 times earnings or 56. This just indicates how impossibly ridiculous the price of 86½ really was. However, it is important to note that it was achieved. Short sellers sometimes think stocks can never get above what they imagine "real value" to be. As a matter of fact, almost every stock at some time or another is over-valued or under-valued, and generally once in its history either grossly over-valued or at an extreme bargain price. Technicolor was over-valued

EVERYTHING WENT RIGHT
Warner Bros.
(Adjusted to Present Capitalization)

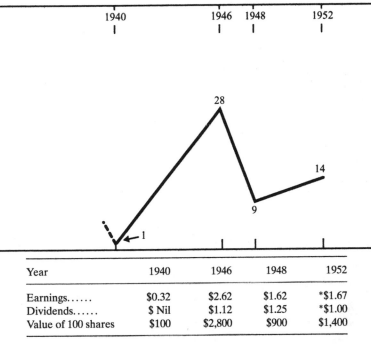

Year	1940	1946	1948	1952
Earnings......	$0.32	$2.62	$1.62	*$1.67
Dividends......	$ Nil	$1.12	$1.25	*$1.00
Value of 100 shares	$100	$2,800	$900	$1,400

*Estimated.

at $40, $50, $60, $70, etc., but that did not prevent it from selling at 86½.

Earnings practically evaporated in 1931, and in 1932, 1933, and 1934 there were deficits. The working capital in 1930, when the stock reached its high, was less than three quarters of a million dollars. Contrast this situation with the real worth when the selling price was $6 in 1941. In that year, the company had demonstrated its success, had a working capital of $3½ million, and actually earned $1.05 per share and paid out $1.00. It was therefore available at

6 times earnings. While the next few years were lean ones, by 1949 Technicolor was earning $2.56 a share and paying $2.

The record shows how very great a part psychological influences can play in market valuations. It also shows that much greater value is often placed on expectations than on reality. Stocks ordinarily make their highs at the moment that the greatest number of people visualize the greatest possible value, and not necessarily at the moment when the highest earnings or highest dividends or highest values are actually achieved.

Warner Bros. sold between $1 and $3 during 1940, 1941 and 1942. An investor in Warner in those years benefited from almost every conceivable helpful factor. (1) The general market rose. (2) Warner's earnings went up. (3) Warner went from a non-dividend paying basis to a dividend paying basis. (4) Warner's financial position improved and the company retired debt and preferred stock. (5) Motion picture stocks were very unpopular around the time of World War II, thus making them very cheap. Investors incorrectly thought that foreign markets would be lost. As time went on, this view proved completely incorrect and motion picture stocks reached the peak of popularity in 1946 when a combination of unusually large grosses and a tax reduction made for record earnings. Since that time, they have lost in popularity because of the threat of television and they've also declined counter to the general market because of declining earnings and dividends.

The record shows how very profitable a stock commitment can be when all factors unite in one's favor.

35

INVESTMENT TRUST INVESTING IS AVERAGE INVESTING

READERS of this collection of articles will end up with one or two points of view concerning investment trusts or mutual funds. Some will emerge with the thought that investing their own money is too complex. They will turn to trusts and funds as the best possible solution of their investment problem. Others, who feel that they can judge the right times to own common stocks and the right times not to own them, may buy and sell some of the listed trusts, particularly the leverage shares, as good vehicles for their purposes.

In August of 1962 the Wharton School prepared an exhaustive study of mutual funds covering almost 600 pages. The conclusion as regards investment companies' performance during the period under study showed that performance records varied considerably, both within funds and among types of funds, but on the average conformed rather closely to the behavior of the securities market as a whole. Many in the industry rated this report as unfair to their efforts. Their conclusions were not broadly accepted. Actually, considering the problems involved in the management of large amounts of investors' money, the results were good.

Funds have their place, and are particularly indicated for the first investor and the small investor.

There are a very few common stock funds, mostly closed end, and mostly leverage type, which during many periods in the past have quite regularly done better than the averages, but even in these cases the results obtainable by owning them only in favorable periods and selling them just before unfavorable periods would be very considerably better than from continuous ownership. It is particularly important to avoid leverage shares regardless of the quality of the management in declining markets.

This is hardly the point. My feeling is that competent investors will never be satisfied beating the averages as it were, by a few small percentage points, even if the funds they bought could do it in eleven years out of eleven. Investment trusts go up and down with the averages and in only extremely rare cases and only for short periods do they go in the reverse direction.

Thus, the investor who truly and substantially wants to do better than drift up and down with the crowd must do his own buying and selling and concentrate on his own selections.

36

DO TAX LOSSES MEAN SAVINGS?

Do you really save money by taking tax losses? *Are you wise keeping stocks that show you a profit to avoid paying the tax?*

All of us hate to take profits and pay the tax involved. If we do we are left with less investable capital for whatever we choose to purchase with the proceeds.

Nevertheless, there are times when it is profitable policy to cash in and pay up to Uncle Sam.

The best reason is if you can recognize extreme overvaluation. It is better to share profits than to have none at all.

Another good reason is if your objective is realized and you feel your stock has reached a final maturity or a plateau of several years' probable duration. Then it is wise to use the lesser amount of proceeds from your sale to reinvest in another direction where you feel things are on the move.

Offset Uncertainty

A good reason, and one not ordinarily given much weight, is to offset future uncertainty by cashing in on some profits by degrees. This way you get an average of variables and imponderables such as errors in judgment, unexpected news, changes in the tax laws, etc.

You may be lucky enough to have a tremendous profit in a stock that still has a bright future and is still reasonably valued. You need some cash but don't want to pay a tax or reduce the size of your investment. The thing to do here is to borrow. This way you can raise money tax-free. The interest you pay is tax-deductible.

Now suppose you own stock at a loss. To the extent that you can deduct it, selling gives you increased capital to try and recoup. You can invest the proceeds plus the tax savings. If you are successful in finding a stock that recovers, a new tax liability will build as it advances. You really have not "saved" any tax. You have postponed it and had the use of tax money interest-free until such time as you realized a profit.

Reluctant Loss Takers

Most investors are reluctant to take a loss. If you are spurred to act for supposed "tax saving" reasons, this will have some favorable side effects. As soon as your stock is sold you are free to stand aside and take an unbiased view of how best to recover. Chances are you will buy some other issue with improved prospects once you are free of your losing stock.

Before you do anything, get a folder on the tax rules from your banker or broker. It is important to know why losses should be taken, if possible, in six months or less and gains longer than six months. There are times when losses should be taken in a different year than profits. Understand about the deductibility of state transfer taxes and how you can deduct interest paid on a margin account. If your affairs are anything other than routine, engage a tax counsel.

Profit or loss, the one important rule you should always follow is that investment factors always come first. They always should govern ahead of tax factors.

If you remember this, your annual check-up can reward you far more because it spurs required investment shifts than because it saves tax dollars.

37

ODD-LOT INVESTORS AREN'T ALWAYS WRONG

ARE "ODD LOTS" FOR YOU?

From 8 percent to 12 percent of actual transactions on the New York Stock Exchange are in odd lots. "Odd lot" means shares issued in less than 100-share amounts. You can buy or sell an odd lot in any amount from one to 99 shares of any listed stock.

Investors buy small amounts like 25 or 50 shares of high-priced stocks when they feel a 100-share "round lot" involves too much of an investment for them in one issue. The odd-lot system allows you the same privilege of diversification enjoyed by those with sufficient funds to have a mixed list of 100-share purchases.

This is a "do-it-yourself" age and you as a small investor probably want to select your own portfolio. You want to learn by doing, which, after all, is the best way to learn. The difference between theory and practice is very wide.

Investment Sample

For example, if you have $10,000 to invest you can buy an odd lot amounting to about $1,000 each of such institutional favorites as International Business Machines, Texaco, General Motors, American Telephone, duPont, General Electric, International Nickel and Eastman Kodak. This would leave about $2,000 to keep in short-term U.S. Treasury bills to use in an emergency, or in case the market declines later and you want to buy more stock.

A more experienced odd-lot investor might take some of the remaining $2,000 to buy $500 each of four less seasoned, more speculative issues.

Odd-lot orders are placed with your New York Stock Exchange member broker. They cost more to fill than round lots, which is understandable. Everything costs more in retail than wholesale; costs more in small packages than in large.

Higher Commission

As an example, the commission on the purchase of a round lot of 100 shares of General Motors at $80 would be $47, or 0.6 per cent of the purchase price. Buying an odd lot of 25 shares would involve paying the "odd-lot differential," or $80^1/_4$ plus the odd-lot commission of $25.06, or 1.6 per cent. Doing it yourself through odd lots saves sales, management, custody and other costs passed on to you when buying investment trusts.

There has been a myth in the market for many years that "odd-lot investors are always wrong." This is simply not true. Odd-lot investors invariably buy more than they sell. As good stocks have gone up over the years, those who have held on to them have profited.

Rarely is one able to use successfully the totals of reported odd-lot transactions as a yardstick for market forecasting. The figures must be looked at in several different ways and carefully tabulated over a period of years. They must be used in conjunction with other technical figures and with the news to be meaningful. I recommend that the average investor completely ignore such forecasts. They are dangerous tools, except in skilled hands.

Odd lots are certainly for you, if you are a small investor or a new one who hopes to eventually become a substantial investor as a result of self-training and market experience.

38

WHAT WOMEN SHOULD KNOW
ABOUT STOCKS

WOMEN OWN MOST OF THE STOCKS—something like $250,000,000,000 worth, counting listed stocks alone.

But women investors go to men for help regarding what to buy and sell. More than 4,500,000 female shareholders are housewives. Many others are professional or career women. More and more they are reading financial literature, turning up at annual meetings, beginning to make financial decisions on their own investment programs.

What should most women know first about investing?

Certainly the qualifications of the advisers they rely on. Look for demonstrated experience, personal investment success, and complete trustworthiness.

If a woman investor is fortunate enough to find such an adviser, she should do everything she can to make his job easy and swift. He is accustomed to work in masculine, businesslike ways.

Maximum Income

She is sure to be asked to outline her objectives. The temptation is strong to reply, "Maximum income." This might imperil the safety she needs and cost her more in the loss of potential gain than the increased income justifies.

A woman investor's first need is quality. She should buy the really good stocks. In good times these high-grade issues should show her a net result of profit, plus income, less tax, that could constitute a maximum gain. In bad times the stocks could give her relative peace of mind.

If I were advising a woman client I would discuss the following:

How will you live? Take for your spendable income an amount equal to $1\frac{1}{2}$ percent of the net realizable value of your security fund each quarter. (Taxes are paid out of capital—dividends are added to it.)

You will be living partly on dividends, sometimes on profits or appreciation, sometimes on capital.

In the long run, if you receive good advice and your stocks are top quality, you will come out satisfactorily.

There is enough protection in taking the equivalent of 6 percent annually out of your fund to care for even several unlikely bad years in a row. As the equity shrinks so will the 6 percent withdrawn from it.

Historically I think the indication is you will do better than had you been a miser with your money or purchased fixed-dollar investments, or had you aimed for income only.

But remember, life is a succession of cycles. Day and night. Hot and cold. Good times and bad. High prices and low. Dividends increased and dividends cut. So don't expect your investments to be the exception to the rule.

Sell Out the Bottom

An essential procedure for all investors regardless of sex is some form of regular methodical supervision. I don't like to lay down any hard-and-fast rules, because they need to be adapted to circumstances. A point of departure might be to sell out the bottom 10 per cent of your holdings once a year and replace with the best you can find at the time. Something like this done annually should help to keep your list in tune with the times and to weed out deadwood.

This is a plan to try in order to stay safe, not to get rich quick.

There are women and women. I have seen my share of their accounts. They tend to be more emotional than practical. Emotions have no place in investment decisions. Trouble is, we all have them to a greater or lesser degree. If the woman investor demonstrates fear or greed this might be recognized in the advice given, the stocks selected, and the policies pursued. A good broker can help with almost anything but cunning. Heaven help a cunning investor.

Yet I have seen two or three women over the years with a special something that makes for success in the markets. Knowledge? Instinct? Flair? Connections? It makes no difference. They should be given their head and encouraged to go on their own. It never pays to argue with success, whatever the reasons.

Women own most of the stocks and will own more.

39

TIP TO THE INVESTOR: ALWAYS WRITE IT DOWN

WRITING DOWN YOUR COGENT REASONS for making an investment—what you expect to make, what you expect to risk, the reasons why—should save you many a dollar.

Years ago, in the early Twenties, I was initiated into writing down my reasons pro and con before making a purchase or a sale. This was suggested to me by an investor who had amassed many millions.

During about 40 years of investing in stocks my major successes were invariably preceded by a type of written analysis. Sudden emotional decisions have generally been disappointments.

Writing things down before you do them can keep you out of trouble. It can bring you peace of mind after you have made your decision. It also gives you tangible material for reference to evaluate the whys and wherefores of your profits or losses.

Quality Not Quantity

I have seen many analyses, some involving many pages of information. In practice, quantity doesn't make quality. When all is said and done, there is invariably one ruling reason why a particular security transaction can be expected to show profit.

Writing it down will help you find it. It will help you judge whether it is really as important as your first inclination suggests. Are you buying just because something "acts well"? Is it a technical reason—a coming increase in earnings or dividend not yet discounted in the market price, a change of management, a promising new product, an expected improvement in the market's valuation of earnings? In any given case you will find that one factor will almost certainly be more important than all the rest put together.

Writing it down will help you estimate what you expect to make. It is important that this be worthwhile.

Of course, you will want to decide how much you can afford to lose. There will be a level at which you will decide that things have not worked out and where you will sell. Your risk is the difference between your cost and this sell point; it ought to be substantially less than your hopes for profit. You certainly want to feel that the odds as you see them are in your favor.

Much More Difficult

All this self-interrogation will help you immeasurably in the much more difficult decision: when to close a commitment.

When you open a commitment, whether it is a purchase or a short sale, you are, so to speak, on your home ground. Unless everything suits you, you don't play. But when you are called upon to close a commitment, then you have to make decisions, whether you see the answer clearly or not. The latter situation is like being stuck on a railway crossing with the train approaching. You don't know what to do—but you have to do something. Go backward, go forward—or jump out.

If you know clearly why you bought a stock it will help you to know when to sell it. The major factor which you recognized when you bought a security will either work out or not work out. Once you can say definitely that it has worked or not worked, the security should be sold.

One of the greatest causes of loss in security transactions is to open a commitment for a particular reason, and then fail to close it when the reason proves to be invalid.

Write it down—and you will be less likely to find yourself making irrelevant excuses for holding a security long after it should have been sold. Better still, a stock well bought is far more than half the battle.

◆ **40** ◆

WHAT IS BETTER: DOLLARS IN THE HAND—OR "IN THE BUSH"?

PROFESSIONAL INVESTMENT MANAGERS today very strongly favor corporations which plow back a high percentage of earnings into research, expansion, plant modernization, etc.

Does this always pay? Or should the investor prefer his tax-nicked dividend check?

I think the answer varies with almost every management, industry and company. It certainly is a major factor for consideration before deciding to buy a stock.

The investor should realize that it is not only the total that is spent but also how it is spent. For every example of a company that has compounded its growth by wise investment of its cash there are several that would have done better to pass their surplus on to their stockholders.

Very rarely one finds a management that can do both. An example is General Motors, which paid out almost 70 percent of its earnings in dividends. It has invested its cash flow internally to maximum advantage. General Motors stockholders have had their cake and eaten it too.

Expected Profits

The normal way for management to look upon proposed investments is to estimate the expected amount of profit. This varies from industry to industry. In any case, it would be unreasonable to invest company funds unless the expected return was substantial. One finds far too much reinvestment that fails to pay off. It is difficult for management to understand that in some cases stockholders are paid off better with their company dead than alive.

Correct judgment of management policy can only come from a full understanding of the problems involved. For example, since 1954, New York Central has invested $453 million to take advantage of the fast changes in transportation technology. The book value of the property is over $1^{1}/_{4}$ billion. Yet earnings in 1963 were only $7 million, and the year before it showed a loss of almost $4 million. This is a long way from realizing much, even for a railroad.

Promised Savings

However, if you dig deeper, New York Central would be another New Haven today if Mr. Perlman, who became president in June 1954, did not follow this course of action. His investment of $453 million over the years promised a potential savings (or a return) of over $300 million, if outside influences beyond the railroad's control had not interfered. Wage increases, employee benefits, retirement-tax increases, excess crew laws in certain states, etc., all contributed to nullify the major benefits planned. The investment was needed to row upstream successfully and keep the Central's head above water.

It will pay the investor well to look beyond the superficialities of figures showing totals put back into business by management. Consideration should be given to the past record. How have plowback expenditures actually turned out?

There is no hard-and-fast rule. Sears, Roebuck stockholders profited enormously by management spending. Montgomery Ward stockholders suffered through management hoarding. Timing is important. Many unwise investments were made by corporate management in 1929. Some very wise ones were made in the early thirties.

The point is that here is an often-overlooked factor which you should include in your analysis of stocks to buy.

41

LAST WILLS AND TESTAMENTS SHOULD BE CAREFULLY DRAWN

IF YOU PLAN to make a will or leave capital in trust for your heirs, you should probably consult with your lawyer, tax consultant, and often your banker. Always remember that these plans have aspects that touch sharply on investment.

From an investment point of view, the most important point is to leave out restrictions. While it is only human to feel that your hard-earned savings may not be invested after you are gone with the success you achieved, you should do your best to select an able administrator; and then don't try to limit investment authority. Your heirs will do far better, most of the time, by making their own investment decisions than by having these forced on them by tight restrictions. Concepts change, and nothing is more disastrous than investments managed by a dead man's hand.

One-Stock Mistake

Years ago a friend of mine made a fortune in the way fortunes are usually made—owning just one stock. When he died he left his estate in trust. His son was to get the income—his grandson the capital, upon the death of his son. The real stickler in his will was the provision that either his original stock be retained or, if it were sold, the proceeds be reinvested only in bonds. As it turned out, the stock that did so well for him reached its peak and turned into a lackluster holding. The son was left with two bad choices: (1) hold a stock with poor prospects; or (2) sell and buy bonds that offered no hope of combatting inflation in an inflationary period.

The provision leaving income to a widow and, at her death, the capital to children, can be a source of trouble. The widow wants high-income stocks—the children lower-paying growth issues. One possible solution is to avoid precise provisions and leave it to the trustee to distribute income and invade principal if necessary. This approach would usually provide adequately for the widow and also allow the trustee to invest in growth issues, thus satisfying the children.

Third Party

No matter how carefully a document is drawn, it is always worthwhile to have a competent third party read over the completed document.

I learned of a trust agreement making the son trustee for his mother. It also provided for him to inherit the residual principal of the trust upon her death. This instrument was drawn by a topflight nationally known law firm. Fortunately, a bank was named as successor trustee in the event of the death of the son. Before the papers were signed, the bank was asked to approve its role. The bank's lawyer found a flaw in the agreement. The son owed an immediate gift tax on capital he might never receive.

The practice of writing your own will in your own handwriting in your own way is almost certain to result in failure to carry out your wishes. Such possible provisions as the little known and not so well understood marital-deduction clause would probably escape the writer of his own will.

Never underestimate the abilities of your wife and children after you are gone. You may never have given them a chance. The instinct of self-preservation is very strong. Many a wife and child who have not demonstrated business ability have turned into good money managers when given the chance.

42

PRICE OF STOCK IS WHAT COUNTS

WHEN ALL IS SAID AND DONE, it is the price of your stock that counts—
or whether it is going up or down.

There is a saying, "A picture is worth a thousand words." One
might paraphrase this by observing that a profit is worth more than
endless alibis or explanations.

What your investments are worth pricewise is obviously vital to
your pocketbook. It is all that really counts. You can't cash in on
what you think they ought to be worth.

Aside from liquidation or valuation purposes, prices and trends
can help you improve your investment record. They are really the
best and the simplest "indicators" you can find. Analysts look at
a great many factors to reach their conclusions. I have a circular
in front of me listing sixteen. There are many more. Some relate to
business and some to money conditions and almost every other area
imaginable.

Traffic Signals

For you who are engaged in your everyday pursuits I recommend
price and trend as your best off-the-cuff market traffic signals. This
can trigger a fundamental analysis in depth.

The great importance of the price-earnings ratio to professionals
and investors generally puts market price out on the end of a lever.
If a stock sells for 20 times earnings and earnings increase by $1
a share, the stock may very well go up $20 a share. Under some
conditions it might go up less. Under others it might go up much
more. Either way, price is the widest-swinging and most sensitive
barometer of all.

As a practical matter, it will pay you to look at the lists of "new
highs" and "new lows." If a majority of the stocks you own are

making new highs you have the right issues for a current move. If they are making new lows it is time to ask your broker or investment adviser why. This policy can often save you money by cutting losses or promoting profitable exchanges.

Check on stocks that make new highs and on quiet stocks that begin to develop plus signs and higher volume. This can help you find new and profitable shares to buy.

One simple way of doing it is to run your finger down the daily stock tables and note the names of the shares that trade more than 10,000 or advance more than a point. If you do this daily you will almost certainly note some developing strength.

Wheat from Chaff

All of these issues won't continue going up. It will be up to you and your broker and adviser to separate the wheat from the chaff. The point is that no important advance or decline can occur without casting its shadow ahead with increased volume and significant plus or minus signs.

One useful fact to remember is that the most important indications are made in the early stages of a broad market move. Nine times out of ten the leaders of an advance are the stocks that make new highs ahead of the averages. The weakest issues are likely to be the ones where weakness shows up individually before it becomes general.

The day is always bound to come when the last and final high or low is made. This is the noontime or midnight of the market. It has to occur. The early buyer or early seller will not be caught. The investor who is late will get a warning by failure of the trend that attracted him to continue.

Despite the hazards, following prices is still the first factor to investment success.

43

CAREFUL INVESTORS LOOK FOR SIGNS OF QUALITY MANAGEMENT

OF ALL THE FACTORS that affect the success of a corporation none exceeds the competence of management. One of the most popular pieces of advice you hear everywhere in Wall Street is to buy into companies with "good management."

In practice, how do you know?

Almost all analyses of individual companies refer to the quality of the management. Comprehensive reports rating the management of leading corporations on varying qualifications are available.

Judging from my experience, you should take all this with a grain of salt.

Ideally you begin by meeting management. However, the door is open to very few, and the ability to assess it is just as limited.

I think as a practical matter you have to begin by looking at the record. If a company's earnings are increasing, this is one piece of evidence pointing to good management. However, results must be measured against others in the same industry. Otherwise, a management which swims with a favorable tide may get more credit than it deserves. Often a superior management fighting bad conditions is unjustly criticized.

Type of Management Counts

You should try to find out the type of management. Is the company in question headed by an old-fashioned entrepreneur who has made management a one-man show? Or does it have good management in echelon depth which can survive the retirement or death of its chief executive?

One aspect of management worth your noting is the extent to which the officers own their own shares. Broadly speaking, it is advantageous for the officers to have a stake in ownership. It makes a difference whether they own the stock because they want it or because they are stuck with it.

You should consider whether they acquired it through inheritance, bought it on option, or bought it in the open market. Likewise, where possible, consider the purchase date and the price paid. The Securities and Exchange Commission releases regular reports on officer transactions.

Close Watch Pays Off

Of the various ways of making money in securities, I know no better way than through a close watch on management. Changes I particularly refer to are those where companies have been in difficulty, their stocks depressed, and general dissatisfaction expressed— and where a new management comes in and invariably begins by sweeping out the accounting cobwebs. Everything is marked down or written off so that the new management is not held accountable for the mistakes of the old. Very often dividends which were imprudently paid are cut or passed. Thus an investor at this juncture often gets in at the bottom or the beginning of a new cycle.

Attempting to evaluate management, even though you can't get all the answers, is worth all the effort it entails.

44

ACT YOUR AGE WHEN INVESTING

WOULD-BE INVESTORS should give some thought to a proper market approach compatible with their age and financial resources.

Shakespeare wrote of the seven ages of man. For investing purposes there are five: the minor; young men up to age 30; those between 30 and 50; those over 50 until they are retired; and retired men. Although I say men, statistics reveal there are more women stockholders than men. However, many more men than women make investment decisions.

All parents who can afford it give each of their minor children the $3,000 a year allowable without gift-tax liability. This accomplishes three aims: parents build up their children's estates, save the gift tax and reduce their personal income tax.

There are legal questions involved which vary in different states. It is well to check with your broker. I think you should select only securities of the highest quality with the most secured outlook over the long term. You may find it difficult to make portfolio changes until your children are of legal age. Therefore, don't select some low-priced obscure stock that you hope will be worth a fortune by the time the children go to college. The odds are heavily against you.

Investment "To Learn"

Young men up to age 30 ought to invest in order to learn. If you are in this age bracket you can afford to take greater than normal risks, although usually you may not have much capital for those risks. Yet this can be a testing period to see just how well you are adapted to money-making. You can't risk everything because your mistakes are apt to be frequent and costly, and you have to leave some reserve for a comeback.

The second age period, 30 to 50, is your real money-making time. If you are hoping to make a fortune, this is the period for it. This is the time to borrow and look for leverage and try to get other people's money working for you.

If you are between 50 and 65 you should be well set in your investment patterns with some measure of success. You are probably eager to hold on to what you have made. Making more profit has less meaning now than in prior years.

It Keeps Changing

If you are like most people in this age group, you are living somewhat in the past and thinking that your investment experience is bound to keep repeating—when actually it is changing. It is difficult for you to change with it.

If you are retired, you may want to keep occupied with your investments—or you may need to engage someone to do it for you. You could do this by buying an investment trust or going to the investment-management department of a bank or to an investment counselor. Either way, you will have peace of mind only if you do not become a back-seat driver, and instead resolve to be satisfied with maintaining an equilibrium in your portfolio.

Don't look for spectacular results at retirement age; be resigned, rather, to receiving average results from whoever manages your investments. Look for steady, adequate income and conservative transactions designed to keep the portfolio from slipping into the loss column.

45

INVESTORS SHOULD BUDGET FOR FUTURE FLUCTUATIONS

EARLIER THIS YEAR, I spoke to a group of business-school students at Stanford. A student reporter, writing an article on my talk, pointed out that the students were eager and that (in his words) I "limned stock strategy" in an illuminating way. But he concluded by saying that it became very clear that "it takes money to make money."

If you are trying to accumulate money to use in an attempt to make more money, the planning, effort, and denial that go into a budget will help you achieve your aim.

I feel a budget should start in almost every case with setting aside each month one twelfth of all "must" items that are not on a monthly cash basis. These would include taxes, interest, insurance premiums, debt maturities, etc. To this I would add a "contingency" reserve for unforeseen or uncovered large lump sums that might suddenly be required.

Next comes your "income" estimate consisting of cash income from salaries, investments, distributable cash from your business, etc. The sources of such items vary for all of us but are easily identified.

Windfall Items

In addition, you may have what I will term "windfall items." If you have already begun to invest, these might be unrealized capital gains or losses appraised realistically on a genuine marketability basis (less a reserve for capital-gains taxes if a profit). They would include realized net cash profits or losses.

While I don't believe in ignoring such changes in your financial status, I certainly advise against counting them wholly as income (if they are on the plus side).

My inclination is to take an arbitrary 6 percent of their total into my income estimate. To illustrate: If your net worth increases $10,000 in a year I think you can add $600 to your income estimate. If it decreases by the same amount, be sure to deduct the $600 as well.

A simple, practical way of keeping accounts and dividing your budget funds is to have a separate bank account for your "must" items and contingency reserve and another for your current expenses. Naturally your working capital investment account will be further segregated.

"Must" Expenses

Now you will come up with your estimated income for the year ahead and your "must" expenses. You have the difference to divide among rent, food, education, transportation, amusement, clothing and everything else.

I did not list "savings" because I prefer to label that part of your budget your "working capital" for appreciation. If you feel you can win in life, invest to build your fortune. If you feel you cannot—save for protection.

Here is where your personal aims and desires—your will to sacrifice or not to sacrifice—come in. Here is where some of us will budget for a better home or car—and lesser "working capital," or the reverse. The worth of your budget is that you decide what you want, and how able you are to get it. Budgeting will bring your plans into focus.

I think the pattern that works best is to be frugal while young and build your "working capital." Spend in the prime of life. Pull in your horns again upon retirement. This program fits your capacity to enjoy and your capacity to afford as closely as most of us can.

And if you can, keep your eyes looking up.

◆ 46 ◆

WHAT TO DO ABOUT LOSSES

"Why did my stock go down?"

You are a most exceptional investor if you have failed to experience the sensation of having one or more of your holdings decline in market price at a time when stocks generally were advancing.

There is an often repeated but rarely observed axiom in Wall Street suggesting that it is good policy to "cut your losses and let your profits take care of themselves." The same philosophy should be applied to checking the source of weakness and leaving your strong stocks be.

I don't think stocks ever go down without a reason. Good investment supervision calls for attempting to find the reason and appraising its importance and longevity.

Perhaps you made a mistake in the first place? Always take into your calculations that stocks sell on expectations. They don't go up for the same reason twice. If your initial purchase was on a widespread expectation of a good piece of news, the actual news itself may not help.

Find the Source

You will want to attempt to find the source of selling: whether it seems to come from institutions, from insiders, from some single source, or is scattered. This will often give you an important clue.

Most likely, you are going to have to look to your broker or investment adviser to determine the facts.

There are going to be times when you cannot determine any visible reasons for a decline. There will be times when some explanation for the fall is available, but the lower price will seem to have taken it into account.

There is no standard answer to such situations. Trends in prices, trends in the news, trends in value—all can and do change. Each situation has to be judged on its own, and in relation to your other holdings.

However, if I were pushed into a general rule, I would say that I think you will be better off liquidating when in doubt. I might express this another way by saying that if the situation isn't strong enough to suggest a fresh purchase, then you certainly should liquidate. You may be "whipsawed" now and then but in the long run it will pay out.

Should You "Average"?

Buying more of something that has started out badly is known as "averaging." I would say that most times this will prove an unprofitable thing to do.

The important attitude is to attempt to develop objectivity. Try to forget you own the stock in question. Try to forget you have a loss. Look at it as if it were a stranger and you were thinking of whether it rated an initial purchase. If so, maybe you are justified in holding. If not, take your loss.

There is a second factor here you are apt to overlook. That is what you plan to do with the proceeds from the sale of an unsatisfactory holding. Sticking with a declining stock can cost you double: first, if it declines further; second, if it keeps you from buying another share that is advancing.

Putting the spotlight on your failures is one of the surest ways of achieving over-all investment success.

47

SEVERAL FALLACIES OF THE MARKETPLACE

I FEEL IT IS NECESSARY to continue exposing the stock-market fallacies that you probably have been quoting in your armchair or commuter seat discussions.

There is an old saw that smugly advises, "You will never go broke taking a profit." This, of course, isn't so. In fact, the mistake you most often make is to take a profit and let your losses run.

If I were going to establish a rule on the subject, it would recommend doing the exact opposite. I have often stated that I don't believe in stock-market rules or formulas. But if you want to use a guideline, "Let your profits run and cut your losses" is better than "You will never go broke taking a profit."

Those of you who subscribe to the latter practice usually mean "Take a profit as soon as you can see it." Thus, the profits generally are small. It also follows that when you have a loss, you usually don't take it. You prefer waiting, hoping the loss will turn into a profit, which could mean a long, long wait. In most cases your losses eventually pile up to a larger amount than the small profits you take.

You will do best steering a middle course. Make a practice of letting your profits run and cutting your losses quickly. Once the profits become substantial it is good insurance to cash in on a proportion of them periodically.

Another old saw one hears in the commuter train is "Never sell America short." In a broad application, this old standby makes good sense. Up to now America has had its setbacks but has always recovered to reach new heights. From that point of view, I have no quarrel with the maxim.

The trouble is in applying it. Most people who use it do so incorrectly, referring to some segment of a given situation: maybe their personal business, or a particular stock they have, or some industry.

An industry can be in a decline, heading for difficulties, even going into bankruptcy. Therefore, to hang on blindly and say, "Never sell America short," is foolish, because America can go right on growing and prospering whether or not this particular business passes out of the picture.

So be sure when you use this expression to think of it as regards our economy, our well-being, and our nation as a whole, and not as an argument to stay with a situation that perhaps you should abandon.

And then there is the widely held view that "Preferred stocks are better than common." The word "preferred" in everyday life always means something that is better. But in investment parlance, preferred stocks are not really better than common stocks. They rank ahead of common in some ways but are far less desirable in others.

The common stock of a sound company that is moving ahead is likely to be far more attractive than the preferred of a weak company that is slipping.

Look into each issue individually. There are exceptions, and these are mostly preferreds with an attractive conversion privilege, or those selling at a discount and coming out of trouble. But in general, don't let yourself be misled.

48

ARE YOU FAST ENOUGH TO SWITCH CAPITAL?

IT HAS BEEN SAID that capital is like a rabbit—it darts away at the first sign of danger! Are you certain you watch your capital closely enough to flee from smoke before it becomes fire?

To do this successfully you must not only be alert to change but ready and willing to act.

More proof of the inexorable nature of change comes from reading one of the newsletters of the First National City Bank of New York. It discusses and tabulates the changes which have occurred between 1919 and 1963 among the hundred largest U.S. manufacturers.

Our largest corporations are not always the most profitable. Sheer size gives no guarantee of profitability or permanence. While almost invariably at some stage in their growth these companies were attractive investments, there is danger if you overstay your market.

Only 49 Left

Only 49 companies that were on the 1919 list are also on the 1963 list. Even these figures, which show less than half as survivors, understate the situation. Comparison of just two dates ignores the turnover. The bank's letter points out that in the interim numerous firms entered and left the group. Many companies can produce a single spurt of growth which cannot be sustained. For example, if the bank added just two additional years—1926 and 1935—28 names that appeared on the list would have been removed by 1948.

Many factors are responsible. It would seem that an unfavorable change in the outlook for their industries was the major cause.

The greatest changes were in transportation companies. It is asking too much to profit from selling horses and buggies in a gasoline age.

It boils down to the always prime factor of management. It takes superior management to adapt to change. And it takes superior management to build worthy successors to follow in their footsteps.

The National City letter concludes that to achieve success and hold it corporations must secure a primary position in growing markets. They must be adaptable enough to shift into new fields that open up and to fill new needs.

It is up to you as an investor to watch the progress of your companies and switch your investments if your managements fail to keep up with the changing times.

None Since '96

The same proof of the inexorable nature of change can be shown in other ways. Earlier a Morgan Guaranty survey compared the stocks that have been part of the Dow Averages since 1896. Continual evolution, shifting investor preferences, and the alterations in the actual composition of business activity have resulted in not a single issue remaining on the list for the entire 68-year period. Only American Tobacco and General Electric are on the 1912 and 1964 list, but both were on and off several times.

One of the least reliable guides to investing is popularity. The transportation industry again contributes many once-popular investments that have vanished or have all but done so. The carnage in streetcar lines and other utilities has been enormous. Likewise in early automobile leaders.

Investors should make a conscious effort to do some switching in their portfolios. I think at a minimum they could switch 10 percent of a list of diversified investments annually. If you own twenty stocks, surely replacing two can only help in keeping your investment in step with constantly changing investment factors.

The wrong industry, a weak second echelon in management, and over-market pricing of transient growth or profits—these are three grim reapers that can damage your investment performance.

49

HOW A BULL MARKET AFFECTS YOUR INVESTMENT THOUGHTS

WHAT MIGHT a bull market do to your investment thinking?

A leading mutual fund managed by a top-flight investment advisory firm says we tend to:

> Congratulate ourselves on being astute investors.
> Think how foolish we were to have been so conservative, how much better off we would be if we had taken greater risks.
> Start stretching—reaching for quick profits under the guise of a "more aggressive" investment approach, which is nothing more than a risky, speculative approach.

I come across this kind of emotional thinking every so often and it certainly might lead to costly changes in policy. Investors who were asking to keep their accounts in the safest stocks when the Dow-Jones Industrial Average was under 575 in 1962 began to talk about stocks with more possibilities after the Dow rose above 800.

The same mutual fund points out that this kind of thinking gets investors to forget long-term objectives, to overspeculate and overtrade and to take poor advice. This fosters a tendency to overcommit funds and to forget that a high level of stock prices often already reflects good news.

Such a change in policy may produce losses rather than gains, can undermine the investment position by increasing risks just when they may be at their greatest and dissipate buying power at what might be the top of the market, and it generally leaves a portfolio a hodgepodge.

Here are the basic rules which this investment-advising firm feels will help to keep your house in order under today's conditions:

—Have a firm foundation of the strongest and best common stocks of companies which are moving ahead and which have shown an ability to do well under all sorts of conditions.
—Include some reserves as protection against less favorable times.
—Stick steadfastly to your long-term investment plan, not modified by the fears or exuberance of the moment.

The application of these comments depends on a reasonably correct judgment as to where we stand in a bull market. Bull markets are not generally recognized until they have run some distance. The great danger is that you are apt to be very cautious in the early stages and then throw caution to the wind when the market keeps going higher and your original opinion seems to be wrong. It is well to remember that most major moves end in what later proves to be considerable over-evaluation. It is at just such times that these restraints are most valuable to an investor.

50

DON'T LET TAX QUESTIONS CLOUD
INVESTMENT DECISIONS

SHOULD YOU INCLUDE short-term profits in your investment decisions, or adhere to the principle of long-term capital gains only? This is a question you might answer too hastily for yourself with a definite "No," because short-term profits are taxed at higher rates than long-term (over six months at present).

I feel that you should consider the reasons in favor of taking "trading" profits, and at times even seek such profit-taking opportunities.

As I see it, investment principles should always outweigh tax considerations. If you have some short-term trading profits in a stock which you feel may go down, it is folly for you to hold off selling in the hope that its price will hold up until after the six-month period. You could end up losing your profit or incurring a loss.

Now and then it may work the other way. There are times when your judgment will be wrong, and waiting to avoid the tax may help you out. A friend told me, "I would never have made the profit I have in IBM if I had not held on to avoid paying the tax." In his case he did not want to pay any tax, large or small, and IBM kept going up over the years.

Very likely he owns some other stocks he did not talk about, stocks that were held because he did not want to take the loss. Some have undoubtedly either declined further or tied up his capital unproductively.

Careful, objective judgment is the only intelligent key to successful investment.

When should you seek short-term profits? At any time you feel the market situation is favorable.

You have heard the old saying, "Make hay while the sun shines." It certainly is applicable to the market. You will find it easier to make money in a sunny market than in a stormy one. It is foolish to let an opportunity slip from your grasp because you have to share too much of your potential gain with Uncle Sam.

It may not even work out that way. The stock you buy for a trading turn can occasionally improve in value and end up as a profitable long-term investment. Thus, the rule of letting investment principles guide you can work in reverse and take you into a lower tax bracket.

Profits are always worth having, in any case. Suppose you are fortunate enough to realize a short-term profit early in the year. Don't think of it purely as a tax ticket. It can open other doors.

As the year progresses you may find a very unusual purchase for important potential long-pull gains. You can now afford to risk a larger position than otherwise because of the cash backlog created by your short-term profit. If you should be wrong and are forced to take a loss you can offset some of the loss with the previous profit and thus get Uncle Sam to share the loss with you.

You should never hesitate to take a profit, regardless of tax, if you feel waiting could endanger your gain. A profit, large or small, is always worth having.

51

STOP ORDERS NEED CAREFUL EVALUATION

WHAT IS NEW that you need to know to safely and usefully employ stop orders?

The "new" comes from their increased popularity. This wider use began about 1960. It came partly from increased publicity about the stop order itself. The use of charts has also grown. The stop order seemed a natural aid to putting some chart signals into practice.

The type of stop order to which I refer can be either a buy or a sell. You can use it either to initiate a transaction or to close one out. Theoretically it appears to be an "automatic" way to cut a loss or secure a profit. You can also use it to attempt to get in a stock at the start of a move.

This is the way it works: "Central Securities" is selling in the mid-90's. You believe that if—but only if—it sells at 100, it will go on to have an immediate and worthwhile move. You give your broker an order to buy "CES" at 100 stop. If the stock trades at 100 your stop order becomes a market order and is executed at the best possible price. This may be 100 or $100\frac{1}{8}$ or large fractions to several points more. It could even be less than 100, though it very rarely is. A sell order works in reverse. There are other varieties of stop orders, but this type is the one most widely used.

Popular Move

Many investors refer to stop orders as "stop-loss" orders. Investors often use the stop order to limit losses, and this is probably its most popular use. In theory the idea is a good one. Deciding at time of purchase, or as you go along, to automatically cut a loss, prevent one, or cinch a profit, is good discipline.

Likewise, a stop order at a supposedly vital "breakthrough" point gets you in, even though your broker could not reach you at the time.

He has your order and he, or the specialist, is on hand to carry it out.

The rub comes from two factors. The stop-loss idea and the chart breakthrough idea have grown too popular. A congestion of similar orders touched off at one time can overaccentuate the price movement of a stock. This can make for a very unsatisfactory transaction when your order is finally filled. In fact, to protect investors, the exchanges have had to prohibit stop orders temporarily on certain volatile stocks.

The second factor is that widespread belief in a certain point on a chart as bullish or bearish greatly reduces the possibility that the concept will turn out to be right. More and more stocks give what traders label as "false" indications. This can result in costly errors if you are a slavish follower of chart theories. The "falsity" of the indication is not known until after you sell your stock and see it turn about and advance—or after you buy it, and see the move fail to develop and turn into a fall instead.

Watch the Crowd

To safely and usefully employ stop order techniques you must give full weight to what the crowd is probably doing. There can be no hard-and-fast rule that always applies.

I suggest considering a "second penetration" if you are uncertain whether a move is valid. After the stops are filled, you can observe whether the movement promises to continue or reverse. This means you might be saved a false move. On the other hand, you will pay more or receive less for the sake of being more certain of your conclusions.

Another way is to try and prejudge a move and act before the key price is breached. You can then stay with your position if it seems confirmed, or close it out if it seems incorrect. Frequently it can be done without loss or at a small profit.

To make money in the stock market you have to either be ahead of the crowd or very sure they are going in the same direction for some time to come.

52

CASH DIVIDENDS MAY SLOW GROWTH OF YOUNG COMPANY

READERS KNOW I am committed to the principle of judging investment success only by the net result. This takes into consideration not only expected income but possible loss or gain in market valuation as well as the effect of taxes and changes in the purchasing power of money.

By far the majority of investors (as distinguished from traders or speculators) tend to look primarily at anticipated income, such as interests or dividends.

There is no denying the fact that for mature companies a cash dividend is desirable and feasible. For young growing companies this is usually not the case.

Case Against Cash Dividends

The case against paying cash dividends has been exceptionally well put to stockholders by Oscar S. Wyatt, Jr., chairman and president of Coastal States Gas Producing Company. At an annual meeting he stated:

"With respect to the declaration of cash dividends, I would like to point out certain relevant considerations upon which has been based the company's present policy that it will not pay cash dividends in the foreseeable future.

"Firstly, Coastal States is still growing, and we are constantly calling upon outside financial resources. If we pay out cash, we have to make up for it by borrowings and that costs the stockholders an interest expense. The payment of cash dividends at this time could actually have the effect of restricting our growth.

"Secondly, by reinvesting net income back into the business, we realize a comparatively high return.

Borrowing Position Improved

"Thirdly, by converting earnings to equity, we enlarge our borrowing position. For every dollar reinvested, there is the possibility that we might qualify for as much as another $3 in borrowed funds, subject of course to having the necessary earnings and meeting the requirements and tests of our various indentures. In other words, every dollar that would be taken out of the business in the form of cash dividends might cost the company three times as much in capital funds needed for future growth."

Mr. Wyatt's reasons in his case are thoroughly justified because the Coastal record of investing its money has been outstanding. The stock was first publicly traded over the counter at the equivalent of $1.67 per share. It has sold above $40 in 1963. Thus, stockholders have gained handsomely by leaving earnings to compound with the company rather than having a part paid out to them for division between their own use and taxes.

What you will have to consider the most in buying non-dividend-paying stocks is whether the company is in an industry and of a type where management can do more with your money than you can. And of course whether the particular management in question has the ability.

53

MIDDLE COURSE HELPS BUYERS TO AVOID MARKET FALLACIES

CONTINUING with our "stock market fallacies," there is one to the effect that the way to make the most profit is "to buy low and sell high." It's a beautiful idea if you can do it. The truth is, no one knows what is low or high.

After the 1929 break, many people who saw stocks set back a great deal thought they were low. They never dreamed they would go as low as they eventually did in 1932. But, by the same token, once stocks started to go up after 1932, many people said, "I won't be caught again; I won't buy them unless they are really cheap." Of course, they have never been at those low levels since. They never became "really cheap."

I have seen people sell stocks which they thought were high, based on what they had been previously, and the stocks went higher and higher. Then news became public that justified the rise, and what had seemed high previously didn't look high any more in the light of new developments. Often the same works in reverse. Perhaps a stock seems low in relation to its dividend. It goes lower and lower. Then the dividend is passed or cut and the supposed "bargain" is no bargain at all.

Two Important Points

Obviously at some point stocks are genuinely "low" or genuinely "high." You may be successful in knowing what that point is if you keep two things in mind. First, remember that stocks invariably become "undervalued" or "overvalued." They overshoot their logical goals or levels. Next, be sure you feel you have a special reason for expecting a turn or change especially when you are trying to buy low. You surely don't want to own a stock that is cheap enough—but stays cheap. So you must feel that you can see improvement or recovery reasonably soon ahead.

"Buy low, sell high" is one of those wonderful ideas which may work out well for those who can learn the ropes. It can be a rather expensive idea if it is just applied as a generalization.

You have heard that "Money is safe." Money is only good for what it will buy. Its purchasing power has been decreasing steadily over the ages. It certainly isn't safe in the sense intended by the hoarder or the frightened widow.

Middle Course

There is a reverse side to this "Money is safe" coin. It is "Keep your money working." This is just as much of a fallacy in its way as thinking that "Money is (always) safe."

You'd do best steering a middle course. Think about money from the standpoint of what you think it will buy now and later. If you feel it will buy more later, hang on to it. If you feel it will buy less, spend it for something you are intending to buy; or invest it if you think investments will be more costly later.

Take "money" and "gold" off their pedestal and learn to think of them as you do of anything else that fluctuates.

54

WALL STREET PROVERBS ARE
OFTEN FALLACIOUS

THE STOCK MARKET is one place where down-to-earth realism prevails.

Yet I am sure you will believe that it has its folklore, and legends—and also its fallacies, myths and misconceptions.

I think it is most important for you to try and separate the real from the unreal, and to examine them—particularly the fallacies—one by one. There are almost two dozen of them that have dangerously wide currency.

One old saw I am sure you have heard many times is that "Stocks recover if held long enough."

The woods are full of examples of stocks of investment grade that have never "come back." Some have vanished entirely.

"Come Back" Fallacy

Stocks such as New York Central were prime investments prior to 1929; so was Consolidated Edison; so was Western Union. There was a time when the New Haven Railroad Stock was the darling of every New England widow and orphan. New Haven has never come back; Central, Western Union, Consolidated Edison are all selling at a fraction of the prices they once commanded.

It should be realized that even when stocks do come back, the original investor benefits very little if it takes the stocks twenty to thirty years to do so. During that period, his life, needs and desires have changed. The value of money has changed. In the meantime, other opportunities have slipped by.

So it is much better to accept a loss, if you can, while it is still moderate—say 10 percent or so. But if the stock really runs away from you, usually it is better to take a substantial loss and start off anew than it is to be tied hopelessly to something which you wouldn't buy if you had the cash.

Short-Term Investments

Someone at some time probably told you that "short-term trading is speculating." I think the idea is fallacious. By "short-term trading" I mean trading from hour to hour or from day to day and occasionally from week to week. I am not thinking, from the tax viewpoint, of less than six months; I am thinking of trading over very brief periods of time.

It has always been my experience that it is easier to tell what lies just ahead than what lies a long distance ahead. It is true that the value of accurate short-term forecasting has been reduced because of the tax rates. It is true that, strictly speaking, short-term trading is speculative. But so is all intelligent investing.

What the people who use this term really mean is that short-term trading is gambling. It is decidedly not gambling if done by traders who know what they are about. It is easier to tell what the weather is going to be an hour from now or a day from now than what it might be a month from now. In the same way it is easier to tell what the market is going to be, too.

Trading is something that takes the whole $5\frac{1}{2}$ hours the market is open each day, *plus.* If you have that much time—and that much interest—and if you also discover you have a flair for it, trading can be very rewarding.

55

INVESTING IN NEW PRODUCTS

IS THERE PROFIT for you as an investor in a new product or service? It all depends.

The mortality in new products which an attempt is made to introduce by a company formed and promoted for that purpose alone is exceedingly heavy. I was tempted to almost go as far as to say they never profit, but I will settle for "rarely" profiting. I know many instances where eventually a new business did succeed, but before this occurred, new capital had to be brought in, much time went by, and the original investors either dropped out, were forced out, or their equity was greatly diluted. Promotion costs alone to finance something with no record of earnings are generally excessive, introducing much "water" into the capitalization. This is a form of investment that involves the greatest pitfalls and highest risks to the investor.

The odds are greatly improved when this is done by an established publicly owned company of good reputation dealt in on the New York Stock Exchange. In such a case funds are either available or can be secured at normal costs. A portion of the probable initial operating loss can be charged off against earnings. Here we find success as well as failure, but the odds are good. Once in a while an enormous success will result.

New products, new designs, and new services appeal to the imagination. Hence they are sometimes overemphasized by management or brokers.

This is especially true of something exotic or romantic. The first question to ask if you are told to buy a stock because of something new is how much contribution to nearby earnings is expected. Very often you will find that it will be an item of expense rather than profit for some years at best. And in other cases you might discover the nearby maximum potential is a very small percentage of the total earnings of a big company.

There are exceptions. A new drug with a high profit margin and protected by patents can be an important earnings factor. There are companies whose products are necessarily always being changed, and here correct judgment can pay off. This would apply to automobile models, motion pictures and television programs, etc. The replacement of an established product by an improved product of the same type can have an early impact on profits. Success here is more frequent.

As in every other investment situation, market action never exactly coincides with realization. The average stock goes up on great expectations. Very often the rise is excessive. It frequently occurs well ahead of actualities. Sometimes the whole expectation is never realized. The new product fails to take on or produce a profit.

Traders can benefit from emotional temporary moves. Investors never can.

There are profits to be made in such situations. To succeed you must as a trader be careful not to overstay your market. As an investor you must dig very deep into the facts.

56

NEWS AND THE MARKET

How CLOSELY do stock prices follow news releases? As an investor is there an advantage in your moving quickly on news?

Expected news is generally discounted. By the time anticipations become actualities, market prices have generally already reached their objective. There is an old saying about this: "The baby is born."

It is the unexpected news, or "bolt from the blue" that poses a much more difficult problem.

A major piece of unexpected news raises three questions: the nature of the news; whether it is good or bad and what is likely to follow; the position of the market.

The position of the market is of paramount importance. An internally strong market will take bad news in its stride. A weak market cannot. In October 1948, the predictions were unanimous and widespread that Dewey would be elected President. The market was up on this expectation. The unexpected Truman victory caused the market to decline immediately. It was several months before it again turned up. A shrewd trader I knew went short of stock the day before the election. He felt that if Dewey won stocks were weak enough to go down somewhat on what investors considered the good news. His reasoning was that if he lost then they would go down faster and further. He was right, and it was the latter that happened.

President Kennedy's denouncement of the steel price advance in April 1962 came at a time when the market was very weak from overspeculation. The decline was immediate and precipitous. Actually, the top had really occurred late in 1961. Stocks would have gone down anyway.

The assassination of President Kennedy in November 1963 merely interrupted an advance that had been gaining momentum since the summer of 1962. The market was in a strong position. The memory of the 1962 decline was still fresh in investors' minds. Despite the fact that the industrial average was at a new high a few weeks before the Kennedy assassination, the internal technical position was strong. There was confidence in Vice President Johnson. Once it became evident that the assassination was an isolated one, the market resumed its upward path.

The news of Pearl Harbor came at a time when market prices were low and the technical situation was strong. Prices declined only slightly and then rallied. They dragged lower for a few months as the war news was unfavorable, but then turned up. By June, when the heavy Japanese loss occurred at Midway, the market was headed for several years of improvement.

If you look back at important turning points, it is very difficult to correlate them with the news. The 1929 top was established on September 3. There was no particular news at that moment. There was plenty of warning in many news items in 1928 and earlier in 1929. The rediscount rate was raised three times in 1928 and finally reached 6 percent in August of 1929. The Federal Reserve had warned on speculation in February. Secretary Mellon had advised buying bonds in March. Call money cost 12 to 20 percent in that month. The 6 percent Federal Reserve rediscount rate was actually recommended in May.

This is the more typical response to news. It takes a long time generally to sink in and be effective. Most of the time it is better to wait and assess the situation. If your investment position is basically attuned to your judgment of market strength or weakness or price trend you will probably be on the right side of the market regardless of the news.

57

A LITTLE INVESTMENT KNOWLEDGE IS NECESSARY FOR EVERY CITIZEN

How MANY INVESTORS are there now in the U.S.A.? The New York Stock Exchange says there are over 17 million investors who own shares of stock.

Actually everybody who saves for the future is an investor, whether he knows it or not, or wants to be or not.

Hence, knowing something about investing is a universal "must."

The moment anyone saves a dollar it starts to be worth more or to be worth less, and the process goes on endlessly.

If you are afraid of the stock market, your dollars might be clipped by a rising cost of living. If you are afraid of inflation and you buy stocks, they might go down. There is no haven where you can divorce your savings from the constant ups and downs of this world and get them back when and where you want them, able to buy as much as when you put them away.

If we want to keep things safe from fire, theft, and similar hazards we rent a safe-despoit box and think it quite normal to pay the rent.

No Value-Insurance

As far as I know, no insurance company, not even Lloyd's, has offered a valid policy to protect your savings against loss of purchasing power. You cannot simply pay a premium and receive in return assurance of getting back your savings fully preserved from the inroads of inflation and taxation.

Investors who put their money into savings banks, savings and loan companies, mortgages and the like not only expect to keep the value of their savings intact but they want a rental (interest) for the use of their money at the same time.

Investors who buy common stocks or real estate expect dividends or rental income and a capital gain or profit as well.

This is an optimistic point of view, but I think it is unrealistic. Most people of experience would probably be happy to settle for getting back the same after-tax purchasing power that they initially put in.

Inflationary Hazard

Those who make fixed-dollar investments or bury their money in the ground have some protection against deflation if liquidity, collateral values and credit are sound. They suffer in the inflationary world to which we have become accustomed.

Those who invest in equities, which means in stocks, real estate, private businesses, etc., don't suffer as much during inflation as the fixed-dollar class. The gains they sometimes seem to realize are seldom lasting or real. An individual's ability to work at a profession or on a job has an equity value. His compensation tends to increase with rising prices but is clipped by the same rising prices and by taxation.

Your best weapons against the forces that tend to clip your fortune are knowledge and experience. Realization of the conditions that exist should lead you to learn more about them. This can be done by reading and talking to those who you feel know more about it than you do.

The acid test is to learn to be a knowing participant in the game of getting ahead of the other fellow. When you feel you are ready to start guiding your own destiny, do it on a small scale and on an experimental basis.

You are going to find it more difficult than you expect, but also more rewarding.

58

DON'T LOOK FOR MANAGEMENT AT BARGAIN RATES

THERE ARE three ways of making money. One is to sell your time. The second is to lend your money. The third is to risk your money.

The investor who buys ordinary common or capital stock makes an equity investment or speculation and is risking his money. He pools it with others in the ownership of a business enterprise for better or worse.

Somebody has to do the work. But I am concerned here with the investors' interest in management.

Obviously, the investor in a public corporation is in the enviable position of being largely able to go out about his own business or pleasure and enjoy the profits and dividends of others doing the actual work and management for him. It is only necessary for him to buy the right shares at the right time, and later sell them should he be in any way concerned over their future. The investor in a private small corporation or partnership usually contributes both risk capital and management and often acts as salesman and does general labor as well. The public investor, however, must be willing to pay for his absentee ownership.

It seems that lately investors have become more conscious of this fact and have been scrutinizing their corporate management from many angles. Does the management itself own a good sized stake in the business? Is it increasing or decreasing? Did they buy it with their own funds or acquire it on option from the company? Are they doing the best possible job? Are their salaries, bonus plans and pensions fair? It is quite proper that investors do concern them-selves with such vital factors bearing on the success of their stock investment.

However, there is a tendency to look with favor on low paid man-agement and with disfavor on the management that seems to get the most liberal financial treatment. This is in my opinion both a short-sighted and incorrect point of view and it is just because so much is written against corporate management and so little for them that I write this.

The important fact for the investor is that his corporations' compensation policies all the way down the line attract and hold the best men. A company is only as good as the men who run it and work for it and who will rise to manage it in the future.

Today our tax laws are such that old-fashioned savings are out of the picture. Both labor and management need, under modern political philosophies, provision for the future in pensions and other similar plans. Each corporation is in competition not only with other corporations but with private business to attract and hold the best executive manpower. Thus, there can be no rule about it—each case must be judged by the investor not on whether management pay is high or low but from the standpoint of what the company is getting at the price paid. Naturally, the size of the business is a factor, too. But generally, the best is cheapest in the end.

To cite one example, no price was too high to have paid Walter P. Chrysler to go to work for the obscure and failing Maxwell-Chalmers Corporation—and build it up into one of the big three motor makers. No low figure, paid the managements of the smaller independents that at the same time fell by the wayside, could possibly have been a bargain.

The same might be said of management ownership. By and large, it's preferable to have the managers of a company own a major stake in it. However, it doesn't follow that the corporations with the highest percentage of ownership management are the most profitable to own by any means. Each one has to be judged on its own merits. If the officers and directors of a company are recent buyers and if they use a high percentage of their own funds, then the situation is most favorable.

The days of secrecy and a smug attitude are over and those in high places who don't realize it will find that investors will shun their shares and thus cause them to sell at lower price earnings ratios and on a higher yield basis. In time, they will find themselves in even more tangible hot water.

Stockholders' concern with the selection and compensation of corporate management should therefore be primarily concerned with securing the best possible men to get the most out of the business rather than the cheapest. In most listed corporations the total top management salaries, etc. is at worst a very small percentage of net income; but the mistakes of corporate officers hired purely on a low price basis can be a very high percentage of net income or even eliminate any net income at all.

◆ 59 ◆

MIRACLE PLAN INVESTING

IN THE PAST FEW YEARS the literature of Wall Street has been increasingly devoted to building a case for systematic saving using equities as the investment medium, and with the idea that the long-term trend of the market is so inevitably up that averaging on a scale down can only result in an eventual substantial profit. Some people call these plans "dollar averaging." I call it "Miracle Plan Investing" because the promises made appear miraculous as well as fallacious.

From a mathematical point of view there is no question but that the combination of systematic saving and compound interest builds up quite an impressive total in the course of time. Money compounded at 6 percent doubles itself in 12 years. If, in addition, you add to the capital annually, the growth is actually more impressive. Thus, in the first instance $1 becomes $2 in 12 years. In the second, $1 a year saved regularly and compounded at 6 percent, becomes almost $17 in 12 years.

These are mathematical calculations. From a practical point of view one is confronted with several problems. One is how to get 6% with safety. Next, there are deductions which are quite substantial, such as income taxes.

When the plan calls for investment of savings in a single selected common stock further questions arise. It is my contention that none of us know what is going to happen to any stock regardless of quality or history. The literature of the Street in 1954 included tabulations suggesting what one might have made in General Motors, duPont, Standard Oil of New Jersey, Eastman Kodak, Westinghouse Electric, or a theoretical group of stocks.

One of these older tabulations, for example, considers Westinghouse Electric from 1937 to 1954. According to this, $1,000 invested annually, or $18,000 in all, would show a value at the end of the period of $41,580. The authors calculate the appreciation including dividends at $23,580 or 131% over cost price. This is something like an average of 7 percent to 8 percent gain a year.

The fallacy in this line of reasoning is first that it looks backwards and not forwards. For example, Westinghouse sold as high as 42 in 1937 and declined to 15³/₄ by 1942. In all these 6 years the fund must have been steadily sinking and would offer very poor results for any one who had to liquidate. It seems to me that the hazards were great, that the plan could be brought to an end prematurely or incompletely. Usually, when stocks are low, they are low because general conditions create a lack of funds for investment. In order to make these tabulations work it is, of course, essential to be a buyer at the low points. This is just sure to be when people are having trouble making both ends meet in their personal budgets. Some of these plans show up very well but they include large amounts of stock bought at the panic levels of 1932. This was a time when people were not paying their rent or their mortgage interest, and when we had enforced moratoriums. It is wholly illogical to suppose that the average person would have the means to keep up his periodic savings.

There is also the matter of faith. It is human nature to feel optimistic and confident when prices go up. When prices go down people begin to question whether they were correct in buying in the first place. For instance, in Westinghouse, earnings in 1946 during the period of this theoretical calculation totalled only 65¢ a share. It would not be hard and only human to feel under the circumstances that it would be wise to stop the plan and cease throwing good money after what looked like bad, even if one had the money in the first place.

Looking forward, which no one could do when the suggestion was made, Westinghouse did a lot better until 1960. In that year, it sold above 60. Three years later in 1962 it was selling under 30. As this is written it is showing some recovery. Hindsight is one thing and foresight is another.

These tabulations showing what could have been made always select stocks and periods which work out well. But, for example, back before the 1929 crash an investor looking forward might have selected such blue chips of that day as New York Central, Western

Union, Consolidated Edison. All three of these looked fine at the time and would have yielded impressive results in the period *ending* in 1929. However, in the period *following* 1929 all of these three issues and a very great many others completely and unfavorably changed their status.

New York Central earned over $16 a share in 1929, paid over $8, and sold above $250. In 1953, 24 years later, it earned $5, paid $1, and sold at an average price of $21. This is typical of what happened to many formerly fashionable stocks. There is absolutely no insurance that it won't happen in the future to many fashionable blue chips of today.

I very strongly advise anyone, who, against the opinions expressed here, embarks on such a program that they select a listed investment trust for their proposed periodic purchase. If you select a good one, enough shifts will be automatically made in the trust portfolio to gear any investment more or less into the average rise and fall of the market and the great hazards of an unfortunate selection will be eliminated.

The hazard of bad timing and inability to stick with a plan will, of course, still exist.

Literature of the Street, for a long time now, is full of opinions that the stock market is going up because it always has. We are told we might have to wait 10, 20 or even 50 years but we are assured that it is going up, surely as we live that long. Another popular compilation supposes the investment of $1,000 in each of 92 stocks from January 15, 1937 to January 15, 1950. The gain here is theoretically calculated at 12.2 percent compound interest. This is lumping market profits and dividend payments together. This is sincerely believed by its authors to be an objective test. They have chosen a period when the Dow-Jones Industrial Averages were very close to the same level at the start and finish. And, they have selected the 92 stocks on a mechanical basis of all the shares that traded a million or more shares in 1936. It came to 27 different industries.

However, the whole idea is purely theoretical and completely impractical. Who has $92,000 a year to invest, through good times and bad? Who can reinvest all dividends and pay living costs and taxes out of other funds? Who can stick to the plan through thick and thin when things look blue? Who is going to have such a placid life that no emergencies will occur?

A genuine investor who had perhaps $500 a year to invest would come up against terrific commission and odd lot costs that are not figured in the tabulation above. As in the other tables, income tax is not figured either. No one can buy the "stock market" or the "averages." They have to select individual stocks.

Aside from the foregoing considerations a completely neglected fact is the changing purchasing power of the dollar over such a long period of time. This occurs in more ways than one. It might just be a plain decrease through inflation or a plain increase through deflation. But it can also be political or influenced by laws. Rationing, for example, limits the value of a dollar. Currency restrictions accomplish the same purpose. Extraordinary large sales taxes, prohibitive tariffs or tiny import quotas all affect purchasing power. It has been aptly said that a bird in a hand is worth two in the bush. Money might be very much more spendable at the time it is saved than at the end of a long 15 or 25 year plan. The value of money changes in an individual and personal way. We spend it one way and enjoy it differently at age 35 than at age 55. All this suggests very careful thought before committing oneself to some inflexible formula on the argument that if you wait long enough, you'll come out all right. I certainly would not want to decide at the point of departure what I was going to do all the way, come what may. I feel that investing is a very inexact science or no science at all. I think it can only be successfully done by feeling your way along, cutting short losses, concentrating on the profitable situations and certainly, above all, avoiding being locked into an inflexible long-term program. Averaging, to me, most of the time means throwing good money after bad. Pyramiding which is just the reverse is far more appealing. It always pays to follow your successes and rarely pays to persist with your reverses.

Back in August 1929 John J. Raskob said, "No one can become rich merely by saving. Mere saving is closely akin to the socialist policy of dividing and, likewise, runs up against the same objection that there's not enough around to save." I must agree with that view completely. However, surviving has to be done by the use of intelligence, not through expecting miracles.

The whole subject of the record of common stocks is being completely and exhaustively studied by the "Center for Research in Security Prices" at the Graduate School of Business of the University of Chicago. It has taken more than $3\frac{1}{2}$ years and involved the recording on IBM tape of millions of pieces of information to provide the material for the first publicly released study.

The conclusions of the study as given in a copyright release in 1963 by the University are summed up as follows: "Over the entire thirty-five year period, 1926–60, the rates of return, compounded annually, on all common stocks listed on the New York Stock Exchange were 9.01 percent for tax-exempt institutions, 8.20 percent for persons in the $10,000 income class, and 6.84 percent for persons in the $50,000 income class."

These figures are valuable as indicating broad general expectations concerning common stocks' investment results. On the other hand, they have no practical applications because no investor is possibly going to own all of the 1700 stocks involved nor act in the theoretical way assumed. Nobody knows what the next 35 years hold in store.

Sound logic and reasoning as to the future is certain to pay off much better than any formula plan.

60

THE STEP SYSTEM

THE STEP SYSTEM: Investment is not an exact science. The best psychologists are usually the best investors; accountants and figure men usually have the most difficult time making book and market values meet. Successful investment is a matter of experience, information, and judgment and not a matter of pure fact or pure formula.

It has been my experience that the most successful investor is the one who has most of his money committed on his most successful ideas and the least amount of money on his poorest.

To express it another way, I have always believed in intelligent pyramiding rather than averaging. It is a rare occasion when it pays to throw good money after bad.

The difficulty with these principles is that they can not be applied by automation, but must be consciously ordered by humans who experience various conflicting emotions, greed and inertia. Theory is one thing and practice is another. Most of us dislike to take a loss and also dislike to pay more for stocks that we missed lower down.

This is where the "step system" comes in. It isn't really a system because I don't believe in "systems" or "methods." It's a good alliterative title.

The idea is that when things go against you in a market and you are not sure of yourself correct the situation a step at a time.

As an example, suppose you buy some stock in the natural expectation that it would advance. You wouldn't have bought it in the first place, I hope, if you hadn't expected it to go up. Contrary to your expectations, it goes down. The situation causes some doubt but you simply do not possess the intestinal fortitude to do what you probably ought to do—that is to take the loss and take another look. Under such circumstances, you can probably bring yourself to sell a portion of your holdings. Later, if things keep going against you, it will be easier, each time you feel there has been a definite "failure" in the action of your stock, to trim a little more. It is surprising how this policy will get people out of declining market who would stay in otherwise. It works just as well getting people into a rising market that they might otherwise easily miss. It's like taking more of a particular kind of medicine if it agrees with you or cutting it out if it doesn't.

Look at the Label

I often walk double the distance to buy a certain candy bar. On the wrapper it says, "milk chocolate—butter—sugar—almonds." Next time you buy a candy bar or a box of candy look for yourself.

Here is the legend on a box I walk double the distance *never* to buy: "Corn starch, invert sugar, pectin, flour, lecithin, invertase, vegetable butter, egg albumin, citric acid, artificial flavoring, cream of tartar, U.S. certified color, gum arabic, benzoate of soda, and sodium acetate."

Some bright candy manufacturer will soon wake up and boost his business with an advertising campaign to teach today's customers the real ingredients that go into his pure and palatable sweets. Look in your own home cook book and see for yourself. Or, some investor is going to sell his company's management the idea that people really will buy more of his brand if it's fresh and made only of the pure and palatable ingredients mother used to use.

Pick of the Professionals

When this section was written it seemed that one perennially read that Amerada Petroleum headed the list of fifty favorite stocks of investment company management. In later years it was displaced by International Business Machines. However, the point can be made with Amerada. The inference implied is that professional management believes that the largest percentage of their funds should be in Amerada. One might also deduce that if the 175 institutions from whose portfolios these lists are compiled were to start off from scratch with all cash, Amerada is the stock they would buy first and Amerada is the stock that they would buy the most of. The same reasoning is popularly applied to the other stocks in the list in the order in which they appear.

It has always been my opinion that most investors have a different philosophy toward securities they already own and securities they are in the process of acquiring. Most of the institutions that bought Amerada were buying equal dollar amounts of other shares at the same time. Amerada went up more and hence at a later date appears in the statements as the largest commitment by reason of the unrealized windfall appreciation rather than by design.

The really useful function of such studies is to note the principal portfolio changes in common stock holdings on a current basis. It is far more important and valuable to the investor to note issues in the list which appear for the first time because of new buying, or issues which advance towards the head because of additional buying. Changes which merely reflect changes in market price are of minor significance. Reluctance to take a profit means something, but nowhere near as much as willingness to make a fresh purchase, or to add at current prices to an older one.

61

DOUBLE DIVIDENDS

How Highly Do You Value Your After-Office Time?

WHAT VALUE do you put on your leisure time? How do you spend it?

The Economic Research Division of the Chase Manhattan Bank in a recent bi-monthly "Business in Brief" discusses "Leisure in America" at some length. It points out that the work week has fallen from 70 hours in 1850 to 40 hours now. On top of this come additional holidays and increasing paid vacations. All this adds up to something like 100 million weeks of vacation during 1964.

The picture is different for business and professional people. It is estimated that 40 per cent of all managers, officials and proprietors work 48 hours a week or more.

Successful men in the top rank work probably nearer 60 hours. The same is true for those few of the business-school graduates who will in time take their places.

"Tex" Thornton, who since 1953 has built up Litton Industries, Inc., from nothing to profits of almost $30 million a year, only a few days ago told his stockholders, "I can't stand useless leisure." Thornton devotes most of his time to business, and this has definitely paid off.

My own observation is that an essential of success is to find what most people label "work" to be really play. Unless you enjoy your job you will neither succeed at it nor give your employer, if you have one, full value.

I know this will be disputed by many who rate their jobs as lowly or distasteful. Yet the Gilbert and Sullivan rhyme, "He polished up the handle so carefully that now he is the ruler of the Queen's Navee," has been proven true in life over and over by many who have risen to the top in numberless different ways.

Whether you use your after-office free time for more work, for "voluntary idleness," play or relaxation, it is certainly as valuable to you per hour as your normal work week. Some think in dollars and cents it is worth more. Most of us forget this. The great "serve yourself" businesses in the U.S.A. could never have flourished as they have if we thought about it. We would not fritter away so many of our few free hours doing chores the clerk or delivery boy should be doing for us.

You are going to have more and more "disposable time" as the years go on. It will pay if you consider what it cost you in labor and what it is worth to you in value. You can use it to work overtime. You can use it to improve your education, for your health, to travel and for many other things.

We are far more lax on what we do with our "spare time" than with the hours we must use to earn our daily bread. Plan your leisure time and get the most out of one of the most important things you work for.

Odd Lots

You can buy from one to ninety-nine shares of any stock listed on the New York Stock Exchange. These less than 100-share transactions are called "odd lots."

They deserve some mention because, until the birth of the Monthly Investment Plan of the New York Stock Exchange, odd lots existed and flourished without benefit of any organized merchandising or method of carrying their virtues to the investing public. The mutual funds in recent years have so much held the center of the small-investor stage that odd lots have practically had to go it alone on their merits.

It is correct to say that the purchase of a top quality investment trust or mutual fund gives the small investor a well-managed and well-diversified equity investment about which he need give little thought or care. If the new investor puts half his surplus funds in such media and the other half in U.S. Government Bonds or in savings banks, he has both an inflation and a deflation hedge and about as much security as anyone can procure in this insecure world.

Odd lots are for the individual with a small stake who wishes a chance to start out on his own. There are still a lot of us in this world who want at least to try to do better than the average. There are also a lot of us who want to learn by doing. The odd lot investment is the ideal medium for such people.

We pointed out earlier in this book that the lowest-per-share price usually bought the most highly priced investment. The majority of the time, an investor obtains better value by buying a 10-share odd lot of a $75 stock than 100 shares of an issue selling for $7.50.

The cost of dealing in odd lots varies with the price of the shares dealt in and the total amount of money involved. A popular transaction might be one where $1,500 was invested in a 20-share odd lot of an issue selling for $75. The commission in this case would be only $20 plus a $1/4$% of a point higher on the purchase of the stock as an odd lot, or an additional $5. This makes $25 in all, or less than $1 3/4$% of the money involved. This is considerably less than the acquisition cost involved in the investment of $1,500 in most funds. Also there would be no annual expenses such as a fund must necessarily incur for management, safekeeping, etc.

Odd lots also permit the individual with a small amount of capital to diversify his funds in the same manner followed by a large investor or an investment trust. At the recent high it cost $10,000 to buy a round lot of 100 shares of General Motors. An odd lot investor could divide this amount of capital into any desired number of parts according to his own preference. If he paid cash, he could receive a certificate in his own name for each of his individual securities and each of the companies paying dividends would forward their checks also made out in his name. He would also receive all company communications directly, especially annual reports. Odd lots thus offer the small investor the same opportunities the large investor enjoys.

Why Buy Quiz

If you want double dividends, double profits, and half losses, try filling out a quiz sheet on every issue you are considering buying.

(1) How much am I investing in this company?
(2) How much do I think I can make?
(3) How much do I have to risk?
(4) How long do I expect to take to reach my goal?

I believe you have a good buy if you think you can obtain an ultimate gain of one and a half to two times the amount invested in six to eighteen months, by risking no more than 10 percent to 20 percent of your investment.

It takes a book to outline how to do it, but here are a few brief ideas to help:

(1) If you are a novice, invest 10 percent of your capital, no more, no less, in each venture. If an expert, you do not need my advice. Experts invest from 20 percent to all the law allows. If you don't feel confident enough to invest a sum that is important to you, better look for something else. If you are right, you want a profit big enough to satisfy your aims.

(2) The gain you expect to make is the heart of your problem. You must see something ahead *that is not reflected in the current price* to bring about the expected advance in price. If everybody expects what you expect, there will be no profit. This is gross over-simplification, but helpful. Following trends is easier than trying to call turns in them. To put it another way, it is more likely to pay off to buy into an advancing situation at a seemingly high price than to attempt to discover when a declining situation will stop declining and turn upward.

(3) I believe in retreating and living to try another day. On high-priced shares you generally will get a run for your money, if you limit losses to 10 percent of purchase price. On low-priced shares, perhaps 20 percent. There will be times when you will sell out 10% below cost only to find the stock come back and make good, but this will happen rarely enough, if you know what you are doing. Limiting losses is like paying worthwhile insurance premiums. The novice can limit his losses mathematically. The expert will have his reasons. The fool will let them run.

(4) Time is the essence of life. Taxwise, six months is the current minimum period. It is hard to see too far ahead. Even a 50 percent gain, if it takes many years to achieve, can become a conventional percentage figured annually.

Try filling out a quiz sheet and you will be surprised at how it will spur your thinking in new and helpful directions.

"The Last Is First"

I was on a two months' vacation and had to double up on a column at a time when I was remote from both the stock ticker and a reference piece of financial data. This pushed me into a discussion of "how" rather than "what" to do.

Most of us logically think that "first" comes before "last" but to the shoemaker—"the last is first." Likewise, most investors think that the stock which is nearest to the low level of its range, or which sells for the least number of times earnings, or sells to return the highest income yield, or which sells at the lowest figure in relation to its book value, must logically be the best buy. To the really successful, experienced and sophisticated, professional speculator "the most expensive is the cheapest."

If you consider a tabulation of a handful of equities in any given group, one can almost blindly buy the seemingly most expensive and make a profit provided you are right on the trend and don't overstay your market. Understand I do not advocate this as a method of investing. I write about it because so many do use the *reverse* of this method, i.e., buying the seemingly "cheapest" with necessarily poor overall results.

The basic reason for this seeming paradox is that the market is always weighing and appraising the shares traded. Ninety-nine times out of a hundred, if one motor stock yields 6 percent and a second one 7 percent, there are points of weakness in the second taken into account by all buyers and sellers in the market, but which escape the buyer who feels high yield makes for a bargain.

The next time you think you see a bargain, take it as a red signal to look further and see if you have missed an important weakness. The next time you feel like selling short some super blue-chip yielding 2 percent, selling at an all-time high and up fifty points on the year, stop and look again. See if these facts are, in reality, green lights reflecting past success that promise even more success in the future.

"When Sell Quiz"

Making a commitment is many times easier than closing one. When you consider buying shares you can avoid a decision altogether, if the situation is in anyway puzzling or not completely to your liking.

But once you own your stocks, the decision as to whether to hold or sell is quite another matter. You are forced to a yes or no answer, no matter how uncertain or confused you may be. It is like having your car straddling the railway track with the express coming down the line. Neither backing up nor going ahead may appeal as a sure way to avoid getting hit. You are on the tracks and the train is coming, so you must do one or the other. Or, maybe you should abandon the car and jump.

If you have a loss in your stocks, then I think the solution is automatic, provided you decide what to do at the time you buy. I am always in favor of limiting losses. In the case of high-priced stocks the limit should be perhaps 10 percent of the amount invested. In the case of lower-priced shares, the limit should be 20 percent of the price paid. The beginner can do this as a mathematical rule. The more experienced can temper the plan with a little judgment. It is when you have a profit that the problem intensifies. It is vital to investment success to let profits run—but not melt away.

Assuming the average reader owns several stocks, the question divides itself into two parts. The first is are we in a bull or a bear market? Few of us ever really know until it is too late. For the sake of the record, if you think it is a bear market, just sell your stocks regardless of any other consideration.

Since 1946 we have been in a market where some stocks have moved up, others marked time and still others declined. Shares and things such as real estate have been in a bull market. Equities have been better than cash. Only equities in industries that have had particular troubles, or equities that have become overbought, have been good sales. At this writing the same inflation climate seems to prevail. Under such bullish circumstances do not sell unless:

(1) You see a bear market ahead.

(2) You see trouble for a particular company in which you own shares.

(3) Time and circumstances have turned up a new and seemingly far better buy than the issue you like least in your list.

(4) Your shares stop going up and start going down.

Not since perhaps 1920 have I been investing in the stock market without knowing that four rules and fifty words will never tell anyone when to sell. They will help if you think them over.

The second part of the question is: Which stock?

(A) Do not sell just because you think a stock is "overvalued."

(B) If you want to sell some of your stocks and not all, invariably go against your emotional inclinations and sell first the issues with losses, small profits or none at all, the weakest, the most disappointing actors, etc. Always keep your best issues for the last.

In a bear market stocks always go 'way below "under valuation." In a bull market they advance 'way past "over valuation." An investor should be guided more by trend than price. Stocks make their lows at that time and point when the greatest number of active investors think the worst of them. The actual low or high point in news occurs many months before or after the market low or high. It is the *expectation* of coming events, rather than the events when they materialize, that moves markets.

Quiz yourself along these lines before you close your next commitment and I think it will improve your average result.

Borrow for Profit

I guess I am a bit old-fashioned because I cannot rationalize the younger generation's popular concept of installment buying. In fact, their entire financial "policy" seems topsy-turvy.

Young people should begin by living within their means and paying rent and letting others supply the capital for their homes, etc. At first, borrowing should be confined to business, investment, or other profit-making ventures if they ever hope to have some capital of their own.

Of course, such ventures may turn out to be losing ones but youth is strong enough to take that in its stride. Youth is entitled to flex its muscles and see just how far up in the world it can climb. It may be that the time will come in a person's life when he will realize his own limitations. These possibilities can never be appraised unless they are tested. Personal borrowing comes later when one knows his status in life.

It makes sense to me to run a risk borrowing for possible gains. It makes no sense borrowing to own a better car or a better house before one's ship has come in or before one knows one's future.

Naturally before one thinks in terms of investment one has to give consideration to the basic necessities of life. Certainly it is necessary to have a backlog of cash for some emergency. Insurance, too, should be a "must." However, only the individual can tell whether he can afford a car or whether he should build or rent a house.

One needs money to make money. The best return one could hope to get owning one's own home might be double bank interest. Young people should look for profits, not immediate income. They should look forward to the day when in their later years income on their capital will support them in the style to which they have grown accustomed without the necessity of selling their time.

Career in the Canyons

Speaking of young men going to work in Wall Street, a career in its canyons has much to offer to those who are really ambitious.

My idea of a young man most likely to succeed is one who takes a job in Wall Street after eating, sleeping and dreaming everything he could get his hands on concerning the subject during his school days.

I see people coming in every day seeking jobs and what they want to know is what are the pay and the hours. Some that inquire by telephone are worried about the extra few minutes on the subway riding south of 34th Street. Such as these might as well forget their futures because they just haven't any.

The particular advantage of working in Wall Street is that you make your living in the same business that you invest your savings. If you are good at one, you are apt to be an expert at both. The usual business or professional man sometimes becomes an expert in his own line but rarely or never at investing his savings.

Different people want different things out of life and the world could not go on if this were not so. But for those who want more coin of the realm and an amusing vocation, and are willing to work for it, Wall Street pays off double. It is demanding—fascinating—rewarding.

How an Ice-Cream Soda Should Be Made

The glass used must be chilled. Many new-day self-styled soda jerks use a hot glass direct from the sterilizer and get a warm drink as a result. The syrup must be chilled. The water must be chilled. Sodas are meant to be taken very cold. Syrup is placed in the glass. Then one scoop and ONLY one scoop of ice cream. Under no circumstances any fluid milk or fluid cream or whipped cream. We are making an ice-cream soda, not a nondescript concoction. The ice cream and syrup are mixed with a stream from the concentrated high pressure soda nozzle. Then the glass is filled with soda and finished off with a few extra high pressure squirts. The syrup must be high grade and used in generous quantity and the ice cream must be rich.

Very few soda dispensers know any more how to mix an ice-cream soda or, for that matter, few know the difference between a milk shake and a frosted. And in California there remain possibly only a half dozen fountains in the State that use milk and ice cream in proper proportions to get a *drink* if you order a "frosted." Most of them use "ice milk," gelatine, and air to get a "thick" stuff that needs a pipe line or a spoon to down and has practically zero real butterfat in it. I hope California fountain practices "go west" towards Korea and do not reverse and move this way. As a matter of fact, I believe the first genuine ice-cream soda was invented in San Francisco by a Mr. Frank Maskey. He and his wife are both dead and the old business was until recently carried on after a fashion by two of their old candy makers.

◆ 62 ◆

A LAYMAN LOOKS AT BUILDING*

THE ARCHITECTS of America have never done a good job of selling the public on what good architecture means. The result is that architecture is the lowest paid of the professions, and our cities and countrysides are blotted with eyesores and impractical and over-costly makeshifts.

Architects should go into partnership. The minimum architectural firm should include an architect, engineer and a business partner. Good architects are artists every bit as much as musicians, authors and actors, all of whom engage financial managers and publicity representatives. I think the architect classes himself as a member of a profession comparable with doctors and lawyers and believes the code of ethics which governs the latter governs him as well. The truth probably lies between the two extremes and, while the employment of business managers and publicity agents will be distasteful to most, the admission of a good business partner to the architectural firm is entirely acceptable from any point of view.

Some of the most successful architects in this country, whose work is the most widely known, are simply good business men first and unfortunately often mediocre designers.

The architectural press does a much better job, but its usefulness is restricted by the fact that it reaches mainly the profession rather than a large public. There is a crying need for a real publicity medium that will teach the need and advantages of good architecture to the public. The occasional articles in national magazines and the popular "home" publications of wide circulation miss the point altogether. They are aimed at women and tend to glorify what might be called

---

* The author was for five years on the Visiting Committee to the Board of Overseers of the Postgraduate School of Architecture and Design of one of our oldest and greatest universities.

"cottage architecture," if that phrase means anything to the reader. They aim at a kind of home-made coziness and comfort miles from the real thing. Their illustrations of homes and rooms uniformly include the good and the bad, which is no way to cultivate good taste. And, of course, being mainly women's publications, they rarely include anything at all tending to raise the standard of the office, the factory or the store, to say nothing of the many other types of buildings that need good architecture.

More business in architecture would mean more architecture and better architecture as the taste of the public became educated and stimulated. The contractor-built home and the inadequate business building would pass.

Architects would themselves produce better work. The proportion of architect-designed buildings that are unfortunate compromises is excessive for the good of the profession. I try to believe the architect had it in him to do better, but, lacking the business judgment to sell his ideas to his clients, prostituted himself to get a job and a square meal.

Anything that brings money and work into architectural offices would improve architectural results. This would bring more money and more work and attract more brains. Thus the profession would be reborn.

I spoke of a third partner—the engineer. If architects are poor business men, I think that can be understood and excused, but being poor engineers is more difficult to understand. Art is the satisfaction of the senses, and why architects should only be sensitive to the impressions of the eye is hard to comprehend. No work of art, or of architecture is complete and real unless it satisfies all senses as well as the sense of sight and unless it is thoroughly functional and practical. In fact, a completely functional design often turns out incidentally to be sound art. But nothing impractical can possibly be good art.

I live in one of the most expensive buildings in the world. I think it would not take long to count how many co-tenants I have living, as I do, on the 34th floor. This building was constructed without regard to cost. The money invested in it was lost long ago. Even the bondholders saw the value of their purchase greatly cut. A firm of internationally known architects designed this building. It was designed with the help of a great staff of hotel managers. Both the architects and the managers had a lifetime of experience designing and managing hotels, though I sometimes doubt it, after visiting and living in hotels all over the world. All through this large building are evidences of money thrown away. But in the one fundamental necessity of proper conditions for bodily comfort in the way of ventilation and temperature, allowing pleasant waking hours and sound sleep, my apartment, if it is a fair example, is completely lacking. Despite the great waste of money everywhere visible, the public hallways have no windows or cross ventilation, obviously to save rentable outside space. However, the economy is a false one indeed. Outdoor air rushes up to the outer skin of this tower, drawing air out of the living and sleeping rooms. The hot, stale air filters through and around doors into the guest rooms and out the windows. In midwinter the atmosphere is usually so hot and stale that one can only try to sleep under a sheet. "Guadalcanal" was my pet name for my quarters in this "luxury" hotel until I moved to another similar room containing a form of out-dated air conditioning.

Now, it is this sort of thing which I think hurts architecture. The traveler leaves his undesigned home and goes to an architect-designed hotel. And, if he found the latter really much better, he would resolve to have his next home architect-designed.

I suppose the point of my "luxury" hotel is not well taken, as surely there must have been an engineer on the job. But I think that he must have confined himself to seeing that the steel frame supported the building and, if he had a business partner, he confined himself to getting the job instead of showing his clients why money spent in some directions would bring returns and thus incidentally help the client and the whole profession.

I am a layman—not architect or engineer—but I can see where windows in the halls and adequate ventilation stacks in the baths, closets or foyers, transoms even if need be, combined with casement windows hung to swing out from the top would have scooped fresh air into these rooms, drawn out stale air and helped to make this building livable and other than the financial nightmare it actually has been since its construction.

Back in 1938 I climbed up the great ruins of Ankor Wat in Cambodia. Here are said to be the remains of a city of more millions of inhabitants than Manhattan. It was interesting to reflect on the reasons for many of the architectural features of the design of the Cambodians. I rarely go into my tower quarters without visualizing some great change that will leave it bare of human habitation for centuries, only to be rediscovered as Ankor was rediscovered. And I cannot help reflecting that these new world individuals will wonder why architects of today designed that building as they did.

If architecture is to successfully compete for the consumer's dollar, it must be real and done with an eye to function so as to produce something that can be properly publicized and sold to the public.

We are told that the future of building is in mass production and prefabrication and that the real market lies in the low income brackets. I believe that to be both true and false. It is true as regards an effort to sell shelter in competition with personal transport as provided by the motor car. But there can be an expanding market for architect-designed homes, offices, factories, stores and various private and public service buildings if architects wake up and take some business men into partnership with them.

The real field for the average architect is in relatively expensive homes plus larger buildings which are practically all architect-designed. In my estimation what the architect accomplishes in homes costing from $30,000 to $60,000 is what will really count in determining whether the market for his services is going to expand. And also what he can do with small privately owned shops is going to mean a good deal. But even in the field where architects must be employed because of size and other complications, a higher standard of work will bring more total work.

For example, a very few modern stores have been designed. But, as these become more common, they will make obsolete the present stores and force additional building.

Are new buildings and homes going to be traditional or modern? They should be first of all functional. There is no reason for us today to copy construction features of the classical architects which were governed by the limitations of their day as to materials, heating, cooling, etc. But, just as I think it impossible to justify our copying of a strictly classic design, so do I think it almost as bad to throw out the attractive features that have lived through the years and can be adapted to be included in the postwar functional building.

The so-called modern and up-to-date architecture I see around the country tends in most cases to be too bare and too cold. If persisted in, this tendency will kill off modernism and functionalism altogether in time.

I think it reflects a concentration on constructional functionalism and a neglect of psychological functionalism. Buildings are built to last and to resist the weather, but they are also built to shelter and contain the human animal. Because a plain white wall will fulfill its constructional function of keeping out the elements does not mean that it fulfills its psychological function. The fully functional wall must also be restful and pleasing to the eye. And walls must also be satisfying to the touch. I think that they must speak to us mentally as well. They must say "this wall was built in an age when good taste and good living and good craftsmanship prevailed." Only too often nowadays they say that they were built in an age when the workman thought only of his union and the employer only of utilitarian needs.

I think I have crossed the Atlantic in most of the well-known boats, and many times I have heard experienced, educated, and sensitive travelers speak in fond reminiscence of the homey wood-paneled smoke rooms of some of the older British ships as contrasted with the cold modernism of the newer express liners. There was much in the "boaty" decoration of the old small ships that was far more desirable than the hotel-like construction and operation of the latest queens of the sea.

The architect must include this human functionalism if his designs are to grow in popularity.

In 1942 I visited the then new Washington Statler Hotel. Here in the new capital of the world, visited by almost everybody of importance in the world, was the newest hotel in the world. One might expect something to symbolize American business and American architecture. Something that might be the most important modern building for many years to come. Something more notable than Ragnar Ostberg's Stockholm City Hall or Frank Lloyd Wright's Imperial Hotel at Tokyo. After all, this is the U.S.A., not Sweden or Japan.

In fact, I feel it should have been a quasi-public enterprise subsidized in the manner of a great liner or any other structure of more than mere commercial importance. Something, among other things, to sell architecture to its guests.

Perhaps I set my sights so high that, when I finally arrived at the plain, undersized midwestern "business man's hotel with a coffee shop" the new Statler so obviously resembles, the letdown was too great. The brilliance of the main dining room at the Savoy in London would be dim next to my conception of what the Statler might have been.

But even if it could not be this and instead had to be the flagship of a famous hotel chain erected on a purely commercial basis, it doesn't seem to be what it should be. The exterior is devoid of required ornament, nor does it achieve distinction through form or fenestration. The inside motor entrance is not dramatized to the extent justified nor is the pedestrian entrance properly tied into it, with the result that cars stop at unimpressive and inconvenient doorways. Commercially, the important fact is that the passerby or the observer of a picture of this hotel is not encouraged to stop.

The room that happened to be assigned to me was functionally inconveniently designed. One expects the combination of a great firm of architects with a great firm of hotel operators to produce a bed light that is right for its purpose. One expects closets designed for clothes of a dimension worn by modern men and women and bathroom fixtures set in the proper places. The thought that came to my mind was that architects should make more use of temporary "mockups" similar to those used by the motor car manufacturers. It is about time that they know some common standard dimensions and, before selecting furniture or arranging fixtures, they should be tried out in a "mock" room.

Foreign visitors will not find much to take home with them from the design of this hotel. Nor will American guests rush back to their home towns to engage an architect for their new building, whatever it may be.

The builders and designers of this Washington Statler have only done what most modern owners and architects have done, and I am not selecting them for special criticism. It does possess many admirable qualities, advances, and innovations. But it serves here as well as anything else as a guinea pig to illustrate what I think is partly wrong with architecture in America, and what must be done to revitalize it.

The greatest threat to more architecture and better architecture is the 1965 "copycat complex." Somebody puts up an all-glass building and then everybody puts up all-glass buildings. What if the glare is so great inside that most tenants draw shades over their windows? What if it costs more to heat and cool them? It doesn't make any difference so long as it matches the new building next door.

Sooner or later somebody will put up something different, perhaps a totally windowless office building. There will be reasons for and against this, but regardless of their validity, unless things change, we will then see this copied all over the land.

The keys to successful architecture are originality and adaptability. Architecture requires new and individual expression. It should be adapted to its site, to its use, to the economics of the day, to modern materials, to the skills of labor available, to current costs, as well as all the other factors that need consideration and make the architect worthy of his hire.

63

INVESTMENT MANAGER'S DILEMMA

IT IS OFTEN DIFFICULT for the layman to measure the ability of his doctor or lawyer. Yet, in the case of the investment manager, clients invariably think they can measure his competency, even if their methods are usually fallacious. The major factor in investment management is the degree of risk accepted to accomplish the result, and this rarely lends itself to accurate measurement, particularly by the layman.

Thirty years of experience in the investment management field leaves me dissatisfied with the results. Speaking broadly and particularly extending over a series of complete cycles, the best that most of the large professionally managed accumulations of capital can do is to slightly better the averages in good times, and possibly decline a little less than the averages in bad times. I have seldom heard of any group of important accounts getting into large amounts of stock at the bottom and out at the top. Another point—the published lists of the most popular stocks, as far as the trusts are concerned, are tabulated on the basis of today's valuations, a sort of tabulation after the fact. If Amerada, for example, was at one time the most popular stock with the trusts, it got that way because it went up the most, rather than that the funds bought exceptionally large amounts at the time of their original purchase.

The problem has two separate parts, the question of investment decision, and the problem of client relationship which vastly affects net results. For example, people who invest money for others have legal and moral responsibilities which often hinder the use of investment practices most likely to succeed. Anyone in a position of trust who buys his clients a diversified list of the best stocks cannot be assailed, even should they decline in price. Let him try a concentrated position in a low-quality issue and he is almost sure to be criticized. His reasons may be well-founded but that will not affect the decision against him. Clients generally want to be fully invested and gener-ally prefer the most popular issues of the day without knowledge as to whether these policies will prove the most profitable or involve the least risk.

Securities are not priced solely on balance sheet or earning state-ment formulas. Investors' psychology plays a very great part in shap-ing market prices and trends. To make matters even more difficult, consumer psychology also plays a large role in shaping the eco-nomics and fundamentals that lie beneath the earnings and divi-dends. We also have unexpected news and occasionally credit strains to deal with.

A logical aim for investment managers in times of inflation is to preserve purchasing power and secure a true profit after taxes and dollar depreciation. Likewise, a proper aim in bad times is to keep liquidity and dollar value. A comparison of results with such aims shows we still have a long distance to go before feeling satisfied.

We can come nearer to accomplishing these goals to the extent that we can cure some of the handicaps listed here. However, it is quite obvious that only in a very small minority of cases will this be possible. Thus, the more practical question is what actually can be done by the majority to improve investment results of the aver-age account under prevailing conditions. The answer seems to lie in wider selling on a scale up and buying on a scale down than is generally practiced. Yet such a procedure is fundamentally opposed to my own basic concepts of investment management as outlined in various articles for years, and particularly in this book.

Another practice that might be studied is how to cut losses before they run into a high percentage of the capital invested. This is easier said than done. The trick is how not to lose good positions selling on declines that later prove to be temporary, and yet get out of positions that really continue to go bad.

If the individual investment manager will stop thinking in terms of striving to have his particular fund decline a few percentage points less than the average or advance a bit more than the average and start to think in terms of making a profit every year, that attitude in itself, if generally adopted, may advance the total results secured by the profession.

64

I DON'T SELL—PEOPLE BUY FROM ME

YOU CAN'T SELL ANYTHING to anybody if you can't sell it first to yourself. This principle, more than any other, runs through my story of how to go about starting in the stock brokerage business as a "customer's man" without customers, and build up to what people loosely call a top securities salesman. Episode by episode, the story is not great, dramatic, or outstanding. No one great coup put it over. It is a repetitious tale of building brick by brick. Yet taken together the achievement is outstanding. I have always wondered why so few achieve something that is so easy.

My career began at the bottom in San Francisco. I had had half a high school education and all my play-time had been devoted to architecture, cameras, travel, and automobiles. I did not at that time even read the financial pages of the papers. At 21 I was catapulted into the securities business when I decided to go to work instead of training for architecture as a profession. The question was what I should do. Sell automobiles or cameras? Books, insurance, real estate, or stocks and bonds? Selling one of the latter was among the accepted fields for untrained beginners those days. I chose bonds. I did not then know the difference between a stock and a bond or a dealer and a broker. I certainly knew nothing about selling except that I did not like the idea. I never learned to like selling and I don't sell today. Instead, people buy from me.

My first job was bond salesman for a retail bond dealer in San Francisco where I was given one day of training. The second day with the company I was supposed to go out and sell. The third day I quit. I quit because I was asked to sell a security I did not believe in. I had no way at that time of really knowing why this security was not good. The commission I was to be paid on this particular issue, however, was suspiciously high. I sensed even then that good things sell, or are bought from you, without a special markup. So I believed that this security was not a good one. Later on my hunch on this particular bond proved correct when the company that issued it ran into trouble. In all the years since then, I have found that same principle to hold true.

My second job was also in San Francisco with a New York Stock Exchange brokerage firm that had a ground floor office in a leading hotel. I was in the bond department behind the counter. Strangers came in all day off the street to ask for information on new bonds advertised by window cards, and it was my job to direct them to a customers' man, give them a circular, or show them a financial manual. Many of these people mistook me for a salesman. There were no rules those days against anyone, even a novice such as I was, taking orders. So I gradually built up a total of about 85 customers in the nine months that I held this position. My selling technique, if that is what it could be called, was to try to guide customers into what I thought were the best securities to own at the time and generally into less of them than they intended to buy. I knew even then that most people are over-anxious to have all their money working, as they term it, by being always fully invested in the market. Actually greater final net returns are achieved by a combination of more conservative purchasing in totals invested with more attention paid to buying and selling the right securities at the right time. A profit of ten points in 100 shares of stock is far more desirable from many angles than a profit of one point in 1,000 shares.

Actually I did not know then which were the best securities, when to buy them, or what to pay for them. I did the best I could. But I was studying all the time, especially reading everything in sight on the subject of stocks and bonds and markets; on investment, speculation, money, insurance, real estate, and economics. My working hours those early San Francisco days were about 12 hours in the office and my studying time out of the office a minimum of four hours. One thing is certain: Success takes time. I often worked alone in that office during an entire holiday on projects that I selected for myself. Such hours were not required by the firm for I never had trouble keeping up with my regular work in a normal 48-hour week.

These events took place about 1921 when the market was very low but going up, and I got along better than might be expected. I was taking orders from clients and trading for myself as well. I made a straight $90 a month as I remember it, plus what I could make in the market. My capital for personal purchases was about $13,000, an inheritance from my father.

From the first I became one of my own best customers. If you cannot successfully practice what you preach, you might as well throw in the sponge. There is a vast difference between the theoretical and the practical, and this difference can only be bridged by taking your own medicine and seeing if you live through it. That is why I say you can't sell anything to anybody if you can't sell it first to yourself.

I was officially in the bond department but my interest very rapidly became greater in stocks. I had a desk between the firm's statistician and the bond man, and I helped each. I liked working on statistical reports and taking orders for stocks with a little fill-in bond trading with local dealers. I always believed in the printed word. This belief, plus my dabbling in statistics, led to my starting to write signed articles for the local newspapers. How I got my first story printed I can never recall.

I think it was in the San Francisco *Call and Post*, Friday, November 18, 1921. The article concerned Liberty Bonds and was about 600 words long. The next clipping I have found is dated December 2, 1921. After that the articles came thick and fast in various western publications. By August 1922, I had my photo as well as a by-line. Also, in January 1922, I devised and had published a large chart on bond prices in the editorial pages of the San Francisco papers. This chart was credited to my firm.

This publicity was helping my firm, as well as myself. It encouraged prospective clients to ask for me, and it made those who already knew me feel they were talking to someone with more than run-of-the-mill knowledge of securities. These first stories were necessarily simple condensations of facts anyone could find in the popular manuals. Still I don't recall much if anything along these lines printed locally at that time. The articles told about an automobile company making automobiles and a steel company making steel, and if a share paid 6 percent I wrote that it paid 6 percent. Anybody could have written these articles if they took the trouble, but hardly anyone did. The only value these items had was that they were an easily read condensation of financial facts, and they helped fill the financial pages. From these articles the readers could get their information in brief form in their daily paper. However, my writing helped me enormously in building a reputation.

Also, the financial editors of those early days became great friends of mine. Men such as Tom Dargie of the *Call* and Oscar Fernbach of the *Examiner* did a lot for me. Naturally, I wanted to do all I could for them. The financial press releases were quite sketchy those days so I tried to give the editors stories, news, and "scoops" of interest to Californians over my firm's privately leased telegraph wire from the East. It was equally natural for them to tell me bits of local financial news before publication. Gradually I became better informed and began to know a few things before they appeared in print. So my progress went, bit by bit, very untheatrically.

This second job might have lasted all my life but I quit again, this time after nine months instead of after three days. As it happened, I left this job for the identical reason that had caused me to leave my first one. One of the members of the firm where I had worked for three days came over and became my immediate superior. At once he tried to enforce the same tactics I had fled from previously. Once more he tried to force me to sell clients securities that I felt were not best for them, and tried to stimulate sales with special commission markups.

So I resigned and became San Francisco manager of the E. F. Hutton & Co. local statistical department. The title was more than the new salary of $110 a month. I had only one assistant under me to manage. I also brought with me to E. F. Hutton & Co. practically all the 85 customers I had acquired during my nine months at the second firm. This transfer, I know now, is not an easy thing to do. Stock brokerage firms sometimes lose employees who think their customers are personal to them. However, departing employees find that these clients are actually not theirs at all when they try to take them to a new firm because the clients prefer to stay on with the old and have a new man service them. My success in this direction certainly proved that putting the customers' interest first paid off.

I have been with my present firm for over forty years, first as an employee in San Francisco, later as an employee in New York, then a *partner*, and when the firm was incorporated in 1962, I became vice-chairman of the board. At any time during those forty years, had any of my associates interfered by forcing me to sell a client something I did not feel was best for him or was too much for him to buy, I would have quit again for the third time. I would quit today under the same circumstances.

Before starting in my new position as San Francisco statistician for E. F. Hutton & Company, I felt I had to make a trip to New York City. The New York Stock Exchange was in New York and so was Wall Street where was located by far the greatest concentration of capital, power, brains, control, and everything that made the whole country tick. I used to be quoted in San Francisco papers under a heading, "Talks By Men Who Know." But did I really know? I thought not, but I knew that the men in New York did and I could learn if I went there and got to know them. I did not expect to do more than visit, however.

I paid for this trip myself and although I had the money, the trip would not generally be considered a prudent expenditure. However, time proved it the best kind of personal investment. I lived most modestly those days. The lowest range of my living costs had been only a couple of years before—$60 a month for room and board. Naturally clothing and other personal expenses were in keeping with this scale. Because the sole purpose of my trip was to meet top people who knew and could give me information, the whole trip would have been wasted if they had not accepted me as one of them. So I bought millionaire's clothes, a $185 suit, not the kind one can afford on $110 a month. Everything else about the trip was scaled at what I thought was the millionaire's level. I felt quite sure that if I could meet the right people I could hold my own with them. I think the style of this trip possibly shortened by ten years the length of time required to make the contacts I achieved. I am convinced I could not have succeeded if I had arrived shabbily dressed and lived in a third-rate hotel. I am just as convinced that even if I had taken a floor in the Ritz, I could not have made the friendships and connections that I did if my intellectual and ethical level had not measured up to my ambitions.

The trip was a great success. I came back from New York with more knowledge than when I left the coast. I knew the sources in New York where, by telegraph or letter, I could gain financial information that I never could have secured in San Francisco. Now I really had something to tell my western newspaper friends that was worth printing in their papers and was not to be had out of books. I could do a better investing job than before. My stories were no longer the obvious and simple ones of the early 1921 days about "automobile companies making automobiles," which anyone could have written had they made the effort. Now they contained news that few others knew. My articles were now of the sort that told of a new model car and how it promised to affect a particular corporation's earnings and thus the market price of its shares. I was starting to have something to sell that could not be bought easily anywhere on Montgomery or California Street.

Facts, even facts that most people don't know, are not enough to guarantee continuous success in the stock markets. Judgment of what these facts mean and the effect they will have is equally necessary. Although my judgment was improving with experience, it was still somewhat sketchy. Fortunately, the judgment of most of my competitors was also rather sketchy so my lack was not the handicap it might have been. However, around this time I suffered the worst loss in the stock market, proportionately to my capital, that I have ever suffered in my life. I lost partly because stocks in general went down a great deal and partly because I was "taken in," so to speak, by a pretty shrewd stock syndicate manager of that day. Nothing that ever happened to me did me more good. I should put flowers on the grave, daily, of the man who fooled me, as a token of all that he saved me later on. The lessons of that 1923 market break taught me what I had to know in order not to get caught in the crash of 1929 to 1932. My own suspiciousness of markets and people that was born in those days has been a potent selling factor ever since. If I am not easily fooled, then neither can my clients be.

When I started on my new statistical job with Hutton in San Francisco, I wanted also to make a sales record. I had an idea that

straight statistical and analytical, or investment research work as
they call it more often nowadays, had a very definite salary top.
When you reached that top, you could go no further. But the actual
bringing in of dollars income to your firm was another story. There
could be no top other than that measured by your own production
or sales success. Although I still disliked orthodox salesmanship, I
did like the fruits of good selling and wanted to achieve them in my
own way. So for the first time I went out after new accounts on my
own.

In those days telegraph connection with New York markets was
irregular and fast service was confined to only a very few security
houses with privately leased wires. I had noted that it was the custom
in San Francisco for the local bond traders to "arbitrage," as they
called it, by concealing rapid changes in the New York market of
various bonds popular in the west. They bought these bonds cheaply
in San Francisco when the New York market stiffened suddenly or
sold them in the west at what seemed concessions in the price when
they knew the New York market was sharply lower. In this way the
local traders handled a few orders at a wide profit per order. I felt
that the best way for me to break into this institutional field was to
give a service that was calculated to bring me a great many orders at
the low standard New York Stock Exchange commission for each.
So I began to keep all the western traders posted on the New York
changes just as a matter of accommodation. Instead of my trying to
grab an undue spread, I told them the story and left it to them to
route their orders my way instead of to the competition. It took only
a few days for me to develop one of the largest bond businesses of
that type in the city. When the others started doing the same thing,
I had the lead because I was there first and had forced them into
adopting my method.

I was very happy and proud of my new connection, and I felt
sincerely that I worked for the best, biggest, and most desirable New
York Stock Exchange member firm in the city. Anything that did not
seem to agree with this opinion annoyed me no end. I was especially
disconcerted by the way in which one afternoon newspaper handled
its record of New York Stock Exchange transactions. The paper had

almost a full page of the important stock tables with the by-line that they had been furnished by a competing member firm and that the figures had been brought west over the exclusively leased private telegraph system of that firm. This happened to be the house where I had held my second position. I felt that people would only know how dominant Hutton was if the Hutton by-line were on that major table each day. Today, of course, all these figures come over the press wires but we had not reached that stage then, and the firm that supplied the tables really had what amounted to the best advertisement in the city.

In December 1923 I started to go about getting that by-line for Hutton. Arrangements of such long standing cannot be shifted by ordinary salesmanship or even through close friendly connections. I had to offer some compelling reason for dropping one house and substituting mine. In San Francisco, the close of the New York markets normally occurs at noon coast time instead of 3 P.M. as in New York City. It occurred to me that if the service were fast enough, this big closing stock quotation table could make the home editions of the afternoon paper. This principal edition was delivered by carrier all through the San Francisco residential districts to the subscribers' doorsteps. The suppliers of the service were so slow that only the late financial editions were getting the closing quotes.

I talked the plan over with the editor and at first he said, "No." But later he said that if our competitors had full notice of our intention and if, after that notice and after their own best efforts to speed up their service, we still succeeded in beating them by a substantial time differential every day for a solid week, then E. F. Hutton & Company would supplant the competition.

So the big race started. Of course we won by a big margin and the shift was made, or I would not be retelling the tale here. We did it because E. F. Hutton & Company actually had better wire service and put an enormous amount of effort into working out shortcut codes for transmission with Brickhouse, who was then E. F. Hutton & Company's star wire chief in New York. We also cut time in San Francisco by such obvious ways as having a motorcycle with engine running waiting for the sheets to come off the wire.

The competition failed to make the grade. Here was selling again without salesmanship, for the situation I created was so attractive that the buyer had to buy.

About this time, I received the first of several offers to move to another house at an increase in pay. This time it was a very big increase. I was offered the co-managership of a New York Stock Exchange office to be opened in Los Angeles at a starting salary of just about as much per week as E. F. Hutton & Company was paying me per month. I told Hutton about it and got a couple of days off to go down and look the ground over. I was also told by Hutton that they were entering into no competition for my services. I turned down this offer of more than four times what I was earning on the theory that success doesn't come from getting the quickest dollar. I felt that working for small commissions per transaction and getting people to buy less shares than they intended if it seemed for their good would in the long run pay off with the largest final totals. I also felt that the right attitude towards a job was not what it paid at a particular time but what it offered over the years. I did well to stay where I was because that Los Angeles office closed in a few years.

A reoccurrence of the trouble with my health that had previously blocked my study of architecture forced me back to New York for medical attention. Once back there again, with my ailment cured, I found it very hard to return west.

It seemed to me that since I was connected with a Wall Street firm, Wall Street was the place to be. I never believed in compromising for anything less than the best. So in 1924 I decided to make New York City my home.

For a man of 24, and an employee of a year or so, I brought a marvelous letter of recommendation with me from the San Francisco Hutton partner. I was given a job in the New York office, which almost overnight became a much bigger one than I had anticipated. This advance happened because I had to do a little pinch-hitting market-letter writing. The firm's market-letter service was outstanding. There was a short page in the morning before the opening and a long page in the evening after the close with flashes of brief items during the trading session. All this information was telegraphed throughout the country over Hutton's privately leased telegraph wires and also mailed out from many cities. My pinch-hitting was so well liked that I was soon on the regular team. In fact, it was not long before I took over the management of the main New York statistical department of E. F. Hutton & Company.

By now things started to roll pretty fast. There is nothing in the whole wide world like printed publicity, nothing like the printed word, at least there wasn't in those days. I was building on both sides of my market letter, which had a very big circulation, a readership of many, many thousands. On the one hand the letter encouraged its readers to seek me out. On the other, its circulation and influence gave me access to primary sources of exclusive information.

I was pretty busy those days talking with my new friends in the eastern press and my new contacts among the members of the New York financial community—brokers, investment trust, investment counsel, bank and, above all, corporate officials.

Yet without new clients and new orders I think my progress would have been circumscribed. I still felt as I had back in San Francisco that this kind of a thing had a ceiling, but getting orders or making profits did not. Clients were coming in pretty fast those days, mainly on their own, to buy something they wanted. I never directly sold them the idea. I tried to help them do better in the market, by making more or losing less as the times allowed, than if they had not consulted me. I tried to keep my clients safe and from doing more than they should. I kept them posted on the latest split-second developments. They got the information from me first and they got it accurately. All my dealings were pointed at the lowest commission per client per transaction, but the aggregate amount made the final total very big.

Most statisticians stayed statisticians and never got any order-giving clients because their approach was academic. "What do you think of General Motors?" someone would ask. "It's a good company," they would answer. That was the end of the discussion. I would answer the question with some others. "Why do you want to know? Do you own General Motors stock? Do you plan buying it? What else do you own? Have you other motor stocks? How much of your capital is invested?" And then they would get a reply that applied to them personally on what they should do and whether I thought General Motors at the price and as things appeared in the market was going up or going down. Such personal attention made another customer every time.

Of course, I was continually looking for more information and more places to make contacts so that I would have greater knowledge of what was going on and more and more investors would have an opportunity to decide whether I supplied a service they needed to buy. I use the phrase "service," but I don't mean I sold anything other than just taking regular New York Stock Exchange commission orders. I felt that if I had information security owners needed, the orders would take care of themselves. So I kept up a very heavy correspondence and made personal calls on corporation officials everywhere. I soon was almost as well posted on the industries that appealed to me, such as the automobile, motion picture, oil, and mining concerns as I was on my own business. I would meet business leaders and try to advise them in the security problems of their own companies. I would ask them for information on their companies in order to appraise the market value and trend of their own shares. They usually needed help in figuring the values in their own stocks to say nothing of their other investments. If they were impressed with my manner of investigation, they believed that my knowledge of other companies and industries and of the market itself was on a par.

As an example, one of my favorite ports of call was Chrysler in Detroit and Walter Chrysler himself in his office high up in the Chrysler Building in New York. I naturally learned a great deal about Chrysler stock as an investment. I made a host of friends and clients. The Chrysler people thought enough of my slant on their product to ask me out to Detroit where, hidden away in a dense woods, they were testing their secret hand-built experimental models of cars to come. Once Walter Chrysler distributed to members of his staff about 40 copies of a long analysis I had made on his new "Airflow" car and what I thought might be done to improve it. This activity was a far cry from the "doorbell pushing" salesmanship and the stress on "PM's" that selling seemed to offer but I was building my business hand over foot.

I remember one top California executive who told me a great deal about his company. I liked it, and altogether my friends and I came to buy and own about 10 per cent of his outstanding shares, which turned out to be a fine purchase. But suddenly this man shut off his information. At first I could not find out what was wrong, but later he told me that I had scared him. "You knew so much about my affairs I wondered what your real aim was," he said. Somehow he feared a sinister motive, such as questioning the quality of his management. Of course, his fears were unfounded, and this was the only time that I have ever encountered such a reaction. Usually after I see the executives of a company, I try to see their competition, their suppliers, and those whom they sell to in order to get a well-rounded and unbiased view of their situation. This procedure may not sound like salesmanship but of course it is. People buy more from "the man who knows" than from any high pressure sales talk that is given them.

Although I always sought a continuing account and not a single order, there were many individual accounts that came to me in various ways. We all have principles although few of us at best can more than adhere to them in a broad way. One of my principles was not to compromise. One day a stranger dropped into one of the western Hutton offices and read a wire of mine advising the purchase of a certain stock—I think it was Colorado Fuel—around $85 a share. He bought it and when he returned to New York it had declined to about $35 a share. He dropped in to introduce himself and see just who it was who indirectly caused him all that misery. After I had told him the story, he took his loss and replaced his investment with shares of Warner Brothers, which in time made up the loss and gave him a profit as well. Later he asked me to help him with various accounts that he held in different houses. I agreed but asked him to sell everything out, close the other accounts, and send over the money. I did not want to do a half-way job trying to pass opinions on securities I had not bought in the first place and was not especially well posted on. He did as I suggested. The move was successful, and we grew to be the closest of friends although I had taken his business as a stranger. Generally I try to refuse business from people whom I already know so well that I dine at their homes socially. I like to do business with strangers, coldly and impersonally, on a value-received basis. Later the relationship often grows to be a friendly, social one.

Buying and selling stocks for people is a retail business. In the days before the Securities and Exchange Acts of the New Deal, stock syndicates were wholesale business. A broker would do many times the volume of business in what the public called "pools" and in what the New Dealers sometimes correctly, I am sorry to say, and sometimes incorrectly called "manipulation."

I will always remember the first such major order and major responsibility that I had. It started indirectly with a study I made of two listed companies competing in the same line. The study analyzed their profits and related their growth and market values. I sent one copy to a director of the larger of the two concerns, who was also a famous banker in the First National Bank of New York City. This was the *crème de la crème* of any and all banks in the country. It was said that the bank's required minimum daily balance to open an account was $50,000. I made a friend of that banker and director and opened an account at the bank. Henceforth, every check I wrote was an advertisement of both financial worth and the best of connections. I also received much valuable financial information from the bank.

The second study went to the head of the smaller company. He invited me to meet him and to come not to his regular office but next door to a private office high up in the tower of a midtown office building. I did not know it beforehand but this man was not only a top corporation official, but a top investor and capitalist as well. The tower office was his private investing headquarters. He was and is one of the most respected, best liked, and widely connected men in the country. I did not know at that time, and maybe he himself did not realize it, but he is the kind that likes to help the young fellow along. I was 29, an age I then regarded as very old, but to him I was a young fellow. He had several sons and sons-in-law in the stock brokerage business, but we got along fine despite the family competition. There are several reasons that may have accounted for our friendly relationship. I tried to give him all the useful knowledge I could, even though an account at first seemed out of the question with all his boys in the stock-selling business. I was honest, but at that time I looked upon honesty as something that went without saying. In this latter respect, I was a bit naive. I did not try to sell him a thing then nor have I tried since that time.

He was the man who brought me my first wholesale order by introducing me to a top oil man from Oklahoma who controlled his own company, which was traded on the New York Stock Exchange. His company needed a sponsor and I got the business. I had never done this work before, but I stayed up nights finding out how to do it. This first syndicate client got a top quality job for his money, and of course it led to similar business for me later on.

This acquaintance with all phases of the investment business also helped me with my private retail work.

A couple of years later this southwest oil executive's business dried up, but I kept him posted nevertheless. Although he never acknowledged any letters, telegrams, or information, I kept on sending him any information pertaining to his business that would be useful to him. One day, a stranger, who was sent by my oil friend, the silent recipient of so much unacknowledged service, walked into my office at 61 Broadway. He said he had been told that "I could fill a little order for him." It turned out to be for 50,000 shares.

One of the largest continuing accounts I ever had, developed in a trivial way. We had an out-of-town broker doing his business through us in New York, and I planned to pay him a visit. Before leaving I checked the various important listed companies with headquarters in his neighborhood. On one I received a peculiar quote from the floor of the Exchange. It was a highly unusual and extraordinarily large bid at a very high price for the shares in question. When I reached my destination, my friends introduced me to the head of the company. He explained his large high bid as a "peg" to keep his stock from declining. The buy order was with a competing broker. It was thought that because so many of the company's employees were long of their own stock, much of it purchased with borrowed money, any decline would hurt their morale and the quality of their work for the company. I made an exhaustive study and presented it to the executive board, showing how no bid, no matter how large, could ever permanently hold an artificial price level and that the trouble eventually would be the greater. Also, I worked out a stabilization program that promised to work, combined with plans to allow the shares to seek their natural level later. Arrangements, too, were made to take the partly-paid-for shares out of the market and finance them privately. The result was that the order was cancelled with the competing broker, and our plan was substituted. Our firm and our out-of-town correspondents did a large continuing business. Our client friends found that the plan worked, and that their deflationary problems were successfully solved.

I recall another exceptionally large continuing order. I was asked to visit a company president who had some problems with his shares. He lived and maintained his office in a city on Long Island Sound and I decided to drive there after the market closed. Because I would arrive about 5 P.M., I was fearful of a dinner invitation, so I left word for the office to call him and leave a message for me that it was urged that I return to New York as soon as our business was over. I arrived, discussed the stock market problem with him, lined up the business, and closed the deal all in an hour. As I started to rush back to my imaginary appointment, he told me how sorry he was because he had planned to have his private chauffeur drive my car back and he was going to invite me to go back on his yacht, dining on deck on our way down the Sound. My business had been successfully concluded so I told him frankly that my phone call was a dodge as a sort of a social block in order not to mix pleasure and business; and that I hadn't known in advance that I would like him so well. So we went on the boat, had dinner, became good friends, and later did much business together.

Another client was in the drug manufacturing business. I recall helping him collect every brushless shaving cream made and trying each one against various trial batches of new mixtures that he was testing. Finally we selected one mixture for consistency, odor, and such qualities as ease in washing off the razor blade and razor. We did plenty of investment for this man who discovered what we knew in our field and of course wanted to favor us.

So there we have the rules for successful selling: faith in knowing that what you sell or what service you render is the best you know how and continually serving people in any way that will benefit them without directly seeking their business.

MONEY FROM MARKET LETTERS

A<small>RE MARKET LETTERS</small> worth reading? Can anyone make any money from using them? How do you go about it?

It depends on who writes them. Good market letters can be profitable guides if properly used.

To evaluate the market letter begin by evaluating the firm that issues it. It must be well established and of the best financial rating and reputation. The most useful letter is individually signed and to be of value must express opinions about the future. It must give a forecast of what the writer expects—not a record of what has already occurred. Statistical compilations of the past are a dime a dozen and require no special quality to be accurate and complete.

Next, consider the individual who writes the letter. He should have a good reputation, be reasonably experienced, well-connected and obviously successful himself.

Granted all the points listed are favorable, the resulting letter will often contain many ambiguities and inconsistencies as well as many basic errors of judgment. The letter, nevertheless, is still worth reading and can prove a real aid to making money in the market.

The key to making profitable use of good market letters is in the understanding of the investor who reads them.

Market opinions expressed in such letters fall into two major types. The viewpoint of the general market level and trend. Is it high or low? Safe or risky? Trending up or down? This type of opinion should be largely passed over unless very emphatic. The market letter writer must say something each day or each week and is apt to be forced into expressions that are quite minor and unimportant to him. The reader should not overstress such routine phrases. He should watch for some voluntary major thought and give that the weight it deserves. Above all, beware the writer who suffers an error in judgment and endeavors to justify himself or talk the market in his direction.

The second major opinion type is the more important and concerns the selection of shares to buy or hold. A market letter writer is certain to be more successful in this direction than in attempting to forecast the general price level and trend. The investor's efforts should again be directed at singling out the voluntary major situations from the forced daily routine. This is usually not difficult to do. More space and enthusiasm will be shown on really important selections. They will be mentioned repeatedly instead of occasionally and casually. Also they will go up. And they may seem either unattractive or already too high to the uninitiated.

A foreign market commentator once very aptly advised his clients that they should "always believe his views especially when they thought him wrong." That was very sound and very profitable psychology. I have often found that those of my market opinions disbelieved by the majority were always my very best. And, likewise, those widely and instantly accepted occasionally contained some flaw in my reasoning.

An important point concerning opinions on individual securities is that sudden silence about them generally means a reversal of opinion. Few well-connected market writers will ruin their good sources of information by broadcasting specific bearish items about individual companies. On the other hand, forthright advisors will never hesitate to privately answer reasonable questions by clients as to why certain favorite issues have suddenly lost favor.

Good market letters are well worth reading and can be profitable guides to the investor who uses them properly. Never expect something for nothing. The investor must match the letter's good points with intelligent interpretation. Many ideas in good letters are profitably used as guideposts to personal research and confirmation.

Following even the best market letter blindly can only result in losses. The reader gives nothing and quite logically gets nothing. The only exception I ever ran across was an investor who bought most everything he thought I really basically liked. If what he bought went down, he sold out. If it went up, he hung on. Over the years this man has made a lot of money and kept it. Perhaps it came from following my market letters. Or perhaps just from following the old axiom of cutting your losses and letting your profits run where they may.

Perhaps in a somewhat different category are the individual security analyses which are distributed by brokers and dealers as well as services and which appear as articles in magazines and papers. Some of these, labeled or intended for institutions, are exceedingly complete and involve visits to company plants and interviews with company officials.

These studies are only as good as the ability of their authors. A recent comment in the *Financial Analysts Journal* is reprinted in the following postscript:

BUY CHESAPEAKE & OHIO—SELL ST. PAUL

LET'S FACE IT. Time is money. Financial analysts exist to discover ways to make money. If they are not using their knowledge to build their own capital, they must get their ideas across to their clients, associates or employers as convincingly as possible.

The best financial analyst I ever knew in my over forty years in Wall Street was Frank Dick. Mr. Dick is long deceased. If he could he would berate me in no uncertain terms for dubbing him an "analyst." Mr. Dick was a most thorough man. When he examined a property he really examined it. What's more he knew what to look for, and what to disregard; what to believe, and what to question. Yet when he had reached an opinion, it generally distilled down into a two-word conclusion: "Buy Chesapeake & Ohio"; "Sell St. Paul."

There are very few analysts today with the reputation strong enough to have their views accepted without their reasons why. Their reasons why should be pointed and brief. Their conclusion clear and unequivocal. Price and trend are critical. The best security bought at the wrong price and time can be a disastrous purchase. A favorable background is vital. The best seed in the world must be planted in spring to germinate. Not winter wheat!

Much of the analytical work we read today is too verbose. It is often descriptive rather than analytical. At times, I fear, its authors are too trusting. The things you hear and see on a "field trip" are very humanly the good things. You must look under the rug. You must get a competitor to tell you about the skeleton that may hang in the closet.

Finally, be yourself. The individual is still the most powerful force in the world.

66

THE IDEAL CLIENT

A BROKER'S ORIGINAL FUNCTION was to execute customers' orders to buy or sell securities for a commission. If a customer gave his order correctly and paid for his purchases or delivered shares sold promptly, that was all that mattered.

Today, this is changed in a large majority of cases. The customer regards his broker as his investment advisor, and, for all practical purposes, almost in a trustee relationship. The way a client acts is of greatest importance to the success of the client's own account. All the clients of a good broker do not do equally well. As the same broker is giving the same advice at substantially the same time to his group of clients, why the variation?

I once had a client actually ask me how I wanted him to act in the one particular of how often to get in touch with me. Would every day annoy me? Would I forget him if only once a month?

You either are an ideal client or you are not, or you are something in-between.

Your investment results are going to vary a great deal more because of your personal influence than whether you buy a security rated "AAA," "B" or even "X."

The answer lies in the varying practical and psychological effect of the different personalities in acting on the information their broker imparts to them and in the strong influence their varying actions have on the way the broker imparts information to them in the future. If ten people deposit $100,000 each with a broker and say "I want you to invest this money for me," the similarity tends to end almost immediately. Each will go on to add something different even though at heart they all have identical aims—namely, to make as much as they can without incurring above-average risks.

But the first of these clients may say no more. And the second may add "he cannot afford to lose." And the third may stress dividend income. And the fourth suggest taking a quick loss if an error seems to have been made.

In actual practice each and every one will say something different. I am, of course, not here talking of different clients of different ages with different needs and tax brackets, but of a theoretical group of accounts all alike as peas in a pod.

The broker would hardly be human if under such circumstances each of these ten accounts didn't start off in somewhat different ways. Some fully invested from the first day—some hardly invested at all—some in-between. And, of course, the list of shares bought would vary as well. Instead of doing the best he knows how, the broker has tempered that best to suit ten different whims.

And once launched on the market sea, each of the ten passengers would treat their broker "Captain" differently. One would have confidence. Another would be fearful. One would offer suggestions. Another would never offer any advice. One would be friendly. One would stay out of sight. Each of these different demeanors could not fail to influence the broker in his handling of each of the ten accounts. Later, as transactions were closed into profits or losses or open positions registered unrealized gains or losses, each of the ten would again behave in a different manner, and again affect the broker who naturally was trying to run each account as near to its owner's wishes as possible. Believe it or not, it is an oft-repeated and easy-to-prove fact, a year later the equities might range from $90,000 to $140,000. All starting with $100,000. All under identical market conditions. And all relying on the same broker.

I say "relying" because there is no point to this story unless the reader accepts the aims of the ten investors as similar and their common idea of relying on their broker's advice.

There is a sequel to this discussion. The "ideal client" is finding it more and more difficult to locate his "ideal broker."

In times gone by most brokers, which in this sense means the partners, officers or registered representatives, in direct contact with the client, were individualists. You might have an exceptional one or an average one or a poor one.

Now the tendency is to regulate their activities to the point that almost all have to fit into a fairly average mold.

The old-time broker did everything for himself. He located his clients. He dug up the information he needed to guide their investment policies.

Now we are moving in the direction where the research department or the portfolio analysis department reaches the investment conclusions and the individual account executive or customer's man just passes it on to his clients.

In this manner, there is more protection against bad individual mistakes, or worse. On the other hand, extraordinary ability or genius is shackled and limited.

67

PERPETUAL PROFITS

AFTER OVER FORTY YEARS in Wall Street I have learned at least one lesson. Opportunity is always here. Everything is always changing. Things look different to people of different ages.

By way of illustration, it was about 1935 when I had the greatest interest in the price of a home. Real estate lagged a little behind other things, price-wise, and that was about the low level for home prices. As a consequence, if I look at a $30,000 house today, it looks high to me. In 1935, a better built one could have been bought for $7,500. To the "young marrieds" just looking for their first home, today's price looks right and the construction looks right. They were not here to see what was offered or what it cost in 1935.

We have to remember, particularly as we grow older, that the same principles apply to the stock market. We can't compare prices with the past. Because of higher tax rates than we used to know or because of less freedom of action, the older generation thinks incorrectly that opportunities now are less than they were in their own imaginary "good old days."

Just as in the case of the young marrieds' appraisal of today's house, aggressive and competent people in the financial world are constantly making plans during their fruitful years and usually bringing them to highly profitable and successful fruition. The age when a man thinks of his first home and the age when a man reaches his greatest success are quite different, but the principle is exactly the same.

We have made a lot of money following this principle. We can recall the growth of Chrysler Corp. under Walter Chrysler's direction from the practically bankrupt Maxwell-Chalmers to a place alongside Ford and General Motors. We remember what "Cap" Reiber did for the Barber Co., and Alton Jones for Cities Service. There were many others. Later it was Bob Young and Al Perlman rebuilding the New York Central that engaged our attention. Tomorrow or next year and the year after another leader will come into his own and another stock will be a profitable purchase for those with intelligence enough to seek it out and faith enough to get aboard. Transactions of all officers and directors and persons controlling 10% or more of voting stock are published monthly by the SEC and can provide a value clue to a management's thoughts on opportunity.

There are opportunities everywhere all the time for depreciating, idle dollars. As the *Christian Science Monitor* puts it: "I bought my baby a thousand-dollar bond today," said the happy young father. "What on earth could he do with the money by the time he grows up?" inquired a pessimistic friend. "Oh," beamed the father, "he'll buy a new suit when he graduates from high school."

We're living in a tough world for misers and a rewarding one for optimists.

68

WHAT MAKES A STOCK "GOOD"?

THERE are three basic elements that overshadow all others in appraising the worth of a stock. The one most commonly used is "quality." Certain stocks are always "good," if quality is the only yardstick. DuPont, for instance, has been one of the best stocks for as long as I can remember. The contradiction is that a good stock is not always a good buy.

For example, important declines since 1929 in the price of duPont were the equivalent of a high of $57\frac{3}{4}$ in 1929 to a low of $5\frac{1}{2}$ in 1932; from a high of 46 in 1936 to a low of $22\frac{5}{8}$ in 1938; $47\frac{1}{8}$ in 1939 to $25\frac{5}{8}$ in 1942; $55\frac{7}{8}$ in 1946 to 41 in 1948; $102\frac{1}{2}$ in 1951 to $79\frac{5}{8}$ in 1952; $249\frac{3}{4}$ in 1955 to 157 later the same year; and finally $278\frac{3}{4}$ in 1959 to $164\frac{1}{2}$ ex a half a share of General Motors stock in 1962.

The second most commonly used measure is "price." People look to see whether prices are "high" or "low." None of us, expert and beginner alike, really knows when high is top or low is bottom.

The third, and in my view most important, element in stock appraising, is "trend." When you buy a stock you want to make a profit. You can only do that if it goes up. You can make money if you buy a stock high and it goes higher. You can lose money if you buy a stock cheap and it gets cheaper. "Trend," therefore, is overwhelmingly the most important element in appraising whether you can make a profit from buying a given issue or not. Fortunately, determining the trend is less of a problem than determining the price level.

The determination of quality can for all practical purposes be almost absolute. Trained analysts can examine balance sheets and income account records and almost invariably correctly label the quality of a security as "Excellent," "Fair" or "Poor" as the case might be. Since 1964, quality has had more meaning than formerly because the trend of the times has been to make it easier for the best to stay best or get better than for the weak to get strong. Thus, with few exceptions, the best investments for income and safety have at the same time been the best speculations for capital gain. The company that has not done well enough to pay a good dividend has also not been strong enough to grow. As is the case in considering stock price factors, trends are likewise most important in security analysis. It is obviously better to select a high quality company that is growing than one that is static, or worse yet, backsliding.

Double Right from Wrong

It has long been my experience that when one sees factors that suggest a movement in the market in one direction and instead the market actually moves in the reverse direction, the unexpected reverse move is probably doubly important.

◆ 69 ◆

A DOLLAR TODAY

LATELY I have been reading a great deal in investor publications of one sort or another that since the Dow Industrial Average is back to 1929 levels, it only goes to show that if you buy stocks and hold them long enough, you are sure, sooner or later, to break even or make a profit. I have been reading that all one needs to do is simply buy and wait, or better yet, if shares decline, buy more.

This is fallacious and misleading talk. It is incorrect on several counts. In the first place, all stocks that decline do not recover. The "Industrial Averages" today are above 1929 levels, but many individual shares are not and never will be at those heights. It might be the stock that you bought that did not come back.

Second, any schoolboy should know that a dollar tomorrow is worth less than a dollar today. I mean, of course, mathematically; I am not referring to changes in purchasing power. For example, a dollar compounded at 6 percent (without consideration of taxes) doubles itself in twelve years. Thus, at 6 percent compound interest, a dollar today is worth two dollars twelve years from now. Or to put it another way, the "present worth" of a dollar payable twelve years from now at 6 percent compounded is just half or fifty cents.

The stock you buy today that declines and takes many years to recover or show a profit, will come back to its original level to find everything changed. The owner, if he was able and willing to hang on, is older. Money has a different value. The buying power will be changed. All this is a speculation no prudent investor wants to take. Therefore, I say when you invest a dollar today, try to look ahead six months to a year-and-a-half if you can, but don't try to see further. You won't be able to. Nor should the investor just hang on blindly.

Invest your money where you can reasonably see anticipated profit ahead. If it develops, accept it. If you have made a mistake, take your loss and make a new purchase where the view ahead seems clearer.

70

THE LEOPARD NEVER CHANGES ITS SPOTS

WHEN CAPABLE AND CONSCIENTIOUS MANAGEMENT arranges to sell securities to the public for new capital their objective is to get the most funds into their corporate treasury at the least cost. In my opinion, the extent to which they succeed is a rather good index to their business acumen as well as their interest in their new shareowners.

The Securities Act of 1933 provides that a public offering of a new issue totaling $300,000 or less can be made with a short-form registration that does not contain much of the information set forth in a prospectus covering larger offerings. In certain circumstances no registration need be filed with the SEC before distribution to prospective investors. It is important to note that the SEC does not pass upon the merits of any securities nor does it pass upon the accuracy or completeness of any offering circular or other selling literature employed by the underwriter. The SEC merely requires full disclosure. If it subsequently develops that the issuer has not made full disclosure, purchasers of such securities have the right of recision. An enormous number of exempt securities have been sold. The Senate Banking and Currency Committee report on its stock market study particularly comments on abuses in this field. They point out that these abuses range from misleading and irresponsible advertising to instances where the promoters have appropriated for themselves most of the money paid for the stocks they sold.

Even so, such offering circulars as are supplied should be very carefully studied. The first point to watch is the schedule showing the price paid by the public, the commissions charged, and the proceeds received by the company. These figures are always given very prominently at the beginning of the offering circular but they rarely tell the story without reference to footnotes and further information to be found inside the circular. In many cases there are additional expenses and their total amount should be determined. Very often the underwriters receive additional stock at a fraction of the price paid by the public or the right to options or warrants permitting the purchase of stock quite cheap at a later date when its market value is known. The real cost of raising the capital can only be calculated by reading every line of the offering circular and between some of them, to see what the company gets and what the salesmen get. My point is, if the amount appropriated for raising the capital is excessive, the issue is undesirable as a purchase on several counts. To begin with, you can only make a profit on the part of your money which actually is invested and not that part which is in the underwriting or selling dealers pockets. They are entitled to their hire of course. But any management that allows them to take more than their hire generally either has a poor deal that no one wants or has neither the ability nor the ethics to watch out for their new stockholders interest.

The next thing to look for in an offering circular is the degree of market stabilization intended. Many of these circulars frankly state that the underwriters may temporarily maintain the market price of the new stock at a level above that which might normally prevail in an open market. In plain language, this means they may support the price for a time while they are selling their shares or withdrawing their support and let the bottom fall out of the market when they are through. Incidentally, salesmen often tell security buyers that they cannot liquidate their purchase while the market is being "stabilized" or supported by the underwriter. This is simply not true. If you do make a mistake and buy a security which you regret, you can sell it if any bid exists.

Another important point to watch is what the original owners or promoters are getting for their property. Very often one will note that they get a great deal of stock for property which cost them very little a short time previous. I have seen statements of assets where actually less than $5 cash was on hand.

Where more than $300,000 is being raised on a public offering, the shares have to be registered. It is then incumbent upon the seller to furnish all buyers with a prospectus. There is very little value to this procedure unless intending buyers read these prospectuses and understand them before they decide whether to purchase any shares. There are times when a buyer has remedies even if he only reads his offering circular or prospectus AFTER he has bought if oral representations made by the salesman are found to be misleading. It is important to know that the SEC neither approves nor disapproves securities offered through a prospectus. The commission, furthermore, does not pass upon the accuracy or adequacy of any prospectus. At the same time, I can say that in most cases, sufficient information is revealed for careful students of investment value to know what they are buying.

Exactly the same points discussed about offering circulars apply to prospectuses. The main difference is that the latter are much more complete. The things to look for are the underwriting discounts and commissions; rights to the underwriter to purchase stock at lower prices or warrants or options granted to them; other expenses; stabilization procedures, etc. These are variously listed in different issues under different captions such as "Transactions with Management," "Arrangements for Offering and Offering Terms," "Previous and Contemplated Financing," "History and Business," "The Company and Its Promoters," etc.

These abuses are, of course, almost always the greatest where the price per share tends to be the lowest They also tend to be the greatest where the amount of money raised is the smallest. So-called penny stock issues, foreign shares, atomic, uranium, oil, electronic and other "romance" issues seem the most profitable field for promoters who are primarily looking after themselves. Intending buyers can save themselves a lot of grief by paying attention to the items mentioned here. If they don't understand them, they can always ask their banker or their lawyer.

Policing Pitfalls

It seems about once a month I am asked on the radio or some place "What is the greatest pitfall for the inexperienced security buyer?" My answer is always the same— "Avoid promotional stocks. Start in by buying the best known, most liquid, most successful and largest listed corporations."

The Securities and Exchange Commission has been formulating some new regulations for the protection of buyers of promotional penny shares. The Fulbright investigation showed the need for additional regulation of over-the-counter issues to bring the requirements as to information for investors more in line with those for listed shares. The Washington hearing also brought out the need for additional regulation of financing in cases that do not require full registration and a complete prospectus. There is also a need, and a most crying one, for state security commissioners to bring their requirements in line with national ones.

In this connection, a great many complicated and controversial proposed regulations become the subject of debate. It seems to me, a very simple solution is to begin by insisting on an initial per share offering price of at least $10 or more.

Informed investors never look at the per share price but at the total price. They multiply the market price by the number of shares outstanding and the total shows the market value of the equity they propose to buy. With this as a starting point they make their analysis.

More often than not, the inexperienced confuse market price per share with value. According to their way of looking at things, Superior Oil is very "dear" at $1,070 and an unknown oil at $1\frac{1}{8}$ is "cheap." Something that sells for a few pennies in their unfortunately misguided ignorance is cheaper still. This is how unsuspecting "suckers" are "hooked." This is where the much-publicized "evils of Wall Street" lie. We of the New York Stock Exchange brokerage fraternity don't call this kind of thing "Wall Street" at all, but rather the use of a fundamentally good name for a false purpose.

We must still keep our sense of proportion and realize that most of our largest corporations were small at some stage in their development. There is a necessity for risk taking at all levels of business. The important point is that the risk is taken by those able to bear it and those that understand it. It is also of equal importance that a substantial amount of the money invested in risk enterprises gets through to the enterprise and doesn't stop on the way in the pockets of a promoter.

The privilege of being listed on one of the two New York exchanges is worth a certain value per share. When the shares of a corporation have a market value of $10 or more, the listing value is a percentage which is small enough to be unimportant. Where the price of a stock is low, it can be as much as one-half the market price. This is one of the reasons why listings under $10 should be denied unless very closely scrutinized for extenuating factors.

71

WORDS FOR THE BEGINNER

BEFORE YOU think of making any kind of investment you should question whether you are ready. You should not rush in on a shoestring. Serious investing should be done only with your surplus money, money left over after you have taken care of your basic needs.

A basic need, before you give thought to investing, is to have an emergency backlog of cash. A new addition to the family can be a financial emergency if not provided for. And we never know when illness or an economic setback may come. You may keep this cash in a cookie jar or the corner bank. Or in U.S. Savings Bonds which you can convert into cash on a moment's notice. How big this backlog should be depends on your age, income and how much importance you attach to security. One good rule of thumb I've heard is that you should have at least enough backlog to cover your living expenses for at least two months.

Now with your basic needs provided for, you can give thought to putting the money that is left, if any, to work for you. You want to make it grow. This is called investing.

Actually, you start investing as soon as you try to get a return from your surplus, such as opening a savings account. Buying a house seems an investment to many. Buying a home is an adventure and will yield your family great emotional satisfaction. Also, it assures you a roof over your head. Viewed strictly as an investment, however, home buying is ordinarily relatively inefficient. The initial purchase price represents only one part of the total cost. You must follow up by spending for repairs, mortgage interest, taxes, and maintenance. And trying to get your money out again can be exasperating, and often disappointing, especially if you are in a hurry.

If, besides all the other fine things a home offers you, it also proves to be a good investment, then just consider it an unexpected bonus! This has been true with the increase in building costs in recent years.

Some of your investing certainly should go into a savings-bank deposit now paying about four and one-quarter percent. This is recommended, not so much for the return it will bring, but rather for its safety value. If deflation comes, you will have a hedge. Your money in the bank will grow in purchasing power. As for the return you can expect, your money compounded in a savings-bank account at current rates will double in about twenty years. In the "thrift" account of a commercial bank, where the interest may be a little less, doubling will take correspondingly longer. If you put your money in a savings-and-loan association it will double a little faster than in a savings bank because these institutions invest most of their money in higher-paying mortgages.

U.S. Series E Bonds should play a part in your investment program for the same reason. They offer safety, and at the same time give you a fair return.

As I see it, U.S. bonds and a savings-bank deposit should comprise the conservative *half* of every moderate-income family's investment program.

The other half should be invested in a business, so that you can share in any profits and growth it enjoys. This is where there is a good chance that your money will really start growing.

One possibility, of course, is to put your money in some neighborhood enterprise. Or into real estate. The other possibility is to invest in major American corporations. This is most popular, by far, with serious investors.

When you put your money in a major U.S. company you know your money is in the hands of trained management experts. Furthermore, at any given moment you can know to the penny what your investment is worth, and you can sell your holdings in a matter of minutes merely by phoning your broker. For the average person most corporate bonds have little to offer that you cannot achieve more simply by buying U.S. Savings Bonds.

—Preferred stock, which stands between a bond and common stock. The preferred share gives you priority over the common in making claims if the company gets into trouble. You have first claim, after bond interest, on any dividends. But your dividend is fixed. And the price of preferred stock ordinarily is likely to grow modestly if at all. Thus, if the company prospers you will find yourself envying the owner of common stock.

—Common stock. This, I believe, offers the average person the best of all possibilities for making your money grow. (Naturally, also, your risk has increased.) The great majority of transactions on the exchanges are in common stocks. Common stock can pay off for you in two ways: by dividends, which are your share of the profits your company makes; and by change in the value of your piece (or share) of the company. This change, of course, may be up or down. It is the total return from both these sources over a period of time that counts.

With common stocks you may double your money in 12 years or 6 years or one year. On the other hand, if you have invested poorly, you may lose most of what you have invested. What actually develops, of course, all depends . . .

It depends on what you buy, when you buy, when you sell. This is why we call stocks "risk capital." You should never invest in stocks unless you are willing and able to share in the fortunes, for better or for worse, of the enterprise or enterprises you have selected.

In the past decade the informed holder of selected choice stocks should have at least doubled his money well within the 10 years. But it was a good, prosperous decade and stocks started up from a low price level. Some stocks, particularly the better utilities, maintain a fairly level price keel and keep paying regular dividends. There are at least 60 stocks on the New York Stock Exchange that have not missed a dividend since the turn of the century!

On the other hand, there are other stocks that give you plenty of action—"thrills and chills," as they say in the sports world. On the "romantic" side, an outstanding example is the story of one of the big oil companies. The people who bought $100 worth of this stock in 1942 were able to sell it 9 years later for $4,000. To mention another example, one major airline stock soared 800 percent in 4 years. Many stocks have doubled in value within a year—and many have shrunk in half.

Such situations, however, are rarely discovered by the moderate-income beginner. As one gains experience, and as time goes on, investment results should improve. The beginner should think of the best long-term investments. Naturally, you should review your investments at least once a year to see if you have any weaklings that need weeding out. But ducking in and out of the market for short-term gains should be left to the hardened professionals. It takes intense study, and strong nerves.

Viewed as long-run investments, the majority of well-known stocks offer many attractive possibilities. On an average, the value of stocks as a whole seems to follow a gradual upward pattern. Over the past 55 years, despite ups and downs, the price of industrial stocks has moved upward on an average of better than 3 percent a year. There will undoubtedly continue to be dips in the future. But, in the long haul, the combination of our increasing population, our rising standard of living, and the seemingly endless depreciation of our money will undoubtedly keep the price curve moving slowly upward.

How do you pick the best investment for your particular needs?

The best place for you to *begin* your buying, I believe, is with the stock of a mutual fund. This is especially so if you are starting with, say, $500 to $1,000. The mutual will help protect you from making "boners" and will educate you to the point where you can confidently push off on your own. It will send you easy-to-read reports on trends in the market and will often explain why it is now adding certain companies and eliminating others. You learn as you earn!

There are more than 100 of these mutuals. Your broker or banker can guide you to a fund best suited to your needs. If you are an aggressive young businessman, you may prefer a fund that gives you a cross-section of fast-moving speculative situations. Or if you are a young couple with an eye on planting seeds for the future, you may prefer a fund that emphasizes "growth" investment.

As you get past the tenderfoot stage of learning, or acquire additional funds, you may become restless with your mutual. For one thing, the cost of investing through a mutual is necessarily relatively high. All that expert guidance and safekeeping costs some money.

The "load" of charges to cover costs of selling the mutual to you runs around 7 or 8 percent.

Furthermore, you may start becoming dissatisfied with the cross-section return which the mutual offers. If the market as a whole goes down, you can be pretty sure your fund of cross-section stocks will go down with it. You may feel you can pick individual stocks that can outperform the averages.

If you do set out on your own, survey all possibilities. Your broker or banker can give you the basic facts you need to know. At a glance you can see how much each company is earning per share and whether its price at the moment seems high or low. Beyond this, however, I think there are several major considerations to keep in mind in choosing your stock. Here are five:

(1) You should decide in your own mind what your aim is. Are you mainly interested—as most investors are—in getting a stock that will improve in price? If so, you will be interested in the company's future potentialities. Or are you more interested in a stable stock that will be sure to pay you a regular dividend? If it is this, you'll be most interested in financial strength and past performance. How many years has it paid a dividend without fail?

(2) There is some security for the beginner in numbers. You will feel safer if you own stock in 4 or 5 companies, each in a different industry.

(3) Choose an industry before you choose a particular company in it, and make sure the industry is essential in American life. Choose an industry that has a future, particularly if you are thinking of a long-term investment.

(4) In choosing a specific company, if you are a beginner, pick a *leader*, whose name is a household word, just as you buy products that have a brand name you have come to trust.

(5) Pick a company with vigorous, farsighted management. Look for the company that attracts topflight executives and is striving, through constant engineering and research, to broaden the market for its products or services.

But remember—don't become so excited about picking stocks that you neglect the conservative half of your investing program—a savings-bank deposit and U.S. bonds.

When you have bought your stock you are in for an exciting time, no matter what happens. Every day you will find yourself flipping to the financial page of your newspaper to see how your stocks are doing. You may even find yourself going on junkets to annual stockholder meetings. Last year some of these were held at company dam sites, airfield hangars, and on company ships. Most now serve lunch, to the special delight of their feminine stockholders.

Even more important, you will feel you are playing an essential role in America's development. Some time ago Irving S. Olds, ex-chairman of the board of the United States Steel, said: "I hope the day will come when every American family will purchase a share of American industry, however small or large that share may be. That, to me, is true public ownership."

I heartily agree. America's future growth depends on the willingness of middle-class Americans to take on the role of owner of our great enterprises.

Invest in America's future! But be careful. Do it prudently. It's your money!

72

MORE ON TAPE READING

THERE ARE 3,772 New York Stock Exchange tickers in operation today. In addition to this there are 650 Trans-Lux tapes and 5,650 other devices for transmitting prices to the viewer.

The true tape reading audience in my opinion is far greater than the comparatively few who can actually continuously watch the tape.

To my mind, tape reading means price forecasting based on interpretation of transactions. Today, I specifically mean forecasting the trend of stocks from understanding the significance of the past in affecting the future.

The broker on the floor of the New York Stock Exchange, be he a commission broker, a specialist, or a floor trader, has the first knowledge of a stock transaction as it occurs on the floor at the post at which he is standing. However, for the position of the market as a whole he must watch the ticker tape shown on the Trans-Lux screens which print transactions at a varying time lag, which depends on the activity of the market at the time.

The person off the floor of the New York Stock Exchange who is able to watch a ticker may even be nearer to the market, tape-wise, than the floor man because in addition to the ticker he may have access to "flashes" from the order room of his broker which, although they are usually a bit behind the actual floor price, still come from many points on the floor instead of just the single spot occupied by the floor member. Most people think of this class as the basic type of "tape reader."

However, from my point of view, anyone who places major dependence on stock transactions in making up his mind whether and what to buy or sell is a "tape reader." I look upon the term as a sort of "nickname" rather than as a precise description. In my opinion, a tape reader might better be termed a "transactions analyst" if the title were not hopelessly cumbersome.

Thus a security buyer who has stock prices placed on his desk once each hour and acts on the information he derives from them, is a "tape reader." I remember such occurrences in my lifetime. Once I was in a hospital in New Orleans. Every hour the local broker gave me the latest prices. I told him what to buy and sell. It more than paid the hospital bill, and it was just as much "tape reading" as if I had a ticker under my eye.

Possibly the largest body of tape readers using my definition are those that look at the daily stock table of volume, opening, high, low and last in their daily newspaper.

There are also those that look only at weekly stock tables.

And there is another great contingent that looks at "charts."

They are all "transactions analysts" to a degree.

I say to a degree because there are probably very few pure tape readers. My definition of a pure tape reader is one that only—*only*—depends on stock transactions for his decisions. The moment he introduces a second factor into his judgment he is no longer a "pure tape reader." If he attempts to find out if the buying or selling is "good" or "bad," as it is called by stock brokers, he is straying from the fold. Tape reading and technical analysis are not the same. The former is a portion of the latter. Technical analysis considers many more factors than pure tape reading.

It must be obvious that consideration of earnings, dividends, balance sheets are far afield from true tape reading.

The true tape reader needs everything that can be known about actual transactions plus anticipated and realized news.

He needs to know about expected news and news as it occurs only from the point of view of judging his transactions. Thus, if a stock is active and strong on no news, it means one thing to him and if it is active and strong on an announced dividend increase, it means another. The true tape reader uses news only to consider its relation to tape action and never—*never*—for itself. If a person buys a stock because of good news he is not a tape reader any more than if he considered other basic statistical security factors. However, if he buys a stock because of its action—*action*—on some news then he can truly be considered to be acting on the tape.

The relationship between floor prices, tape prices, stock tables and charts is that they are all used in the same way by those that analyze transactions. The tape reader carries in his mind what the chart reader writes down to remember. Both are motivated by the same forces.

I felt I had to emphasize this relationship even though I am going to keep as near to the actual tape as I possibly can today.

What is the value of tape reading? I think its value is very good if it is used along with other factors to help reach an accurate investment conclusion, or to trigger an investment investigation.

I said "investment" deliberately and not "trading" or "speculative." The analysis of transactions should not be confined to what is commonly known as a "trader" or "speculator." The final determination of an investment is the difference between the price at which it is bought and the price at which it is sold. To ignore the importance of past and current price and volume action as a factor in determining future value is either ignorance or prejudice. The value of the tape in bringing potential investments to one's attention is also very great.

I am departing here from "pure tape reading" as defined previously because as a practical matter there is very little of this actually practiced and even less is profitably practiced. However, the investor who knows whether the stock he intends buying or the stock he is holding acts "badly" or acts "well" according to tape reading standards possesses a most valuable aid to success in his security transactions. I for one would not buy nor hope to hold any security that acts "badly" unless I satisfied myself as to "why" and felt that the depressing cause was temporary. Note, I qualified my statement when I said "hope to hold" and I did this because as a practical matter we all find it relatively more difficult to close a transaction than to initiate one. Partly this is a matter of personal psychology and partly a matter of tax dating and other such considerations.

The investor who watches tape factors to get ideas for new investments to be investigated in broader ways is sure to latch on to some very profitable ideas.

The meaning of a "new high" or sudden activity of strength may be very fundamental and well worth checking. I have made many exhaustive studies of individual securities just through such a thing as "seeing something start on the tape." Sometimes they have led to important long pull profitable positions. Sometimes they have led to blanks.

Tape reading therefore to the well rounded security investor can be both a dinner bell and an alarm bell.

It is no real digression to say that investment management is not an exact science. The published reports of institutional investors prove that. How many are "out" of the market before a fall? Believe me, they would like to be. How many buy into individual situations that turn sour before they can do anything about it? I do not know whether in this uncertain life, medical, military or political science is any more or less correct in its views. If an investment account shows up badly the owner knows it. If a patient dies, no one can tell the proportionate parts played by nature and the physician. However, I am sure that if it were generally accepted that tape reading was a basic factor in investment analysis, I think our institutional records would improve.

As it is, tape reading is a bit beyond the pale. It is something you don't do at all in some circles, or at least do it in private. That is very unfair, but it is true.

Tape reading in my opinion is a very essential factor to consider for all investors of every type.

Now what about the "pure" tape reader who considers nothing else in reaching his conclusions? I feel that very, very few can succeed if they make a fetish of tape or chart reading to the exclusion of other basic factors. I have seen it done. I would not advise most people to try.

Aside from the very few people mentally equipped to succeed, actual, constant observation of the tape requires time. Conclusions are more likely to be short term than long term, hence tax factors are currently unfavorable. The great demand for increased investment research from the customers of New York Stock Exchange member brokers and the emphasis placed on six months capital gains by today's tax laws are factors that tend to increase buying and selling commissions to the higher levels required to care for a statistically-minded, six months clientele. The expensive amount of time required by the many first time investors also has put pressure on increasing commissions. The day of the sophisticated tape reader who was in and out of the market constantly may come again but that is certainly not the condition now. Spreads between bids and offers on the floor are undoubtedly wider than they might be, due to the same influences. The amount of capital that can be profitably employed by watching the tape exclusively is also rather limited with today's narrower markets.

Hence, pure tape reading is somewhat rare along with real vanilla beans, freshly squeezed orange juice, and other pleasant common-places of yesterday.

How do you go about learning enough of tape reading to really improve your investment performance?

It is easy to mention books which cover several hundred pages on the subject of tape or chart reading exclusively. I have scanned most of them—studied none of them.

You won't find much more in *The Battle for Investment Survival* than you will find in my talk today about "double tops," "head and shoulders," "triangles" and "rectangles," to mention a few, because I believe in very few of these ideas.

I have not "researched" or done any studying or refreshing skull practice for this talk. My reason is I do not believe in such methods. I buy and sell stocks every day. It seems logical to me that the most useful tape reading ideas will automatically float to the top and occur to me. If I have to dig them out or jot them down and catalog them, they can not be so vital. If I forget an important point today maybe it isn't important at all.

Using this system or lack of it, the keyword that first comes to my mind when I think of analyzing security transactions is *"compare."* No action of any stock, no chart, no high or low, nothing of this sort is of any value whatsoever unless compared with the action in other directions. Everything in tape reading is relative. Relative to other stocks and groups, and relative in point of time. The second keyword refers to time and is *"when."* It makes all the difference in the world *"when"* something happens.

Speaking first of individual movements, you should compare the stock in question with the market as a whole and the group to which it belongs. This is essentially easy to do. We spend a great part of our lives comparing in order to arrive at decisions. Do the same in the stock market. Compare, and for buying purposes, give first consideration to the best. You can compare stock movements over a period of years. Which issues advanced the most? Which made tops higher in 1946 than in 1937 and are higher now than in either year? You can also compare support or bottom levels. And naturally recent levels. Which stocks are higher now than when the market made its previous top?

Such observations are only the starting point. Next, I believe in departing from pure tape reading and inquiring into why. What are the chances of persistence of the trend in being?

There is no rule about anything in the stock market save perhaps one. That rule is that the key to market tops and bottoms or the key to market advances or declines will never work more than once. The lock, so to speak, is always changed. Therefore, a little horse sense is far more useful than a lot of theory.

However, in a broad general way the averages work in favor of those that assume the trend in being will continue until proven changed. This applies both for the company in question, industrially speaking, and price trend of a stock, tape-wise.

"Never argue with the tape" is one saying worth thinking about.

In order for the trend in being to change direction there has to be a change in the influences that caused the trend in the first place. Those who can detect this change before it occurs and becomes generally evident are gifted with powers of analysis and foresight of the very highest order. For most of us detecting the change after it has occurred but before it has proceeded too far is still a very profitable and to many an attainable goal. I think on the average it is better for most of us to be late and sure than to be early and doubtful. Many, who thought that various levels on the way down after 1929 to 1932 were buying or turning points, lost the most. The late buyer who came in after 1933 and up quite a bit from the bottom, did quite all right.

I believe in pyramiding, not averaging. That means I believe in following up one's successes and minimizing one's failures. Or as the saying goes, "cut short your losses and let your profits take care of themselves."

I believe stock prices mean something and when I see a portfolio of diversified shares I automatically want to sell the bad actors and buy more of the good. However, as I am not a pure tape reader, I use this tape indication as a reason to try and determine why some of these stocks are weak and some are strong. I do NOT necessarily think those that are low are cheap and those that are high are dear. They might be. In fact, they MUST be ultimately because the "top" is high and the "bottom" is low. But absolute tops and bottoms occur infrequently, hence at most in-between times when one considers the market, the reasoning I indicated is more apt to be correct.

Next to comparison comes timing. When something happens is all-important. The FIRST new highs for the year after a weak spell usually mean a lot. After scores of shares have been making new highs, the addition of new ones is meaningless.

Volume of trading is also an important factor. It is difficult to define in positive terms. If you are driving a car you can get to your destination more quickly at 50 mph. than at 10 mph. But you may wreck the car at 100 mph. In a similar way increasing volume on an advance up to a point is bullish and decreasing volume on a rally is bearish, but in both cases only up to a point. There are a great many varying circumstances. Experience is the best teacher. Observe the variation in volume, and in time you will learn what it indicates.

As I mentioned previously, patterns of trading behavior are endless. You will have to study a book if you wish to have a knowledge of them and it will be up to you to decide to either partly use or discard that knowledge. There are very few patterns that are actually useful. You will find that they occur logically and that you will note them even if you have never heard their name or had them called to your attention.

I will say on thinking it over that perhaps after all there is one valid reason for meticulous study of popular tape and chart notions. It resembles the need for news mentioned before. A good tape reader knows the theory of how the masses tend to interpret any particular action at any critical moment. The reflection of this on the tape— whether it makes a normal anticipated impact on a stock or a greater or less than estimated impact is important. At least it is important where a very elemental and widely spread tape sequence is involved.

An abnormal follow-through in such cases gives a good tape reader a useful clue to add to his other conclusions.

Recording and remembering what you see on the tape is the greatest difference between tape reading, chart reading, and simply keeping a numerical record of prices and volume.

So far we have not stained our fingers with ticker tape ink but I must say that for a competent person with a retentive memory it does supply the most complete picture of the market. In the first place, it is "live." Charts for example are "canned" or "on film" in comparison. It's a real case of "See It Now." A moving tape picture of the market also gives several other types of information not readily available elsewhere. You see approximate transaction volume as it occurs. I say "approximate" because there are items such as "floor stopped stock" that are not printed and of course a percentage of odd lot transactions are hedged and thus are not printed. You see approximate sequence. That is, sales in the general order in which they occurred. This is very valuable because it is essential in making some of the comparisons mentioned before. If the motors advance you know by watching the tape which particular motor started first and which was the most active. You can see how sustained a movement might be, or the change in activity on a reversal. You can see if some issue seems in supply under cover of strength elsewhere. That is comparison again. And of course you can see how active the market really is by how fast the tape moves or how much of it falls behind actual transactions.

Oh, direct tape reading is wonderful if you have the time and know how. It certainly can be rewarding. But it has its drawbacks as described previously. Few of us have the time and as a selected occupation, taxes are against it. Direct tape reading has a tendency to focus your attention on the very short term. A critic might say it tends to have you fail to see the forest for the trees—but the truth is that the trees it may show you can be rewarding enough if time and taxes, commissions and floor spreads were not so much stacked against you.

The average investor has to depend more on charts or tabulations for his analysis of transactions and I favor the tabulations over the charts. For most people charts have a peculiar way of appearing simple and it is very costly to find out that they are far from it. Just plain records of what you wish to remember in the way of unusual activity or dullness or important high or low points supplies most people with all they require.

In conclusion, remember, investment analysis and advance or inside information are useless unless weighed on a current market price basis and considered against the general market trend and in relation to expected persistence of that trend. I mention this because most of the analysts I have met do not seem to know it. That is why they earn as little as they do. More attention to transaction analysis would increase the accuracy of their investment conclusions. The margin clerk looks at market prices not at book values, price earnings ratios or income yields. Be sure that you pay some attention to them as well.

73

WHAT'S THE VALUE OF WATCHING "TAPE"?

THE NEW YORK STOCK EXCHANGE stock price ticker system has spread to over 700 cities in the Continental United States, 6 in Canada, 3 in Switzerland, 2 in Puerto Rico, and 1 in Hawaii.

Years ago, these tickers printed the transactions as quickly as possible after they occurred on paper "tape." Now 80 percent are projected on Trans-Lux screens and many others reproduced on closed-circuit television. Something between 30,000 and 40,000 of the New York Stock Exchange member personnel watch the progress of the market in this way. In addition, most member offices have facilities for clients who wish to watch the market themselves.

Why do people watch the "tape"? What use do they make of this effort? Can "tape reading" be profitable?

In these days of electric quotation systems, the first use of the tape is probably to check the proper filling of orders. The tape's major value is its use as a means of helping to determine the trend of prices.

This is perhaps more of an "ancient" art than a modern one. Stock tickers were first introduced in 1867. They were at first most valuable for relatively short-term investing. The coming of the income tax cut the ranks of tape readers. Increased commissions and changes in market participation had the same effect.

Nevertheless, the tape is invaluable even today. Few have the time to watch it the full $5\frac{1}{2}$ hours a day. From 1922 to 1936 I had lunch at my desk so as not to miss a foot of it. I wish I had time to do this now. Most investors who rely partly on the tape deal with a broker with similar ideas whose business it is to watch it continuously for his clients.

Profitable investment comes from a combination of superior interpretation of research, news and market action. The tape is a much better source of market information than the daily or weekly stock lists in your newspaper or any "charts" you may construct or buy.

The tape is the only source of market transactions that comes to you "live." Judging the market this way involves the time something happens, the volume of transactions when it happens, and the comparison of action with the market as a whole or with other stocks where some relationship exists.

When you watch the tape you see all these factors spread out in front of your eyes just as they occur. You see what stock starts to move first. You see how active it is. You see how strong or weak it is in comparison with others. Much of this has to be conjecture when using tables or charts.

The tape watcher who knows what he is doing is in a way as much ahead of the chart reader as the business executive who gets key figures quickly from his computer as compared with his competitor relying on unassisted manpower.

The tape can help you fill orders to the best advantage. It can strengthen or question your judgment derived from analysis or in other ways. It can give you ideas on stocks to investigate. While essentially short-term in its initial impressions, it often leads to more advantageous handling of six months-plus investments.

It is time that we saw a renaissance of tape reading. Thoroughly understood it should prove far more rewarding then the current "chart" fad.

74

IMPORTANCE OF EQUITY INVESTMENTS

Outline of a talk given to students at the Wharton School of Finance and Commerce, University of Pennsylvania:

You students soon will be entering the world of security investment. It has changed drastically since the day when I began some 35 years ago. I believe the change has been unquestionably for the good of investors. And the place of the stock broker has altered enormously, elevating quite high in standard and public opinion. There are four vital factors you should bear in mind while shaping your careers: (1) Be proud of your profession and conduct yourself accordingly. (2) Learn to count in value units—not just "money." (3) Prepare to see equity investment become as widespread as savings accounts and insurance. (4) Think more in terms of today and tomorrow—not yesterday.

At the outset I wish to point out that I carefully differentiate between an investment banker, a security salesman, and a stock broker. I am a stock broker. To me the term is synonymous with being an agent or at times even a trustee. An investment banker ordinarily is a wholesaler who buys securities at wholesale and sells them directly or indirectly at retail. A security salesman simply sells the securities owned by the firm for which he works. But a true broker doesn't wholesale or retail anything, nor does he sell any security owned by his firm. He is an agent who goes out and fills an order for the client to buy or sell at a commission. I know that in actual practice today these terms and others are used loosely and interchangeably. As I use the term, broker, I mean "broker" in the dictionary sense and in no other way.

Years ago, the broker was simply a means of filling an order. These orders came from relatively sophisticated, wealthy, and informed sources or from gamblers who were putting the legitimate machinery of the financial world to improper use.

Today, the stock broker has evolved into a type of investment counselor. His financial position is important. His ability to transmit and fill orders and finance them is important. However, his major importance is his ability to advise his client on investment matters. This means that his research department is important and his contacts are important. But, above all, the essential qualification is his ability to interpret what he learns in a practical, everyday market sense.

Most of us look with respect on the help we receive from our family doctor. It is just as important to have a knowing, reliable family broker. Physical health and financial health are very closely related. The modern field of psychosomatic diagnosis proves that— if it needs any proof. The stock broker's role, therefore, has grown in importance and will grow even more in the future. It stems from the necessarily ever-widening circle of security investors created by a better understanding of what fluctuating dollars and increasing taxes mean. Equity investments held by savings banks, insurance companies and pension funds are beginning to prove to the masses that equities have a place in everyone's savings program. The stock broker's increased prestige also stems from his own growing up and realization of his new responsibilities.

I may hold a prejudiced view, but I think that a good broker can give better advice than a good banker or counsellor lawyer. I believe this because the broker is more in the middle of things. He is not trying to advise from a remote observation post.

To my mind, a broker can be a good adviser only if he maintains the position of a true and unbiased broker. As long as he does this, he can be in fact, in law and in spirit a true agent and trustee of his client.

There is a place for the salesman working on special compensation. He may sell mutual funds or new issues or special offerings or secondaries. If the seller sticks to selling and the broker sticks to being an agent, the client is best served.

A good broker, from a career standpoint, derives another great advantage, this time inuring to his direct personal benefit. In a manner of speaking he is in a position to do well for himself investing his own money on a full-time basis, as compared to men in other fields who have to make a spare-time job of investing or get someone else to do it for them.

The "big change" in security investment practices today is the current re-realization that the value of money is forever changing and for sometime now in the direction of losing value. Sound security investment policy favors dollar obligations in times of sound money and shifts to equity shares in times when money is losing value, as it currently is.

Security investment which, at the beginning of my career, was exclusively for the classes, is now accepted for the masses.

Generally speaking, bankers and lawyers, as well as dad, mom, and the boss, have been cautioning against the "dangers" of buying stocks. *It is time now someone warned against the dangers of NOT owning stocks.*

The stock market crash of 1929 is still popular as a warning of what can happen to security investments. It has been a long time to wait, and to me *time* is an important investment factor, but it is true that stocks generally are worth more now than in 1929. Many individual stocks surpassed their 1929 tops in 1937—eight years after the break. Others did it in 1946. And still others last year.

I would not be proud if I made an investment for you today and it took until 1992 for you to get even. All other things being equal, which of course they are not, $1 to you at average age of perhaps 21 today is of different value than it might be 36 years from now when you will be 57. But nevertheless stocks did come back from the 1929 crash even if it was a long time.

But what about money? It's former value never came back. You don't expect to hire a carpenter for what George Washington paid when he built Mount Vernon no matter how long you wait. In fact, history shows the longer you wait the less your money will be worth. Of course, we have had periods of rising money values and we will have such periods again. Right now, however, as far as I can see ahead, there is no real sound money on the horizon.

An important point for young investors or brokers-to-be is to be as watchful of fluctuating risks in cash, bonds, or insurance as you are cautious of losing money in the stock market.

We do not live in a riskless world. Let us admit that risks exist in everything we do and however we invest.

How much can you earn in the brokerage business? My experience is that, as you are dealing with money, pre-tax earnings should be above average. Your savings or inheritance can be managed on a long-term capital gains tax basis to better advantage than by those engaged in other pursuits.

Drawbacks might include the fact that the stock brokerage business is an ownership management business and fundamentally the capital for the business is supplied by the partners. In times past, one could lift oneself by one's own bootstraps saving enough to keep increasing one's participation in the firm. But now taxes make that rather difficult, though not impossible. There are no "management options" in the brokerage business as in the field of corporate endeavor.

75

WALLFLOWER STOCKS

IT IS CHARACTERISTIC of the novice investor to want to run before he has learned to crawl, or walk. Tell a beginner to buy one of the best-known listed investment trusts as his first equity venture and you will get a look of scorn for such kindergarten ideas. Talk to the inexperienced about the market pitfalls in new promotions, unseasoned, small, or relatively obscure stocks and get brushed off for your pains. The blue-ribbon roster of America's most successful corporations might be good enough for our best-managed institutions, but somehow fail to interest the tyro.

The primary reason for this is that the investor regards familiarity with contempt. He feels that "everybody" knows, for example, that "General Motors is a good stock." He incorrectly thinks that to succeed he must buy something "new," something "special," or something "exclusive" with him. The fact that the most successful corporations are more or less also the most popular stocks—"The Favorite Fifty"—is against them, in his view.

The fact of the matter is that new investors have next to no chance in the world of success unless they begin by buying the best and only the best. There is substantial income and good prospects right among our most successful corporations. General Motors paid the buyer in 1955, 5 percent plus, depending on when he bought. The stock sold for $18 in 1953 (adjusting the price for various stock splits) so the buyer more than doubled his money based on prices in the summer of 1955. The stock sold for $9 in 1949 so the buyer in that year doubled his money in four years and quadrupled it in six. And it sold for $5 in 1941. The average buyer at average prices has received better than 7 percent from General Motors in ten years. In 1955, the stock was split 3-for-1. While the figures would be different the same principles would hold good if recalculated for 1965 and the years preceding.

The important point is that size and success are not a hindrance to continued success as many inexperienced investors are inclined to think. Under the economic and political conditions existing since 1933 and prevailing today, exactly the reverse is true. It is far easier for the strong to grow stronger than for the weak to acquire strength.

Nevertheless, there are investors who cut their eye teeth on investment trusts. Then they graduate to selecting a diversified list of odd-lots for themselves. Even later they advance further and succeed in confining their investment list to a lesser number of the best opportunities. Finally, they get to the point where they feel they want to buy something "special" for themselves. They think that special opportunities lie among smaller companies that can grow faster, or in romance shares involving mining, oil exploration, automation, electronics, uranium and atomic ventures. There is this strong feeling that something not so well known and not yet listed on the New York Stock Exchange, offers more.

To those who think along these lines I will say that for every one that rings the bell, literally thousands fail. Many of these types of shares are like the vacant lots in "Mosquito Manor," sold to the ignorant and unwary by real estate sharpies with the promise that they will be the "Grand Central" zone of the future.

However, there is money to be made by the experienced in a small minority or special situations. The hazards can be vastly reduced and the opportunities greatly increased if the would-be buyer of this sort of thing lets the institutions that have the staff and investigating ability do the initial selecting. One way to do this would be to watch the best investment trusts and when a relatively obscure speculation appears in their portfolio for the first time, then the investor should check into it. For example, Kerr-McGee was published for the first time in the Lehman Corp. Portfolio in December, 1950, and sold at $15 in the month following the publication of the Report. Considering a 10 percent and 33 percent stock dividend since that time, the shares in the summer of 1955 were worth $75.

Another way this may be of value is if one of the lesser-known stocks is suggested to you for purchase, first see if it has been bought by any trusts. If it has not, better forget it. Realize that mere ownership by a trust or several trusts does not guarantee you profits, but it does perhaps mean you will get a real run for your money, which most likely would not be the case otherwise. The big trusts spend millions to investigate such shares and riding on their coat-tails should reduce the risks by an enormous percentage.

Any New York Stock Exchange member firm's research department can help you in several ways. They can tell you whether any particular issue you are considering is owned by a trust or not and by which one. They can tell you what the trust paid. Often they know why it was bought and what its current value and prospects are. They can tell you of new and first purchases of this type share, as the trust reports are published. They can execute your order as your broker and agent to buy at the lowest possible open market price and at the lowest possible commission fee.

76

MORE DOUBLE DIVIDENDS

Investment Clubs

Investment clubs have grown like mushrooms, but far too many have proven to be toadstools in practice.

There are two major problems when considering an investment club. The first is whether the group promises to make a better investment record than the individuals could by themselves. Certainly sheer numbers do not guarantee success.

Investment clubs must be formed for a sound reason, not on the theory that there is safety in being a sheep.

Some practical reasons are:

(1) To secure better service from a broker by having one large account instead of many small ones.

(2) So an uneducated group (used here in the investment sense only) can secure the services of an experienced management committee.

(3) For experts in different investment lines to pool information.

The second major problem of an investment club is its legal setup. Most investment clubs are partnerships, unincorporated associations, or joint ventures. This means unlimited liability, and in some cases it may mean dissolution upon the death of any one member. It means that each individual's proportionate part of all realized income or profits of the club is taxed as his individual income. However, this is an unpalatable arrangement. So, often, papers are drawn to attempt to limit the effect and operation of a general partnership relationship. An effort is made to limit the liability of the partners as between themselves and to limit the power of placing orders, handling the funds of the club generally, as well as to restrict the amount to which the managing agents of the group can make commitments.

The result is certain to muddy the waters. A tax question is constructed that might result later in double taxation in the event the group is held to be "an association acting as a corporation." The broker handling the orders is never really certain whether the person or group entering them has the proper authority. The limitation of liability is apt to prove relatively dubious. In my opinion, all investment clubs should be corporations, because the corporate form gives them exactly the suitable form for all involved. Basically, the aim must be knowledge—not simply association. The success of the club hangs either on a varied and wide expert membership, or a group of beginners who are being shepherded by a professional.

The Twelve Wealthiest Men in Wall Street

It was a top flight editor who told me: "Of course you are one of the twelve wealthiest men in Wall Street."

When I told him it was not so he continued with "If not— why not?" There was the implication that he was disappointed in me.

To become one of the twelve wealthiest men in Wall Street, you must be born with an exceptional brain. That is the starting point. Without it the other requisites are of little value. This brain must have the courage to accept risks. It must be willing to borrow up to the hilt. It must know the knack of using other people's money. It must figure how to use its financial resources. It must have a cerebral hemisphere devoted to minimizing taxes, and it must want to be wealthy very, very badly— much more so, perhaps, than it wants to be healthy or happy. A portion of your brain might be gifted enough to figure out how to make a profit but other portions might not be willing to take the risks or to capitalize on the idea. Therefore, it must be obvious now that "total net worth" is not in itself a final measure of "total financial ability."

To know what one really wants and be able to get it, is a far more commendable goal.

Buy the Stock That's Suited to You

Why is it that certain types of shareowners are always trying to bring about changes in the shares of corporations they own? They originally selected the investment, but perhaps they should have selected companies which were better suited to their desires. When one reads the accounts of their proposals at annual meetings or studies them in proxy statements, one wonders why they would not profit more by switching into issues they approve than attempting to alter the whole course of a giant corporation.

In the canine world, we have watchdogs and hunting dogs—Affenpinschers and Komondorocks. One can not make a toy do the work of a mastiff. It is precisely the same in the stock market We have all common stock capitalizations of the most conservative kind and very speculative high leverage capital structures. We have steady businesses and growth industries and decadent ones—regulated and unregulated. There are also industries, requiring heavy annual additional capital investment for survival and others that can lift themselves by their own bootstraps.

In the period 1946–56, Dow Chemical returned an annual dividend income of about $2\frac{1}{2}$ percent. It was an ideal growth equity for top income bracket shareowners. During this time, the market value of its shares had appreciated almost 600 percent.

American Telephone, on the other hand, had paid a different kind of shareowner, interested in steady income and stability, over $5\frac{1}{4}$ percent per year. There had been no growth in market value from 1946 to 1956; in fact, there had been some depreciation.

Actually, in those same ten years, the total operating revenue of the American Telephone Company was up 153 percent and the net income was up even more, or 234 percent. The rub came in that the per share earnings were up only $29\frac{1}{2}$ percent. This was partly due to the nature of the business as a regulated public utility engaged in an industry that requires vast capital expenditures. A second reason for the smaller per share growth in net was that obviously the more paid out in dividends the less growth in per share net, because undistributed earnings available for capital investment are thereby reduced. American Telephone stockholders have always had the privilege of reinvesting what remains of then dividends after income taxes in additional shares of American Telephone.

Thus, during that time, Dow Chemical with a ten-year average dividend payout of 44 percent fitted one type of investor and American

Telephone with an average ten-year dividend payout ratio of 83.7 percent fitted another type. In between are thousands of companies offering every investor just exactly the type of situation he seeks.

Another point to watch is that the experience of the last ten years is not necessarily going to be the experience of the next ten. American Telephone changed its spots beginning about 1958 and became a growth stock. Earnings went up. Dividends went up. The stock was split. The price went up.

Like the young ladies who are always going to "train" their fiancés after they are married, investors would be better off to pick the right one in the first place.

The Case for Federal Time

On January 1, 1965, members of the New York Stock Exchange maintained approximately 3,559 offices; 415 of these were in the Pacific Coast states, with California, of course, in the lead with 371. Thus perhaps 10 percent of the Stock Exchange business originates in California.

The investor in California who wants to know what is going on finds himself waking up for phone calls at 6:30 A.M. Pacific time if he wants to be posted on news and opinion a half hour before the market opens. Recently it has been even worse with a month of "daylight time" in the East and none in the West.

"Widespread confusion," reported the *N.Y. Times*, due to the changes of time in many areas. It is bad enough to have four major time zones. It becomes worse when some communities adopt "daylight saving time" during the summer. But now it becomes impossible when the multiplicity of local time systems across the country end their daylight time on varying dates.

The worst example is undoubtedly California. Here is a great state which, because of geography, is three hours "behind" New York City. This is on an adoption of true sun time. It means that when business men in the west wish to telephone to business men in New York at 9 A.M. Eastern time it is only 6 A.M. Pacific time in San Francisco or Los Angeles. It means when business-men fly east and west in less than 8 hours their entire personal sleeping and living habits are upset. The loss in dollars and in health is stupendous.

The National Time Research Institute, through its President, Mr. Robert F. Kane, states that the cost of "chaotic time" to the television industry alone is more than $2,000,000 a year. Mr. Kane says that current time inconsistencies are like having narrow and broad gauge rail tracks operating across the country.

There are two reasons for this mess. The first is that our time systems are archaic and adjusted to the old days of slow communication. Today universal telephone service, private telegraph wire systems, radio, TV, and super-fast air transport make us all neighbors and bring our interests close together.

It is true that the individual interests of the farmer, the business man, the theater, etc., clash. But it is time each group buried its self-interest for the common good.

This is best done by *national time* fixed in Washington, D.C., for the entire country and over-ruling states, counties and local communities. Let Washington consider all interests and let all interests accept a common compromise which is the best for the greatest number.

Let me suggest that broadly the new Federal Time can be changed twice a year, as many do now with a Federal Summer Time and a Federal Winter Time. The change, however, will be on the same dates everywhere in the nation and effective in the biggest city and the smallest hamlet. I think some thought might be given to reducing the number of geographical time zones perhaps to two, or at most, three.

In these modern days of increasing artificiality of life—of synthetics—deep freezers—artificial illumination—it should not be too difficult for those of us at the farthest ends of the stick to adjust ourselves to an unnaturally early dawn or late dusk. The gains would be incalculable.

There should also be fewer time zones in the world. In the United States, a western zone and an eastern zone would be ample. This would make the maximum difference between the coasts just one hour.

Travelers who cross too many time zones in modern jets find their systems of waking, sleeping, nourishment, etc. completely upset. If something isn't done can you imagine what will happen when the new super-jets come into being a few years hence?

In Washington the House Interstate and Foreign Commerce Committee began hearings on time legislation in 1964.

How Growth Stocks Grow

It is all very well to buy "growth" stocks, but before doing so it is essential to know what you are paying for them, where the growth is expected, and the anticipated rate.

True growth stocks can grow through growth of earnings and through growth of investor regard. *They can also decline through decrease of investor regard.* That is why careful analysis and pricing is essential.

Millions have been lost by generalization. Growth of gross may not mean growth of net or growth of investor regard. It may mean new financing and it may mean straining of profit margins and lower net or possibly red ink. For example, airline gross has grown every year as far back as I can recall. But the decline in airline stock values from the 1945–46 highs to the 1948–49 lows was remarkable. Look at a few. American, 19⅞ to 6⅛, and it was 1955 before they went back to the 19⅞ price, or a wait of nine years. Braniff, Capital, TWA, and Northwest at the end of 1955 were still far from their highs of 1945–46.

It is only with the coming of the jets that airline revenues and stock prices have made headway again.

Using the minimum amount of caution, one should compare current prices with current earnings and get a current price-earnings ratio. This is the index of current regard. Then decide the rate of growth anticipated for earnings and the same for the price ratio (if any) and project a future market price. Compare this with your projection for the Dow-Jones Averages. If it is substantially greater you may have a true growth stock.

Growth in market price is the aim.

An interesting example of the past is ALCOA. In 1949, it sold at 11 and its price late in 1955 was 75. This is an increase of 580 percent. Earnings increased 240 percent from $1.10 a share in 1949 to an estimated $3.75 a share. The significant increase however is the earnings multiplier, the price-earnings ratio. ALCOA sold for ten times more than it earned in 1949 but in late 1955 it was selling at twenty times its earnings. If the earnings were priced at the 1949 ratio, the shares would have been selling for 33¾ instead of 75.

This illustrates the great importance of "investor regard" as a factor in the rate of growth in the price of stocks.

Obsolete Stocks

Not so long ago, Ernie Breech, the then very dynamic mainspring of Ford, said: "In my opinion, the main goal of product engineering in any consumer goods company is obsolescence. Our job at Ford Motor Company is to render obsolete every car on the road—not merely by superficial changes but chiefly by dramatic and fundamental engineering and styling improvements."

In our competitive world, it is the job of every competent industrial manager to make obsolete the products or services of his competitors. Today's corporate manager seeks to render his competitor's product obsolete by making a superior product at a lower price and merchandising it in a better way. What is more, this competition crosses industry lines. The television set maker is not only striving to take business away from a competing TV manufacturer, but also from the movie maker. He hopes to increase his take of the family spending budget by channeling the funds that might be spent for the movies, into a $99 second portable TV set.

Stock market-wise, it means that every investor should be on the lookout for obsolete stocks in his portfolio. The best way to go about it is systematically. At least every so often, check over the list and sell the stock that shapes up as the least attractive. Replace it either by increasing the position in the stock already owned that then appears to be in the best position or by adding something new which appear to be better than anything already owned.

Stocks Are Good for Everybody

What concerns me today is the spirit that seems to prevail that "stocks are good for everybody." I agree with this but with the proviso that they are only good if the right issues are selected, in the right amounts and at the right time and price. It is vital to us in the security business and vital to the survival of capitalism in this country that shareowning keeps its good name. It could set us back years if a sizable proportion of the new first investors became disillusioned in any way.

In this connection, some of the remarks of Mr. Frederic W. Ecker, President of the Metropolitan Life Insurance Company, in an address on "Variable Annuities," before a Texas Life Convention in Dallas, are pertinent.

Common stocks are widely recommended as inflation hedges. For that matter, much of today's homeowning rests on the inflation theory. In years gone by, the moment one bought a home it was worth a quarter to a third less. Today, buyers blithely believe that it will always be worth more. Here are some of the things Mr. Ecker says about inflation: "If ... one will examine the price situation in this country in periods other than those affected by war, one will see that there have been long periods of time when the general trend of prices was stable or downward. While in certain other periods there has been some upward movement, it has been slight indeed, except in periods of war and its aftermath."

Another point made by Mr. Ecker concerns the currently popular argument that in effect the dollar averaging theory largely eliminates the risk in common-stock purchases. He says in part: "One is bound to question ... whether such a theory will stand up in practice. From our experience we know that in a period of depression many individuals, due to reduced income, are not able to keep up even their life-insurance premiums. How much more difficult it would be to keep up payments on a contract which, in most instances, would not be nearly so essential as a life-insurance contract! Yet, this would be just the time when, to make the dollar-averaging theory work, it would be most important to continue payments—when presumably common-stock prices would be low and any given sum would purchase more shares. Furthermore, even among those who possessed the income to continue their payments, many would not. Human nature being what it is, people in a depression period tend to lose confidence and to question the desirability of continuing to purchase common stocks when the prices of such stocks are continually falling." This is only one of the several hazards involved in dollar averaging.

Mr. Ecker points out that there have been at least eight periods since the turn of the century when the stock market, as measured by the Dow-Jones Industrial Average, has dropped as much as 40 percent. It has happened before and of course will happen again.

A final point made by Mr. Ecker throws some doubt on the popular idea of a supposed correlation between the stock market and the cost of living. Mr. Ecker admits that over a long period of time such figures look pretty good but he feels that they are unduly smoothed out in their method of compilation. He presents a table to show many times when this was not the case, such as, for example, in 1909–1910 the stock market dropped 27 percent while the cost of living remained unchanged. From March to December 1914, the stock market dropped 36 percent while at the same time the cost of living increased 3 percent. Again, from 1946 to 1949, the stock market fell off 24 percent and during that same period the cost of living increased 29 percent.

The point is that because we had considerable inflation between 1939 and 1951 and before that between 1914 and 1920, it doesn't mean that we must necessarily have it between 1957 and beyond. And likewise that the successful stock-market rules of the last ten years do not necessarily guarantee success in the next ten years. If I were forced blindly to choose between locking my savings in Standard Oil of New Jersey or locking them in cash, I would choose the Jersey. Better yet, I would prefer to choose and be able to change my mind.

Investment Efficiency

Every commitment in securities involves a risk. It is either for better or for worse, but practically never neutral.

To gain the greatest potential profits with the minimum risk of loss an investor must keep his portfolio alive. If he agrees with the premise of the first paragraph, then an investment program must have the stocks that have the greatest potential for profit. It must not have a residue of issues that failed to live up to initial promises.

Keeping deadwood pruned is perhaps one of the most difficult personal psychological decisions. A great deal has been intelligently written about limiting losses to a certain number of points or a certain percentage of the investments. But perhaps one should go further and cut out stocks that fail to perform on a time basis. In other words, if the investor expects action and doesn't get the action, he should consider liquidating.

Many investors incorrectly feel that if they sit with a sleeper little harm is done. However, I do not look at it that way. As long as any stock is held it involves a risk and tangibly affects the ratio of equity to cash reserve. Thus, it directly prevents the purchase of something else. In recent markets, even steep rallies have been highly selective. The rally leaders can and do move up 10 and 20 points while the sleepers mark time and get nowhere.

Thus, every stock should contribute to the appreciation prospects of a fund, just as every oarsman must carry his own weight in a boat.

Short Selling

Quite a few readers have written in and asked for a chapter on short selling. It is easy to argue that if you adopt a philosophy of making money out of rising prices, why not do the same when prices are falling?

The difficulty comes in that there is a difference between theory and practice. In my opinion only a very small percentage of investors can even bring themselves to attempt short selling. Most of those that do, go about it in precisely the wrong way. They generally sell short the stock that has advanced the most. More often than not, there has been a good reason for the advance and the strength might very well be bullish rather than bearish. More often than not, they select an issue with a small capitalization or small floating supply and an issue which is popular with other short sellers. All this leads directly into losses.

The proper procedure in selling short should be precisely the reverse of buying for an advance. Technically, a good short sale should be an issue which is overbought—this is another way of saying an issue which is overpopular and has too many buyers. It should be an issue with a large floating supply and a large capitalization and with very few or no shorts in it. The list of shorts is published monthly in the leading financial papers. It should be an issue that is in a downtrend, perhaps near its low or making new lows. It should be an issue where lower earnings and lower dividends are anticipated but not discounted. All this adds up to something which few people can bring themselves to sell.

Bearish information, incidentally, is much more difficult to secure than bullish. In many cases, officers of corporations who of necessity must be of a constructive nature in order to succeed just don't believe that unsatisfactory developments will continue for long. There also is a feeling that talking about bad news makes for worse, so if they do realize the situation, the tendency is to conceal it. Even where an analyst correctly uncovers unfavorable developments it is generally impossible to broadcast it. Doing this results in the loss of valuable contacts. Bad news, therefore, must be sought in private because it is not popular with everyone.

Rather than include a chapter on short selling, it seemed more appropriate to insert these few words of warning, so that readers will understand that the basic difference between theory and practice is against the short seller. It is not as easy to be a successful short seller as it may seem.

Blue Chip Gambling

In fabulous Las Vegas I noted around the roulette table stacks of "blue chips" and "red chips," the two colors Wall Street hears the most about. But there were also stacks of yellow and green and lavender, etc. Being Wall Street trained, I thought the "blue chips" were valued highest, and was surprised to learn that the chips were valued at what I wanted to pay for them, color being no consequence except to identify each owner.

Many "blue chips" in Wall Street represent first-rate corporations but the market valuations represent only what the net judgment of buyers and sellers happens to be at any given moment. Maybe it is "15 times earnings" one year and "30 times earnings" another and then later, perhaps, "15 times earnings" once again. These market valuation changes are usually far greater than any earnings or dividend changes. The safety of a genuine "blue chip" corporation may be unquestioned—but the stability of its market price may not.

Nevada is a legal and good place to gamble, but the New York Stock Exchange is not. Securities traded on the Exchange should only be bought and sold on an investment or speculative basis. Gambling is a game of a slot machine.

Security investment or speculation should only be made as a result of an intelligent study of the facts. These facts concerning the past and the present lead to conclusions concerning the probable future. The odds in gambling are sometimes known, but are always against the gambler. There are varying degrees of risk involved in gambling, in investment and in speculation, but that does not in any way make them similar. The odds in security transactions can be calculated broadly by the educated and experienced investor. They should be in the investor's favor as far as facts and reasoning indicate, or the transaction should not be made.

There are a few "investors" who attempt to use the facilities of the security markets to gamble. The Exchange and all its members attempt to discourage this.

Funds that are used in gambling serve no useful purpose. There is simply a change of ownership with a "cut" for the house and for the government.

Funds invested in securities go to build up our productive facilities and our defense powers. They strengthen the purchasing power of our currency. This is true even where no direct new financing is involved.

Some investors are like sheep; they select stocks because they are dear. They seem to feel that anything so expensive must be choice. Others turn the other way and buy stocks that seem cheap—shares selling so low they look like sure bargains. Both approaches are superficial.

Investors and speculators alike must seek out "true-blue" corporations that stand up under informed analysis. Then they should consider the price and, if it seems fair, buy. If the price appears high, it may be necessary to look further for some other justification that may have originally been missed. If it is found, all well and good. If not, the shares should be left alone.

If the price appears very cheap, check for some demerits that might have escaped analysis. Nothing is truly cheap unless it is good. If a double check brings out no flaws perhaps there exists a real bargain, sleeper or special situation. With so many investors looking, such a situation is difficult to locate.

No Storm Cellar for Investors

The 1955 Fulbright study of the stock market was aimed partly at warning investors against the dangers sometimes prevalent in equity investments. Who is there to warn investors of the dangers sometimes equally prevalent in fixed-dollar value investments? Or in just hoarding cash?

The facts are that cash, bank deposits, the investment-type of insurance contracts, bonds, mortgages, and all other forms of fixed dollar value investments have treated their owners quite badly for many years. People who invest their savings in this manner knowingly sacrifice both income return and hope of profit for safety which is not forthcoming.

The greatest loss has been in purchasing power. The rise in the cost of living since 1914, the start of World War I, has considerably outdistanced interest received net after income tax. Furthermore, dollar bond market prices have gone through several periods of sharp decline because of war financing, impaired credit standing, higher interest rates, forced liquidation during business recessions, etc. The bond buyer has not received the safety he expected.

Precise timing in converting equities into cash or into the very highest grade short-term paper has of course paid off. But this requires a high type of speculative foresight. Likewise, precise timing and pricing in buying bonds at depressed prices or at the start of upward trends has equally paid off. But again, this takes both superior understanding and a speculative point of view.

It is time more people realize that all of us are investors the moment we have surplus earnings to save for future use whether we buy stocks or avoid them. Stocks go up and stocks go down and savings held in other forms likewise buy more or buy less as the value of the dollar changes.

The following table is reprinted with the permission of the First National City Bank of New York. The table does not show how fortunes are wiped out by explosive inflation but rather what happens to the average investor whose money is in bank accounts or fixed-income types of securities such as bonds, mortgages, or insurance policies, in a period of supposedly "safe, slow" inflation. The politicians would have us believe that a 2 or 3 percent increase in the price level each year is good rather than bad. Labor leaders who want high dollar wages would have us believe the same thing. The actual figures, below, show that the careful individual knows this is not true and must try on his own to offset it.

RATES OF INTEREST AND DEPRECIATION OF MONEY

Country	Indexes of Value of Money 1953	Indexes of Value of Money 1963	Annual Rate of Deprec. (comp'd.)	Rates Offered* 1963
Venezuela	100	92	0.9%	N.A.
United States	100	88	1.3	4.00%
Canada	100	87	1.4	5.06
Switzerland	100	84	1.8	3.25
Germany	100	82	2.0	6.00
South Africa	100	82	2.0	4.75
Australia	100	81	2.2	4.58
India	100	78	2.4	4.68
Netherlands	100	77	2.5	4.22
United Kingdom	100	77	2.6	5.59
Sweden	100	73	3.1	4.45
Japan	100	72	3.2	N.A.
France	100	66	4.0	4.97
Mexico	100	59	5.0	N.A.
Brazil	100	6	24.4	N.A.
Chile	100	5	26.3	N.A.

Note: Depreciation computed from unrounded data and measured by reciprocals of official cost of living or consumers' price index. N.A. not available. *Interest rate on bonds with at least 12 years to maturity. Source of rates: International Financial Statistics of *IMF.*

Over a lifetime, common stocks have basic advantages over fixed-dollar investments. They benefit from growth and human effort. They enjoy a certain amount of compounding of savings by reason of reinvestment in the business of retained earnings. They are hurt less by inflation, and inflation is politically always more popular than deflation or even sound financial policies. Nevertheless, there are times when people pay too much for them or incorrectly appraise the future.

When people ask me whether to buy stocks or wait, I know that I can do them as much financial harm telling them to wait in a rising market as telling them to buy in a falling one. The idea that buying nothing, or staying on the sidelines is "safe" is completely fallacious.

There is no storm cellar on this earth for investors save one—that is, knowledge of what you are doing.

77

NEVER ACCEPT WITHOUT CHECKING

I THINK I started writing about securities I liked as far back as 1921. I started at the same time reading what others wrote about securities *they* liked. The first one I ever wrote was about United States bonds which in those days were called "Liberty Bonds." The ones I wrote about were gold bonds totally exempt from all taxes except state and inheritance. Their yield to maturity averaged about 4 percent at the prices then prevailing.

I vaguely remember around that time selling Goodyear Tire & Rubber First Mortgage 8 percent bonds at a discount and each and every one was payable at 120 percent at par. Those were the days when the private investor received a good return for the use of his money. The high take-home income that was left bought plenty because the cost of things was low and the cost of living was low. The loss to the conservative dollar saver from artificially lowered interest rates, increased taxes and the decreased value of money has been astronomical.

Shortly after the United States bond story, I started writing for a column then known as "Talks by Men Who Know." One of the earliest subjects was the ailing and failing Maxwell-Chalmers automobile company. I said Walter Chrysler, who was just taking over, would rescue it, and he did.

In all these years reading what others wrote about securities they liked, I never accepted their ideas without checking. Some were interesting; some were not. It seemed logical to me to look up those I liked and see if I agreed. There is always a time lag between when something is written and when something is printed and when it is read. Markets change, situations change, and opinions change. All these factors have to be considered. I think the present feature column of the "Commercial and Financial Chronicle" is one of the most valuable sources of ideas I know and I read it religiously. I think to act on it blindly would be a mistake.

I think the caption of the column "The Security I Like Best" is a fine one but it can mean many things to many people. To begin with, it runs every week, and who among us can possibly think that a "security I like best" at the "time I like best" at the "price I like best" can all occur week after week. I consider myself very lucky if once every year or two I can find in conjunction all the elements that make for an ideal stock purchase. The time to put forward such an idea is when it occurs rather than when space for its printing happens to be available. With this in mind, I think I have to look at the caption as having a little literary license and the reader will do well to do the same.

I think, too, it is logical to ask "best for what." In my day, I have had stocks I liked best for the backbone of an investment account. I have had stocks I liked best for those who insist on income. I have had stocks I liked best for those who want some special tax advantage. In fact, I am sure every contributor who responds with a story when asked is thinking of it in one of these ways. It is only once in a few years that any of us really have a stock we like best on all counts taking the strict dictionary meaning.

78

HOW TO GET THE MOST OUT OF YOUR INVESTMENTS

THE INVESTMENT EXPERIENCE and view of "inside Wall Street" given in *The Battle For Investment Survival* covers a wide and varying field.

It can be valuable to the individual reader in precise proportion to his success in appraising his personal resources, abilities, opportunities, and aims.

There will be many who should learn from this book that trying to find their own way in Wall Street will prove unprofitable. They will benefit, however, by what they save rather than by what they make. I do not think anybody with savings in excess of their emergency backlog, however, should avoid owning equities. The modern investment trust gives the person with no knowledge of investment whatever a very safe, satisfactory and rewarding stake in the future of our country. It should be realized that most people who feel themselves incapable of selecting securities or dealing with the stock markets are usually equally incapable of making other types of investments. The simple system of splitting investable savings in half between government bonds and top quality investment trusts is an ideal solution for this type of person. The government bonds are a reserve against hard times and deflation. Investment trusts are a stake in good times and a hedge against the rising cost of living. Both the bonds and investment trusts are a protection against promoters and swindlers of all types in all fields— real estate, general business, or securities. This combination in my opinion is basically a much sounder approach to the problem than salting everything away in some form of dollar investment such as cash, bank accounts, mortgages, savings and loan deposits and bonds.

Most readers of this book will feel that they can go further on their own. What they do and how they go about it will vary a great deal, depending upon many personal factors, such as age, wealth, goal, ability, contacts, and occupation.

The important point is that someone with a full time occupation of his own should not attempt a professional type of short-term trading which itself requires full time attention. It is essential that the ideas selected from the book match one's personal proclivities.

In the course of forty years as a stock broker, as well as an investor, I have seen all types of people and all types of accounts in action. Some have made money—some have lost it. A few almost always made money in the stock market. I have even seen fabulous fortunes built up. While I have seen many losses I have luckily not seen much in the way of complete catastrophe such as attracted so much publicity in the 1929–1932 period.

So, do not be "afraid" of Wall Street. Losses in other directions simply do not get the advertising Wall Street losses receive. They are just as real, however.

I believe that whenever possible the time to run risks is when one is young. It is also the time for testing and appraising one's own abilities. This means taking a job which seems to have a future. It means living relatively frugally and renting a home rather than buying one. All one's efforts should be pointed in one direction, which is to build up capital. When I was young I invested on margin and looking back, I am glad I did so. I had a lot to gain and really little to lose. It is time enough to be conservative and safe after your ship has come in and when you have much more to lose and less to gain. It is also time enough to be conservative if you find your efforts are not successful and that saving rather than building is your obvious course.

I know as I write this that only a few who try will succeed. This is equally true of every phase of life and is certainly not an argument against trying.

There will be the practical question of how to go about it. Those few young readers of this book who are making a career in some form of the investment business will naturally try completely on their own. The majority of readers engaged in different businesses or professions will simply have to make investment an avocation or, on their own, find someone successful to help them.

Occasionally among their families or friends they may know an outstandingly successful person who can help them or who has connections of his own available for introduction. Where this is not the case, it comes down to searching for the right person in the investment business itself.

I lean to a broker rather than the average banker or investment counselor, not because I happen to be a broker myself but because the objective of most of the readers of this book will be capital appreciation. The objective of bankers and most investment counsellors is orthodox diversification for income, safety and moderate growth.

Incidentally, this does not necessarily mean always attempting to find somebody at the top of the business. Often such a man being older and having achieved success is no longer as free to devote himself solely to investing for appreciation as he could do in his accumulative years. Executive duties and other activities deprive him of his time. An investor seeking help in this direction must conduct himself correctly or he will not be quick to find it. Time is money, particularly in the higher income brackets.

Actually, the greatest portion of a broker's efforts should be devoted to determining what to do. In other words, what to buy— what to sell—when—etc. Once these decisions are reached translating them into policy for individual accounts is very simple. Thus, whether or not a top man can handle an account does not really depend, as most often thought, upon the size of the account but upon the amount of time which will be required to satisfy the client.

Most people outside of Wall Street incorrectly think "insiders" find profits easy to secure. Everybody has heard the story about the brokers owning the yachts rather than the customers. If Wall Street profits were easy to secure I am sure that those who have the key would willingly share it with all whom they come in contact with. This book is called *The Battle for Investment Survival* because protecting and increasing capital is in fact a "battle." In addition to experience, flair and contacts, matters like this need uninterrupted time and attention and also a need to succeed. Thus, success can often very likely be achieved if one finds some bright young broker who is going up in the world and with his help can go up with him.

Going back to the subject of selecting assistance, I apply this principle personally when venturing into fields that are unfamiliar to me. At times, I have applied it to investing in the theater, in real estate and in oil ventures.

It is equally applicable to personal matters. Years ago, I needed medical assistance. I could not operate on myself any more than I think the butcher, the baker or the candlestick maker can invest for himself. I turned my attention to appraising a half dozen surgeons before making a decision. The success of the operation resulted from my being fortunate in choosing the right doctor among the six.

The success of many accumulative programs similarly comes from the correct choice of someone in the field with whom to consult.

The type of investor I find in the majority are those who have achieved some degree of success in their own careers and who make the handling of their funds a major avocation. This is seen most often starting at about age 35. I think it is a very fundamental and worthwhile thing to do. I can only guess at the time which is required by many of this type but perhaps it is at least an hour a day. Anyone who can successfully save money or inherit it will be exceedingly well paid for giving at least this much time and attention to his affairs. In fact, it can make the difference between actually losing money and making a great deal of it. This is the man who can make the most use out of this book.

If the first period of an individual's investment life falls between the ages of 21 and 35, this second period runs from 35 to 50. After 50, people are more apt to be on the defensive. However, if they are successful in the manner indicated they will know that the best defense is a good offense. Thus, actually there will be less change in the way they do things investment-wise than in how much they do. The successful investor may show less interest in his mature years but his very success will have taught him not to change his basic tactics. Thus, investing for retirement as it is often termed, in real life is not much different for the successful man than investing for appreciation.

Some people feel there is safety in numbers. They always check the opinion of one person against that of another. I don't find this works out very well. A banker, for example, is very apt to disapprove of a list worked out by a broker. The difference may be one of objective, which is as it should be, but yet the banker may simply disapprove because it doesn't fit his personal patterns. Thus, in the final analysis, no matter what one does the investor when selecting help must depend on his own judgment.

As a broker myself, the question I am asked frequently is, "Do you know something good?"; or, perhaps a variation, "Let me know when you hear something good." I don't think the people who ask this will get much real help or find much real lasting success in Wall Street. Wall Street is not a place to try to make an isolated profit. Rather it is where one goes to set up a continuing and consistent investment or speculative program.

Another question that I am asked frequently is, "How do I make a killing?" This can be done but it involves a great deal of risk all along the line. To make a killing these days one needs to buy the maximum amount of the most volatile high leverage shares using the largest amount of credit. This means that if a person is wrong he will lose with the same supercharged speed as he had hoped to gain. In other words, he runs the risk of being "killed" as well as of making a "killing." It is also something that one probably will have to do for himself. It will take a great deal of effort to find a conscientious and intelligent broker who will share the moral responsibility of guiding such a program.

In closing, let me repeat that this book is principally a chronological review of what I have experienced and witnessed in the field of investments. It should be very obvious that the methods outlined are not equally useful to every reader. It has been said that "one man's meat is another man's poison," and this quotation is completely applicable here.

However, every reader should close the book knowing more about the hazards of preserving capital and why the book is entitled, *The Battle for Investment Survival*. To quote again, "forewarned is forearmed," and a knowledge of true investment objectives and the great difficulty in their achievement is half the battle and of great value in itself.